SCIENCE, TECHNOLOGY AND SOCIETY IN CONTEMPORARY JAPAN

This book explores the dynamic relationship between science, technology and Japanese society, examining how it has contributed to economic growth and national well-being. It presents a synthesis of recent debates by juxtaposing competing views about the role and direction of science, technology and medical care in Japan. Topics discussed include government policy, the private sector and community responses; computers and communication; the automobile industry, the aerospace industry and quality control; the environment; consumer electronics; medical care; and the role of gender. This is an ideal introductory text for students in the sociology of science and technology, the history and philosophy of science, and Japanese studies. Up-to-date research and case studies make this an invaluable resource for readers interested in the nature of science and technology in the twenty-first century.

Morris Low has taught at Monash University, the Australian National University, and is currently a senior lecturer at the University of Queensland. His other works include the recently completed *The Historical Dictionary of Japanese Science and Technology* (forthcoming), as well as special issues of the journals *Osiris* and *History and Anthropology*. **Shigeru Nakayama** taught at the University of Tokyo before becoming Professor at Kanagawa University. A leading historian of Japanese science, his previous publications include *Science, Technology and Society in Postwar Japan* (1991). **Hitoshi Yoshioka** has taught at Wakayama University and is currently Professor at Kyushu University. He has published extensively in Japanese, including *The Social History of Atomic Energy* (1999). This is his first book in English.

CONTEMPORARY JAPANESE SOCIETY

Editor:
Yoshio Sugimoto, La Trobe University

Advisory Editors:
Harumi Befu, Kyoto Bunkyo University
Roger Goodman, Oxford University
Michio Muramatsu, Kyoto University
Wolfgang Seifert, Universität Heidelberg
Chizuko Ueno, University of Tokyo

This series will provide a comprehensive portrayal of contemporary
Japan through analysis of key aspects of Japanese society and culture,
ranging from work and gender politics to science and technology. The
series endeavours to link the relative strengths of Japanese and English-
speaking scholars through collaborative authorship. Each title will be
a balanced investigation of the area under consideration, including a
synthesis of competing views.

The series will appeal to a wide range of readers from undergraduate
beginners in Japanese studies to professional scholars. It will enable
readers to grasp the diversity of Japanese society as well as the variety of
theories and approaches available to study it.

Yoshio Sugimoto *An Introduction to Japanese Society*
    0 521 41692 2 hardback 0 521 42704 5 paperback
D. P. Martinez (ed.) *The Worlds of Japanese Popular Culture*
    0 521 63128 9 hardback 0 521 63729 5 paperback
Kaori Okano and Motonori Tsuchiya *Education in Contemporary Japan:
    Inequality and Diversity*
    0 521 62252 2 hardback 0 521 62686 2 paperback

SCIENCE, TECHNOLOGY AND SOCIETY IN CONTEMPORARY JAPAN

MORRIS LOW
University of Queensland

SHIGERU NAKAYAMA
Kanagawa University

HITOSHI YOSHIOKA
Kyushu University

CAMBRIDGE
UNIVERSITY PRESS

PUBLISHED BY THE PRESS SYNDICATE OF THE UNIVERSITY OF CAMBRIDGE
The Pitt Building, Trumpington Street, Cambridge, United Kingdom

CAMBRIDGE UNIVERSITY PRESS
The Edinburgh Building, Cambridge CB2 2RU, UK   http://www.cup.cam.ac.uk
40 West 20th Street, New York, NY 10011–4211, USA   http://www.cup.org
10 Stamford Road, Oakleigh, 3166, Australia
Ruiz de Alarcón 13, 28014, Madrid, Spain

© Cambridge University Press 1999

First published 1999

Printed in Singapore by Craft Print Pte Ltd

Typeface New Baskerville 10/12 pt   *System* QuarkXPress® [PH]

A catalogue record for this book is available from the British Library

National Library of Australia Cataloguing in Publication data
Low, Morris Fraser.
Science, technology and society in contemporary Japan.
Bibliography.
Includes index
ISBN 0 521 65282 0 (hbk).
ISBN 0 521 65425 4 (pbk).
1. Science – Social aspects – Japan – History – 20th
century. 2. Technology and state – Japan. 3. Technology –
Social aspects – Japan – History – 20th century. 4.
Science and state – Japan. I. Nakayama, Shigeru, 1928– .
II. Yoshioka, Hitoshi, 1953– . III. Title.
303.4830952

Library of Congress Cataloguing in Publication data
Low, Morris Fraser.
Science, technology and society in contemporary Japan/Morris
Low, Shigeru Nakayama, Hitoshi Yoshioka.
p.   cm.—(Contemporary Japanese society)
Includes bibliographical references and index.
ISBN 0-521-65282-0 (alk. paper).—ISBN 0-521-65425-4 (pbk.:
alk. paper)
1. Science—Social aspects—Japan. 2. Science and state—Japan.
3. Technology and state—Japan. 4. Technology—Social aspects—
Japan. I. Nakayama, Shigeru, 1928– . II. Yoshioka, Hitoshi,
1953– . III. Title. IV. Series.
Q175.52.J3L68   1999
303.48′3′0952—dc21   99–35364

ISBN 0 521 65282 0 hardback
ISBN 0 521 65425 4 paperback

Contents

Part III The International Dimension

Part IV Science and Technology for the People?

Abbreviations

AEA	(United Kingdom) Atomic Energy Authority
AEC	(United States) Atomic Energy Commission
AIDS	Acquired Immune Deficiency Syndrome
AJEI	Australia–Japan Economic Institute
ASEAN	Association of South-East Asian Nations
ATR	Advanced Thermal Reactor
CD-ROM	Compact Disk Read-Only Memory
EMAS	Eco-Management and Audit Scheme
ERA	Engineering Research Association
FBR	Fast Breeder Reactor
FEO	Federation of Economic Organisations (also known as *Keidanren*)
FRG	Federal Republic of Germany
FS-X	Fighter Support Experimental
FY	Fiscal Year
GATT	General Agreement on Tariffs and Trade
GNP	Gross National Product
HIV	Human Immunodeficiency Virus
IAEA	International Atomic Energy Agency
ICOT	Institute for New Generation Computer Technology
ISAS	Institute of Space and Aeronautical Science/Astronautical Science
ISO	International Organisation for Standardisation
ITA	Industrial Technology Agency
JAEC	Japan Atomic Energy Commission
JAERI	Japan Atomic Energy Research Institute
JAFC	Japan Atomic Fuel Corporation
JAIF	Japan Atomic Industrial Forum

JAPCO	Japan Atomic Power Company
JIS	Japanese Industrial Standards
JNSDA	Japan Nuclear Ship Development Agency
JSC	Japan Science Council/Science Council of Japan
JUNET	Japan University Network
JUSE	Japanese Union of Scientists and Engineers
KDD	Kokusai Denshin Denwa
KEK	National Laboratory for High Energy Physics
LDP	Liberal Democratic Party
LSI	large-scale integration
LWR	Light Water Reactor
MHD	Magneto-Hydrodynamic
MITI	Ministry of International Trade and Industry
MS-DOS	Microsoft Disk Operating System
NAMCO	Nihon Airplane Manufacturing Corporation
NASDA	National Space Development Agency of Japan
NEC	Nippon Electric Company
NGO	Non-Government Organisation
NHK	Japan Broadcasting Corporation
NIEs	Newly Industrialised Economies
NISTEP	National Institute of Science and Technology Policy
NSF	National Science Foundation
NTSC	National Television Systems Committee
NTT	Nippon Telephone and Telegraph
ODA	Official Development Assistance
OEM	Original Equipment Manufacturing
OTCA	Kaigai Gijutsu Kyōryoku Jigyōdan (later known as the Japan International Co-operation Agency)
PCDD	polychlorinated dibenzo-p-dioxins
PNC	Power Reactor and Nuclear Fuel Development Corporation
PVC	polyvinyl chloride
QC	quality control
QCC	quality control circles
R&D	research and development
S&T	science and technology
SCI	*Science Citation Index*
SDF	Self-Defence Force (of Japan)
SDPJ	Social Democratic Party of Japan
STA	Science and Technology Agency
STC	Science and Technology Council
TRON	The Real Time Operating System Nucleus
UNCTAD	United Nations Conference on Trade Development
USSR	Union of Soviet Socialist Republics
VLS	very large-scale integration

Figures

Tables

Acknowledgements

The literature on Japanese science and technology (S&T) has grown greatly during the past decade. This introductory book provides a window to that literature. We would like to thank the series editor Yoshio Sugimoto and Cambridge University Press editor Phillipa McGuinness, without whose encouragement and patience this book would not have been possible. We are also grateful to Maxine McArthur, Yoshioka Yayoi and Yasuko Gower for research assistance, part of the support extended to the project by the Division of Pacific and Asian History, Research School of Pacific and Asian Studies, Australian National University, where much of the manuscript was written. In the final stages of preparation of the manuscript, the assistance of the Department of Asian Languages and Studies, University of Queensland, and the Centre for Cross-Cultural Research at the Australian National University were important, as were the comments of anonymous reviewers. The efforts of manuscript editor, Lee White, and friendly cooperation of Cambridge University Press Editorial Controller, Paul Watt, were crucial in shaping the book in its current form.

Romanisation generally follows that found in Masuda Koh (ed.), *Kenkyūsha's New Japanese–English Dictionary*, 4th edn, Tokyo, Kenkyūsha, 1974. Elongated vowels are indicated by lines over the vowels. Japanese family names precede given names in the text unless the person has been a long-term resident overseas. The names of the authors of this book are, however, given in Western order for ease of reference.

Since 1949 the yen was fixed at 360 yen per US dollar. In 1985 the yen was allowed to appreciate, rising from 260 yen to 130 yen to the dollar by 1987. Since then the exchange rates have fluctuated. In June 1999 the rate was 122 yen. Amounts in US dollars given in the text are those provided by the sources cited.

In Chapter 1 we reprint parts of S. Nakayma and M. F. Low, 'The research function of universities in Japan', *Higher Education*, vol. 34, no. 2, pp. 245–58, with kind permission from Kluwer Academic Publishers ©. We would also like to thank Kuramoto Masaaki (Japan Foundation of Public Communications on Science and Technology), Miyahara Masanobu (National Science Foundation, Tokyo Office), and Asaka Takenaga (Research Institute of International Trade and Industry) for permission to use copyright material in tables and figures. And finally, we are grateful to Diane Harriman for compiling the excellent index.

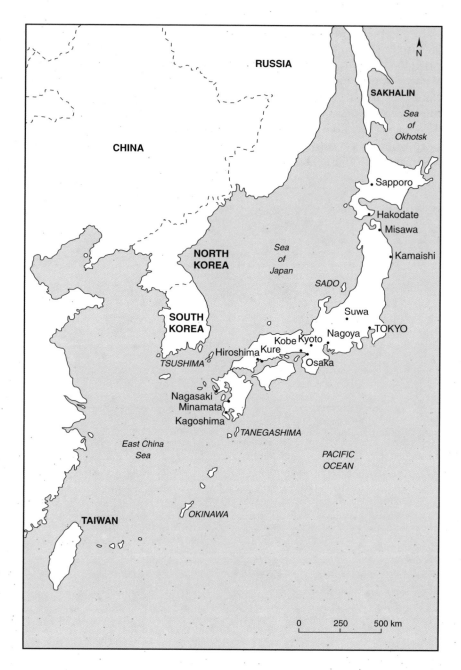

Japan and neighbouring countries

Introduction

When people think of Japanese science and technology (S&T) a number of images come to mind: Japan as borrower and imitator; Japan and war; Japan as a resource-poor island nation; and Japan's government control. It is generally agreed that these are all important factors in the development of technology in Japan. In studying Japanese S&T the inevitable question arises as to why the Chinese were not able to meet with the same type of success as the Japanese. This is especially puzzling given that the Japanese have borrowed so heavily from Chinese culture in the past. The Japanese, it has been suggested, have exhibited a greater willingness to borrow from other cultures, whereas in China where Confucianism was more rampant, and respect for the past and one's elders more ingrained, the development of S&T was stifled. This is not to say that neo-Confucianist doctrine has not influenced Japanese culture, but the Japanese seem to have reconciled this with their need to learn new ways. Sugimoto & Swain (1978, 1989) have viewed Japan's history as a combination of domestic development and waves of Chinese and Western influence. How one balances the need for indigenous development against the relative ease of foreign borrowing appears to have been a problem throughout Japanese history.

Japan has a long history of borrowing foreign technology, and there has been a military imperative behind it. Samuels (1994, ix) argues that insecurity is the key to understanding what makes Japan tick. The indigenisation of technology, diffusion of it throughout the economy, and efforts to encourage Japanese enterprises which could take advantage of the technology are seen as having been fundamental to national security since the late nineteenth century. The Japan found by Commodore Perry (who headed an American expedition to Japan in the 1850s) had little means to support modern warfare but things changed

1

with the Meiji Restoration. The slogan 'Rich nation, strong army' illustrates Japan's commitment at the time to create factories that could, among other things, produce modern weapons, with the help of foreigners. Westney (1986, 1987) has described how Japanese military institutions led the way in adopting Western organisational patterns and hiring foreign advisers. The Japanese government played a leading role in the adoption of Western technology with the Engineering Ministry (Kōbushō) spearheading the effort from 1870 to 1885. Large numbers of foreign engineers were brought into Japan during this period. As Japan learnt from the foreigners, they were replaced by Japanese. Private companies gradually took over responsibility for the borrowing of foreign technology, although some important military industries like shipbuilding and railways were either owned or sponsored by the government. The last years of the nineteenth century and the beginning of the twentieth, saw the establishment of associations between large companies such as those between Toshiba and General Electric, Mitsubishi and Westinghouse, and ITT and Nippon Electric. Inter-firm transfers of technology between the United States and Japan have been important ever since.

Military hardware improved during the nineteenth century with the use of railways, the telegraph, and development of weapons. These improvements were not, however, systematic applications of scientific knowledge. It was only in the twentieth century that the connection between scientific knowledge and economic and political power was finally demonstrated, and the concept of science policy was born. It is not surprising that its origins have been of a military nature.

The link between knowledge and power was demonstrated to governments and the military during the First World War. One of the lessons Japan learnt from that war was that nations had to be able to supply themselves during wartime with adequate quantities of raw materials and manufactured goods. Reliance on other countries was seen as a sure way to defeat. Japan's status as a great power was shaken by Germany's defeat in 1918. Germany had far more formidable forces than Japan and yet the country had been vanquished. The Japanese Empire began to be reorganised in a search for self-sufficiency, a search for economic security. In the two decades after the First World War Japan made impressive strides toward a self-sufficient Japanese Empire. Manchuria, for example, had been completely absorbed into it. The Japanese made the mistake, however, of antagonising the West before self-sufficiency was actually achieved. Although Barnhart (1987) has found that army–navy rivalry played a far more important role in propelling Japan into war with the United States, Japan's fundamental war aim was to establish the

Greater East Asian Co-prosperity Sphere as a self-sufficient and powerful unit with the Japanese Empire at its centre.

After the Second World War a strategy was put forward by bureaucrats and administrators in the government which favoured the importation and adaptation of overseas technology. Industries with world market potential were targeted for development. With the outbreak of the Korean War in June 1950, Japan became a supply base for the United States military. As tension mounted between the United States and the Soviet Union, Washington developed a world strategy that included a resumption of military production in Japan in order to rearm the country and to secure a source of military supplies for other Asian nations. Despite resistance on the part of the Japanese and their desire to create a 'rich nation without a strong army', the militaristic aspects of Japanese science and technology and their economy remain.

Peck (1976, 527) pinpoints three distinctive features of Japanese technological development in the postwar period: (1) high returns from importing technology in terms of exports and productivity; (2) extensive government controls over importation of technology; and (3) clever use of management, investment and domestic research and development (R&D) to capitalise on imported technology. From 1952 to 1960 extensive government controls were administered by the Ministry of International Trade and Industry (MITI). The government aimed at making Japan more self-sufficient in materials such as chemicals and iron and steel. Between 1960 and 1965 imports of technology became more oriented toward consumer goods and potential exports, and in the period 1966 to 1972 imports of technology were increasingly those of improvements to technology where the technology had been imported previously. The importation of technology is the most striking feature of postwar Japan, but considerable gains were obtained from Japan's domestic R&D. Japan's economic recovery did not depend on pioneering R&D which led to new products, though the situation is now changing.

Japan is committed to becoming a science and technology-oriented nation. Government expenditure on R&D at time of writing continues to increase. This book explores the relationship between science, technology and society and its contribution to economic growth and the well-being of the Japanese people. The form and content of S&T are governed by class relations/power hierarchies in society, and it will become obvious to the reader that projects which are promoted by the government tend to serve the interests of the dominant groups in society. What will emerge time and again in the chapters that follow is a complex interplay between values, interests, knowledge and power. The world of science and technology is not very different to that of society. There are strong similarities between scientific practice and other forms of social practice. Furthermore, technology can be viewed as a social system rather than a mere artefact.

Where have readers gone previously to learn more about science, technology and society in contemporary Japan? There are various specialist books and articles in the English language that have appeared over the last two decades (see Bibliography). Shigeru Nakayama's *Science, Technology and Society in Postwar Japan* (1991) is one of the few that provides a sense of the big picture. Nakayama views the development of S&T in Japan in terms of the dynamics of the relationship between the interests of four social sectors: academic, public, private and citizen. The present book builds on the framework of Nakayama's work and suggests that the relationship has grown somewhat fuzzy, with blurring between the divisions. Like Tessa Morris-Suzuki in her important study *The Technological Transformation of Japan* (1994), we are also interested in understanding the process of technological change that these four sectors contribute to. Morris-Suzuki adopts an original approach by emphasising the role of social networks of information in innovation. And like us, she is mindful of the social costs of rapid technological change.

Readers of this book can supplement their reading by referring to a number of useful introductory studies. Takatoshi Ito's *The Japanese Economy* (1992) is an easy-to-understand textbook treatment of its subject. Although a little dated now, and lacking a discussion of the Asian economic crisis of the late 1990s, it provides a solid treatment of economic issues. For an overview of Japanese industry, Tomokazu Ohsono's *Charting Japanese Industry* (1995) provides a handy guide to corporate structure and industrial structure in Japan. And if one's interests specifically concern S&T, any one of the editions of Jon Sigurdson & Alun M. Anderson's *Science and Technology in Japan* (1984, 1991) will provide a good overview of the organisation of S&T in Japan. For a more academic study of issues relating to R&D, readers can turn to Martin Hemmert & Christian Oberländer's *Technology and Innovation in Japan* (1998).

This book presents a synthesis of debates and arguments relating to science, technology and society and the chapters characterise debate surrounding S&T in terms of opposing positions. The reality is that there is often no single answer to a particular problem; this book shows different points of view. What is deemed a success by one group may be viewed as a failure or disaster by another. The structure of the book reflects our attempt to make a balanced investigation of the topic. We deliberately juxtapose competing views to show the diversity of opinions about the role and direction of S&T in Japan. Often scientists will lobby for an emphasis on basic science (that is, openly accessible scientific research of a fundamental nature which is published in academic journals) as opposed to applied science (that is, scientific research often carried out in private laboratories and aimed at developing fundamental ideas into industrial applications and commercial products). Industrialists tend to show greater interest in applied science. Competing views on the development and uses of S&T may arise from different moral values, political interests, disciplinary background and scientific claims. Power, ethical values and social arrangements often affect the way policy is formed and implemented. Governments can have explicit policies, sometimes formalised in laws, which dictate certain choices. Much of the book looks at Japanese government policy which has attempted to promote certain aspects of S&T. Individuals and organisations influence the policy process, and citizens, scientists and private firms also make specific choices or preferences known, using moral arguments to support their case. Policy-making and implementation contest the validity of facts and certain values, whether they be economic or scientific in nature.

Many of the case studies found in this book show how choices are made by the government, corporations and other organisations. One group will often seek to increase its own power at the expense of others. Economic realities, too, can determine the way policy is formulated and implemented. Since the end of the Second World War the industrial landscape has changed dramatically in Japan, as has its place within the world economy. With the challenge of the Asian economic crisis in the late 1990s, there is pressure on the Japanese economy to continue to change.

The book is divided into four parts. In the first part, we look at some features of what can be described as the Japanese model of R&D. It is useful to consider Japanese S&T in terms of features, issues or ideas which are often thought of as opposites. The first chapter contrasts basic research with applied research. While there is a blurring of the divisions between the two, it is possible to differentiate the sites of such research. Applied research still tends to be found more often in corporate laboratories, and basic research can often be found in government research institutes and universities. Some commmentators cite the Ministry of International Trade and Industry's (MITI's) R&D projects and Japan's science cities as good examples of cooperation, but Chapter 2 suggests that competition can, at times, get in the way of cooperation, and may actually have been one of the motivating forces for the involvement of the private sector in such projects.

Part II looks more closely at S&T and its role in promoting economic growth. Quality control, discussed in Chapter 3, has long been hailed as a contributing factor to the success of the Japanese automobile industry, but commercial concerns have not always underpinned science and technology-related activities in Japan. This can be seen in Chapter 4, where the government, especially the Science and Technology Agency (STA), has often championed the development of domestic capability in nuclear technology, frequently without due attention to its commercial feasibility which is of prime importance to electric utilities. In contrast, the popularity of consumer electronics in postwar Japan shows how growing affluence has been reflected in greater use of electric appliances. Another symptom of economic growth is the growth in environmental problems. We see in Chapter 5 how in recent years issues concerning global environmental problems have received more attention than local pollution.

We are increasingly living in a global world, and confining our study of Japanese S&T to activity within Japan's borders ignores the external forces which have long shaped the direction of S&T in Japan. The third part of the book examines the international dimension of Japanese science and technology. The question of domestic development versus the importation of technology came to a head in the FS-X fighter plane controversy, described in Chapter 6 in the context of the aerospace industry. Some of the tensions can be traced to differing visions for science and technology. Chapter 7 argues that what has often been called 'Japanese' S&T is increasingly becoming global, and is difficult to label.

While it is convenient to speak of entities such as 'Japan' and matters such as 'Japanese' S&T, we should not forget the controlling importance of people and how much of what has been done by the government in terms of S&T policy has theoretically been done for the public interest. We suggest in Part IV, however, that much of what occurs might be better described as being for the 'national interest' as defined by some of the powerful actors who determine policy in Japan. While the 'information society' holds much promise there is, as discussed in Chapter 8, potential for people's lives to be controlled, in terms of technological choice, nature of their work and surveillance of their lives. Social control can be highly gendered and despite some reforms, Japan is still very much a patriarchal society – the key decision-makers are often male. Chapter 9 looks at how men are still often favoured over women in the science and technology workforce, a tendency which became even more pronounced during the Asian economic recession of the late 1990s. Women are frequently more active in social protest, but men were certainly to the fore in the sometimes violent dispute surrounding the construction of Narita airport, an airport which has still not been completed. Chapter 10 describes this drama, and shows how the history of the airport's construction reveals that national interest has been pitted against local interests. Attitudes to public participation in policy-making are changing in Japan, and local residents are slowly becoming more empowered and more able to resist or oppose contentious projects such as Narita airport, which involve deeply entrenched, vested interests. This can be seen in Chapter 11 where we examine changing attitudes to medical care and the human body. We discuss how the concept of informed consent has been slow to take root in Japan, due to the powerful medical community, and a long-standing patient–doctor relationship which favours physicians. The Japanese public has increasingly become aware that it cannot rely on the medical system or corporate Japan to look after its interests. There are mixed views on organ transplants and the validity of brain death, and oral contraceptives have been very slow to be introduced. The cultural context of medical care in Japan is different, for example, euthanasia occurs under conditions which are different from elsewhere.

While there are no easy answers to explain Japan's relative economic success, this book shows that without considering the contribution made by people and society, any cost–benefit analysis must surely be flawed. The pairing of opposites discussed in each chapter often results in a dualistic relationship which is sometimes fraught with tension. This accounts for some of the dynamics of S&T in Japan. While things are in flux (and what this book describes will change), the chapters provide an accessible way of framing discussion of the relationship between different sectors in Japan and their differing views on where S&T should be headed in the future.

PART I

The Japanese Model of Research and Development

CHAPTER 1

Basic versus Applied Research

The Role of Corporate Laboratories and Universities

Introduction

Asia's dynamic growth has been attributed to state-encouraged market strategies and what has been described as the Japanese model of development. While the Asian economic crisis of the late 1990s has prompted many to criticise the Japanese model, the general assumption behind much Japanese R&D is not very different from the assumptions made for R&D elsewhere. Basic, discovery-oriented research is often pursued in the hope that novel technologies might be generated, and in turn lead to the development of new industries or products. However, in addition to science-based technologies such as nuclear engineering, there are other advanced technologies found, for example, in the car industry, which owe much less to basic science and more to workshop engineering. The dividing line between S&T, basic and applied research, and what one can deem the most appropriate sites of R&D, is a fuzzy one. While science tends to be equated with basic research and technology with applied research, both tend to justify themselves by the potential economic spin-offs (Ziman: 1984, 113–19). The likely benefits mean that large budgets are allocated to research that promises to produce economic advantages.

The old, now discredited, linear notion of innovation from discovery or invention to commercial product alluded to above (Elzinga & Jamison: 1995, 586) has been used by American journalists who have argued that Japan has emphasised applied research over basic research, free-riding on American basic science to make up for a lack of creativity and ideas. How true is this? This chapter first outlines the organisation of S&T, describes some features of R&D in Japan, then examines two types of R&D sites: corporate laboratories and universities. What is their role in Japan's research effort and is it good or bad?

The Organisation of Science and Technology in Japan

On 4 December 1998 the Japanese government submitted a supplementary budget for the 1998 fiscal year (FY) in an attempt to help the Japanese economy recover from its depressed state. The budget included allocations for science and technology-related activities which, along with earlier allocations that year, would have amounted to 4163.2 billion yen. This represented an increase of 38.7 per cent over the previous year's science and technology budget of 3002.5 billion yen. Table 1.1 compares the initial 1998FY budget with that of the previous year and gives some indication of the government entities involved in science and technology-related activities in Japan. Figure 12.1 (in the Conclusions) shows

Table 1.1 Science and technology-related budget according to ministry and agency, 1997FY and 1998FY

Ministries and agencies	1997FY (total) (billion yen)	1998FY (initial) (billion yen)
Ministry of Education, Science, Sports and Culture	1289.0	1311.1
Science and Technology Agency	734.5	740.1
Ministry of International Trade and Industry	472.2	492.8
Defence Agency	175.3	144.2
Ministry of Agriculture, Forestry and Fisheries	100.9	104.2
Ministry of Health and Welfare	91.5	95.1
Ministry of Posts and Telecommunications	57.7	60.5
Ministry of Construction	38.9	39.5
Ministry of Transport	23.1	23.1
Environment Agency	18.0	19.6
Ministry of Foreign Affairs	13.0	12.4
Ministry of Labour	4.3	3.9
Ministry of Finance	2.2	2.4
Ministry of Justice	2.0	2.1
National Police Agency	1.5	2.1
Science Council of Japan	1.3	1.3
Economic Planning Agency	1.1	1.0
Ministry of Home Affairs	0.8	0.9
National Land Agency	0.5	0.7
National Diet	0.6	0.6
Hokkaido Development Agency	0.2	0.2

Source: Miyahara: 1998.

the proposed bureaucratic structure intended to come into being in the year 2001.

By January 2001 it is envisaged that the government's twenty-two ministries and agencies will be reorganised into a Cabinet Office and twelve ministries (see Figure 12.1). For reasons which should become clear after reading this book, the Ministry of Education and the Science and Technology Agency will be merged into the Ministry of Education, Science and Technology. The Ministry of International Trade and Industry will remain and will be renamed the Ministry of Economy and Industry. The Environment Agency will be upgraded into a ministry, and the ministries of Labour and Health and Welfare will be merged into the Ministry of Labour and Welfare (*Japan Times*: 1997a).

Technology Transfer: A Free Ride?

The claims of Japanese free-riding also includes the assumption that the Japanese do little creative work on the innovations that they might borrow. It is a useful argument in order to elicit further bargaining power during US–Japan trade negotiations, and to encourage the Japanese to open their markets to foreign goods, but it does little to heighten our understanding of the development of S&T in Japan. Japanese engineers counter with the claim that if that is the case, then American industrialists should utilise their own science.

Whatever position one wishes to take, we can say that the process of so-called free-riding is not necessarily free and easy. There is an element of truth in the claims in so far as the Japanese are very good at borrowing from other cultures, but the claims neglect consideration of the complex process in which public, private and academic sectors are involved in developing those ideas and commercialising them. The infrastructure for this has been built up since Japan's opening to the West in the late nineteenth century, the foundations date perhaps from the seventeenth century, and the infrastructure continues to be developed.

Why does the literature fail to show how difficult this process is? International technology transfer usually takes place in two stages. The first is the transfer from advanced countries to the public sector of developing countries, and the second is from the public to the private sector in those economies. Up to the 1960s historians of modern Japanese S&T tended to emphasise the first aspect of the state-centred approach of early Meiji Japan. Those who were engaged in the state enterprise of technology transfer were samurai élite, who were proud of their enlightened endeavours and were not shy about talking about them. Historians of S&T were drawn to the efforts of the samurai, given the historians' fascination with what is deemed 'original' and operates on a large scale. Of less interest was the effectiveness of the technology in the real market, an area examined more usually by economic historians.

In the 1970s a movement critical of science emerged in Japan, and revisionist historians of S&T appeared who re-examined the simplistic emphasis on original and grand achievements and found that many efforts to introduce technology had failed as market-oriented private technology. Technology could not be effectively transferred merely by a directive from the central bureaucracy. The technology that could best survive in the local market was intermediate technology carried out in the private sector by traditional craftsmen, like Gaun Tokimune and Toyoda Sakichi. This has been largely hidden from the historical account.

Tessa Morris-Suzuki (1994) advocates delving further into this via the 'social network approach', which starts at the opposite end to the state, namely the outer edges of society: local governments, trade associations and the like. Technology transfer was not so much a top-down hierarchical process but rather a weak horizontal process with the centre being much less significant than originally thought. Another thesis of Morris-Suzuki's is that 'technology is locally-bound and thus dwells in the periphery rather than the bureaucratic centre'. The network approach serves to connect literature on the state-centred public technology with the revisionist approach to private technology. Once imported knowledge is poured into the nodal points, it flows effectively into the whole network.

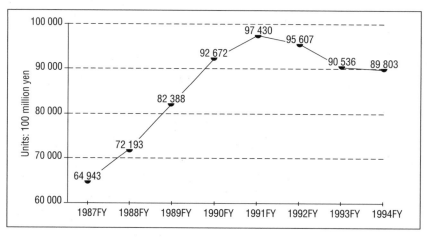

Figure 1.1 Trends in private sector research and development funding, 1987FY–1994FY
Source: MITI: 1996, p. 173.

It is abundantly clear that the introduction of foreign technology is no free ride. With the licensing of key technologies which helped fuel postwar Japanese economic growth likely to become more difficult, Japan is faced with a dilemma. But Japan has been creative in commercialising technology and no doubt Japanese researchers will continue to have innovative ideas. Who will do this? And where can they be found? Private sector R&D funding has varied over the years (see Figure 1.1). Despite the economic recession, the late 1990s saw annual increases in private R&D expenditure (Figure 1.2). The private sector has been responsible for about 80 per cent of Japan's total R&D expenditure; this helps account for the large proportion of R&D that is of an applied or developmental nature (Figure 1.3). Japan has previously lagged behind other major industrialised nations in terms of the government funding of R&D and in terms of the percentage of gross national product (GNP) (see Figure 1.4). Odagiri & Goto (1993, 103) explain that this has been partly due to the smaller defence-related expenditure compared to that of other countries. Even when such expenditure is excluded, total government R&D expenditure has been smaller.

If we look more closely at where the funds are directed we can see that government funds, not unexpectedly, are directed at government research institutions and universities (Table 1.2). The amount of government funds devoted to industrial R&D is very small (1.2 per cent) while the private sector finances most industrial R&D itself.

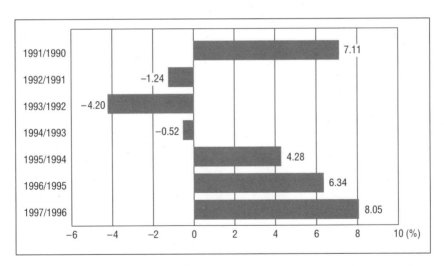

Figure 1.2 Private research and development expenditure compared with the preceding year, 1990–1997
Source: STA Today: 1998, 9.

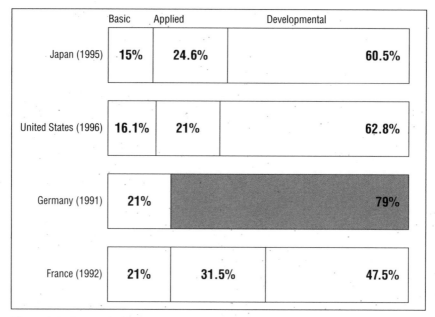

Figure 1.3 Research funding of major industrialised countries according to type
Note: In the case of Germany, applied research and developmental research
proportions are not able to be determined separately.
Source: STA: 1997, 125.

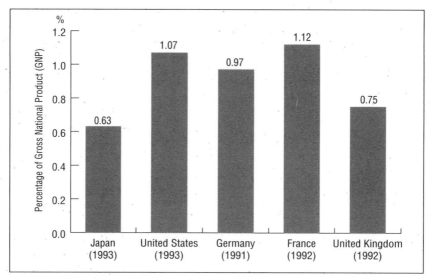

Figure 1.4 Government research and development funding as a percentage
of GNP
Source: MITI: 1996, 187.

Table 1.2 Japanese research and development funding according to sector, 1994FY

Source of funds	Sector receiving funds	Amount (units of 100 million yen)	Percentage share of total funds distributed by source
Government	Government	12 195	99.4
Industry	Government	66	0.5
Government	Industry	1 072	1.2
Industry	Industry	88 506	98.6
Government	Universities	13 855	50.3
Industry	Universities	638	2.3

Source: MITI: 1996, 188.

The slow but increasing internationalisation of Japanese R&D is perhaps another manifestation of the privatisation trend, as well as evidence of a lack of confidence in the research function of Japanese universities. Admittedly, a change in attitude on the part of the Ministry of Education and industry is occurring that results in a blurring of public and private activities and an increase in research funds to universities. But if students are not attracted to careers in S&T, as is the case now, such university–industry cooperation may be in vain.

The Privatisation of Knowledge

In the industrialised countries of Europe and North America most research after the Second World War was conducted under government sponsorship and direction. In contrast, in Japan research laboratories run by private companies began to play a larger role from the late 1950s and into the early 1960s. The beginning of the 1960s saw an increase in scientific and technical research world-wide, and even businesses in the United States increased research funding during this period, but the increase in privately-funded research laboratories in Japan proceeded more rapidly still. Also, whereas the percentage of government subsidies for private research was high in Europe and North America, in Japan government assistance for private research amounted to about 2 per cent of the whole, the remainder of the costs being borne by the companies themselves (Nakayama: 1995).

In the late 1950s it was usual for Japanese companies not to differentiate between researchers and technicians, and to assign posts according to personal suitability after employment commenced. Graduates and graduate degree holders of the new university system were not evaluated highly by those who had studied under the old system, and research posts were not greatly distinguished from those of technicians' in terms of pay and rank. The resulting shortage of research personnel meant that plans to increase research funding were unsuccessful, revealing the lack of appropriate corporate infrastructure to support the increase in research activity.

From about 1956 'technological reform' became the slogan of the times in Japan, and in the post-Sputnik world after 1957 international interest in S&T increased sharply. There was also an international boom in central research laboratories at the beginning of the 1960s, encouraged by management theories such as those which debated the correct percentage of research investment to profit. In the favourable economic climate of the early 1960s it was common for large companies to purchase land and amalgamate their scattered research facilities into one main laboratory. A central research laboratory became a kind of status symbol by which companies might attract talented personnel.

In Japan, large companies were prepared to pay twice the wages of the public sector to lure capable researchers and technicians from national research laboratories and universities. In the central laboratory boom of the early 1960s companies in the electronics and chemical industries took the lead in importing technology, and their expenditure on research was far larger than that of other industries. Because it was expensive to adapt imported technology, activity in research and the establishment of central laboratories was confined to large companies. At the central laboratories of mechanical engineering companies 'reverse engineering' was the main form of research, where imported machinery was dismantled and copied. The chemical industry, on the other hand, relied on the method of using technicians from abroad to supervise implementation of new machinery and techniques.

The main purpose of a central research laboratory was to promote development of technology original to the company, and companies such as Hitachi that were committed to these goals succeeded in attracting excellent research personnel. During this period, however, most central research laboratories began by importing as much foreign technology as possible, then they absorbed and adapted this technology to fit their own needs.

In the early stages of the central research laboratory boom many researchers left universities and national laboratories to join private companies, and a number of theories were propounded about the percentage of the total profit which should be invested in R&D. In 1964, however, reduced economic growth led to budget cuts in research and a slight decrease in the number of research personnel. Many results of the research conducted at central research laboratories were not immediately utilised in production because of an orientation to basic research, and criticism arose because the laboratories were perceived as not realising their full potential. It took until the 1980s for the central research laboratories to prove their practical use, leading to management recognition that R&D funding should be included in budgets as a matter of course and should not be subject to the economic situation of the time.

Japan is strong in the 'private' science of company laboratories which tends to be applied and developmental in nature, and much weaker in the 'academic' science practised at universities and affiliated institutes (Nakayama: 1989). In recent years, Japanese firms have attempted to move more into areas of basic research, conducting such research in central research laboratories and carrying out new product development where the products are manufactured. James L. Bess (1995) suggests that about half of the research budget of large Japanese firms goes to the central laboratory, and the remainder is allocated to the decentralised manufacturing plants. Job rotation facilitates links between the central laboratories and the plants.

If we look at postwar R&D in other industrialised countries, it has been dominated by a trend towards the nationalisation of science, or the public funding of R&D, as formulated by Vannevar Bush in *Science: The Endless Frontier* (1945), Bush's response to President Roosevelt's request for a postwar science policy. Japan and the former West Germany adopted the opposite strategy of privatisation of science. With the advent of the Reagan administration, since 1981 American policy has moved towards privatisation, and federal spending on industrial laboratories has often been curtailed (Slaughter: 1993). Although subtle differences in language make international comparisons difficult (Narin & Frame: 1989), it is clear that public research expenditure has been declining throughout the world since the 1980s. It is also obvious that the Japanese have been leading the trend towards privatisation (Japanese Government, Science and Technology Agency: 1992, 169).

The privatisation of knowledge has led to the relative impoverishment of Japanese academic science (Japanese Government, Science and Technology Agency: 1992, 194). The research funding per capita of academic science as practised in the university sector has stayed flat since the early 1980s, while funding for other types of laboratories has doubled in some cases. Part of the reason can be found in the Ministry of Finance's policy, since 1983, of stipulating that the budget requests of ministries do not exceed that of their allocations of the preceding year. University funds have thus grown very little, but grants-in-aid for scientific research have increased. There is, however, a great disparity between average sums awarded to university-based researchers and those at national research institutes, which receive much higher grants (Yamamoto: 1993, 177). This tends to show that the privatisation trend of Japanese science does not so much refer to the privatisation of academic science as to the much better-funded state of private science.

Is the prevalence of private science a positive thing? The response depends on who answers. The Japanese government has often been criticised by Japanese academics and Americans for the low government funding of basic science, compared to the funding offered by the private sector. This neglect of academic science has been noted since 1970 and led to the accusations of free-riding on American science. The budget of public universities, where most government-funded research occurs, has failed to keep up with inflation since that time.

Japanese academics have always been dissatisfied with the poor state of university budgets, especially when compared to those of the United States. On the other hand, the American scientific community tends to recognise more of the strong points of Japanese academic science than does the Japanese community. Who, then, criticises the Japanese basic science effort? It seems that overseas critics are primarily concerned with trade and technology-related conflicts between the United States and Japan. They claim that American intellectual property has been virtually given away or stolen by Japanese manufacturers.

If we are to view the debate in a more 'objective' light, there needs to be agreement on parameters and some empirical evidence. Although it is difficult to distinguish between basic and applied science, for our purposes we take basic science as being work published in academic journals which are accessible to anyone capable of reading such material. The number of such articles per capita provides a good indication of scientific productivity. Not surprisingly, the United States is the most productive nation, with more than twice the scientific productivity of the Japanese per head of population. However, America's share of the global production of such knowledge has actually dropped from 38.2 per cent to 35.6 per cent over the period 1973 to 1986. The European share is slowly decreasing too. In contrast, the Japanese share has risen from 5.3 per cent to 7.7 per cent over the same period (Science and Technology Policy Research Institute: 1991, 44).

Such statistics must be considered with caution. The source of the data may be somewhat skewed towards the United States, since much of the scientific literature is written in English. This ignores literature on locally relevant subjects such as geology and ecology, which tend to be written in languages specific to the country in question. We could turn to a different indicator to obtain a more favourable result for Japanese science. Tominaga Keii has attempted to measure the productivity of individual institutions cited in *Chemical Abstracts*, including Japanese language articles with English abstracts which make up 30 per cent of total Japanese works reported in the journal. In 1976, when the counting began, the most productive institution was Tokyo University, followed by Kyoto University, University of California, Berkeley, and Osaka University, in that order. In 1979 the order of ranking was Tokyo, Kyoto, Osaka and Berkeley. In recent years the share of contributions by Japanese institutions which are included has gradually increased to such an extent that in 1991 the first four places went to Japanese universities, namely Tokyo, Kyoto, Osaka and Tōhoku, followed by Berkeley and the University of Wisconsin, Madison. Again, a word of caution. These placings and the number of contributions on which they are based are, perhaps, only an indication of the large size and concentration of resources in certain Japanese research units. There may well be a strong correlation between research productivity, the age and prestige of an institution, and the amount of funding directed to it. Aspiring graduate students may be attracted to an institution for these sorts of reasons. For example, the top eight universities that were established before the Second World War confer 80 to 90 per cent of Japanese doctorates in science.

There has been a gradual increase in the quantity of Japanese academic research. Admittedly, this may not necessarily reflect an increase in quality or creativity, but it does signal an increase in basic research, which Americans have chosen not to acknowledge adequately. There are perhaps other reasons for their criticism of the Japanese. Let us consider the competing views and try to account for them.

1 *Public Sector Argument.* A guiding principle of science policy in the postwar period has been the claim that basic research is essential for technological innovation. The Vannevar Bush ideology of science has been most prevalent among American science policy-makers, while Japanese bureaucrats, such as those in MITI (Johnson: 1982), do not share such concern for the primacy of basic science. It should be pointed out that while the American military-industrial complex has supported basic science as a sub-system of public science, the Japanese MITI-industrial complex has shown much less interest in promoting science, basic or public.

Furthermore, it can also be pointed out that the science policy of the American-led Occupation Forces in Japan during 1945 to 1952 was to encourage an emphasis on applied science for immediate economic recovery and to promote the view that basic science was a luxury (Nakayama: 1995b). This policy was not adopted by the Ministry of Education, but it was more or less taken up by MITI and other ministries.

2 *Academic Argument.* Before the Second World War even the United States was accused by Europeans of an undue emphasis on practical

applications, and depending too much on basic research originating in Europe. The lack of basic research in postwar Japan is perhaps a feature of the transition from a scientifically-developing country to a developed country. Viewed in this way, Japanese basic research has started to grow only recently.

3 *Private Sector Argument.* The rapid postwar Japanese growth in private science has overshadowed public and academic science. Sooner or later the Japanese structure of science and technology will converge towards an international or American standard.

4 *The Argument of a Historian of Science.* Rather than bemoan the situation, we might better interpret Japan's postwar experience as having created a new type of structure of S&T, one which is dominated by strong private science and weak, large-scale, public and academic science.

Arguments 1 to 3 may seem to conflict with argument 4, but in reality all offer meaningful interpretations, and their accuracy can only be assessed in the future.

The Matter of Quality

Is the quality of Japanese scientific research good or bad? It may be some time before an original idea is developed into a commercial product or a theory shown to be accurate by experimental data. Japanese scientific contributions have so far been less influential than American contributions in terms of citation, but generally attract more international attention as time goes on. This has been the case in fields such as electronics, agriculture and food science, and organic chemistry. These are fields where Japanese industrialised science is prominent.

Perhaps the problem is that foreign academic researchers are seeking out published academic papers rather than the unpublished, industrialised scientific findings of the private sector. Whatever the case, in the fields mentioned above Japan exceeded the United States in 1985 in terms of the frequency of citation, according to a study based on *SCI (Science Citation Index)* (Japanese Government, Ministry of Education: 1991). This database includes approximately a hundred Japanese journals out of a possible 4000 science and technology journals published in Japan (Hicks et al.: 1992, 116).

In most fields, Japanese scientific research has come close to the world average, but in terms of the frequency of citation there is still a large gap of 70 per cent between Japanese and American papers (Negishi & Adachi: 1991). It is, however, difficult to assess the contribution of industrial laboratories to publishable academic research. Some research based on interviews with company scientists suggests that much of their work is published in the Japanese language as conference papers (roughly three-quarters of total publishable outputs), so that they are rarely suitable for citation in international journals (Hicks & Hirooka: 1991). Conference presentations can be of variable quality whereas articles submitted to journals need to reach a certain standard.

Internationalisation

The extent to which Japanese scientists have been internationalised, and thus share their know-how with the rest of the world, can be measured by the language used in publishing their research output. According to a poll conducted by the Japan Science Council, 42.3 per cent of academic scientists write their major works in English, while 37.7 per cent do so mainly in Japanese (Japan Science Council: 1991, 34–5). In science departments, more than three-quarters of Japanese academic scientists write their papers in English. In most of the social sciences and humanities, as well as in the more local sciences of ecology and geology, however, researchers write in Japanese for a Japanese academic audience. Most scholars have never written in English. This has been mainly due to the difficulty of translating their subject-matter into English. As a result, their work never enjoys the international recognition which it might deserve.

The number of citations may not necessarily reflect the importance of a paper, but may reflect the social system in which science is practised. Scholars in most social sciences, humanities, and the local sciences form their own citation groups in the Japanese language and entirely different approaches to the discipline and scholarship occur. Some may claim that they are better equipped to gather information world-wide as they are able to read major European languages without much difficulty, in addition to comprehending Japanese and often Chinese sources. But those who attempt to make Japanese scholarship available to an international audience find the task is a formidable one.

Most Japanese academic researchers are willing to invite foreigners into their faculty and graduate schools; 88.7 per cent of non-scientists agree to the appointment of foreigners as faculty members, while 72.8 per cent of scientists also agree. This difference may be interpreted as reflecting a greater need for foreign languages in non-science fields.

Considering Japan's geographical and cultural isolation from the West, it is not surprising to find that there is much less international collaboration between Japanese and foreigners in terms of the number of co-authored articles. In 1984 only 6.7 per cent of articles by Japanese were internationally co-authored. Furthermore, Japanese collaborations were mostly limited to American scientists (Luukkonen et al.: 1992, 116). In certain contexts 'internationalisation' can merely mean a strengthening of US–Japan relations rather than an opening-up of dialogue with the rest of the world.

The private industrial laboratory, where the bulk of Japanese R&D occurs, is even more isolated. While a typical American corporate laboratory has an average 7 per cent international co-authorship, for a Japanese corporate laboratory the figure hovered around 2 per cent for much of the 1980s, though it gradually increased to 6 per cent in 1989, reflecting the trend by Japanese industry towards internationalisation. It also shows that despite the hype, 'internationalisation' in Japan has tended to be fairly superficial and mainly aimed at improving language skills and increased familiarity with foreigners. Hence the frustration of Americans who wish to learn from Japan.

As Japan reaches the twenty-first century, politicians and members of the scientific community have become more convinced than ever that restructuring and investing in R&D infrastructure and international cooperation will be the key to Japan's future. There are plans to have at least one foreign researcher in every research unit or laboratory in Japan, and some go as far as calling for foreign researchers to make up one-third of the total number of researchers (Tanagaki: 1998).

The University–Industry Relationship

Overseas students may attend Japanese universities to learn from Japan but the reality is that much of the S&T knowledge is held by private corporations. Japanese corporations have long regarded the country's universities as providers of human resources for their own in-house research centres and production sites rather than as places to go to have research done. Indeed, many Japanese companies have turned to American universities for basic research before their own (*Economist*: 1986; *Business Week*: 1984; *Business Japan*: 1986), and until 1989 Japanese companies had spent more on American universities than those in Japan. Thus, internationalisation of R&D may be prompted more by a lack of confidence in the research function of Japanese universities than a desire to share knowledge with other nations.

How did this situation arise? The tendency to oppose anything which might be construed as linking research to private profit was the product of student unrest in the late 1960s and Japan's postwar academic culture. It has only been since 1983 that national universities have been able to jointly undertake research with private companies. Joint university–industry research is slowly increasing but it has been a long time coming. The increased blurring between academic and commercial research interests, as well as the intense competition between the United States and Japan in technology, have been singled out as major factors for this change in attitudes and policies (Koizumi: 1993).

There is some empirical evidence of this transformation. Between 1983 and 1987, national university–industry joint projects increased from 56 to 396 (Kinmonth: 1989, 488). To see this quantitatively in terms of publications, university–industry co-authorship increased over the period 1984 to 1989 from 16 per cent to 21 per cent. During this time, Japanese corporations shifted the focus of research expenditure for university cooperation from the United States to Japan, as the result of the 1989 abolition of a law that had discouraged Japanese public universities from being involved in profit-making private ventures. Since then, it has been possible for public universities to openly admit to accepting donations from private industry. Those in engineering-related fields are more willing to accept such funds than their colleagues in science, who still cling to the ideals of academic freedom where they are free to select their own research topics. And as for industry, even though the climate for university–industry collaboration is gradually changing, the private sector is still reluctant to trust the research capability of Japanese universities, as evidenced by the lack of science cities with a truly dependable university as their hub. It is only exceptionally good university scientists who are sought out for their advice by Japanese industry and provided with support.

Japanese Graduate Programs

We have so far established quite a complex picture of the state of research in Japan and come to the realisation that 'quality' is often relative. Let us next take the viewpoint of a 'consumer', a graduate student, and attempt to measure the strength of academic science in terms of education, mainly at graduate school level. The prewar Japanese graduate school was rather superficial, lacking links to any degree program and only providing a shelter for unemployed academics. In the postwar period, the Occupation Forces intended to reform it by modelling it after the style of the American graduate school. Unfortunately, the Japanese scientific community did not have a very deep understanding of the American graduate system and the postwar reforms remained underdeveloped. Academics who have experienced the American system firsthand in the postwar period have pushed for further reform of the Japanese system but it was only as late as 1982 that teaching fellowships were officially approved.

The Japanese graduate program was developed as a training ground for academic science. Under the control of the Ministry of Education, it did not develop into the professional schools that the industrial world desired. In the meantime, other ministries, such as MITI and the Science and Technology Agency, which were dissatisfied with the purely academic nature of the Japanese graduate school, tried to establish a new style of professional school at graduate level. Such attempts were opposed by the Ministry of Education and the plans were never realised. This inter-ministry conflict could also be seen in many other areas as well.

The industrial world was slow to recognise the value of the American style of graduate training, as industrial leaders were graduates of the old system and tended to look down on the product of the new American-oriented system. Thus, the Japanese industrial community has for some time failed to recognise the value of the new graduate schools that were established in the 1950s. However, in the early 1960s, with the boom in S&T, industry began to appreciate the higher levels of graduate training and hired master degree holders. Companies enrolled their newly-recruited bachelor degree holders in master degree programs or built strong ties with bright graduate students by providing industrial fellowships. The loan of laboratory and office equipment to academics by Japanese firms also served to form informal links between the university and industry sectors.

This is not to say that many Japanese and Western corporations viewed graduate training in universities highly in those days. Bachelor degree and master degree holders were treated in a similar way, master degree holders being judged a mere two years more senior on the pay scale. Despite this lack of financial incentive there has always been a tendency, on the part of students, to aim for higher educational qualifications though there is some doubt whether this will continue (Arai: 1992). In Japan, the best time for employment prospects for students is immediately after graduation and usually before they reach the age of twenty-five. Those who go on to graduate school or study overseas for lengthy periods are sometimes seen as going against the system and risk damaging their future job prospects. Many major Japanese firms prefer to hire their future managers and engineers from fresh university graduates rather than recruit older engineers with experience obtained elsewhere (Sakakibara & Westney: 1985, 5).

Higher education at the graduate level depends on the academic sector, which is far more poorly equipped than industrial laboratories. Schools of engineering produce about 13 000 master graduates per year (Japanese Government, Science and Technology Agency: 1992, 201) of whom 80 per cent are recruited to work in research laboratories of private enterprises. However, PhD programs are still not well developed and private industry has yet to fully recognise the value of doctoral degrees. Hence, those who complete master degrees tend not to go on to PhD programs but prefer to find permanent positions in private corporations. However, company engineers of academic orientation can write PhD dissertations using the much better equipment found in corporate laboratories. By submitting these dissertations to universities they can obtain a PhD degree without any coursework. In the 1990s, conferrals of this type of thesis-PhD outnumbered PhDs with a course-work component. This trend could lead to the eventual collapse of coursework-PhD programs. The entrance quota for PhD programs are not generally filled by native Japanese students, so the remaining places can often be given to foreign students, mainly Asian students from China, South Korea and Taiwan. Some engineering departments have aggressively recruited top engineering students from Asian countries in order to make up for the shortfall in numbers. Scholarships are used to attract such students and some teaching is now done in English to over-come the communication gap. These students now dominate a number of Japanese PhD programs and admission to graduate programs has become more competitive. Two of the spin-offs of this situation have been an increased number of publications, and higher quality (Normile: 1993a).

The increase in thesis-PhDs reflects the diminishing attractiveness of university graduate schools to young researchers. Overall, it appears that native Japanese doctoral students are decreasing. Students are being wooed by the private sector and, given that salaries do not increase markedly upon obtaining a PhD, there is not a great deal of incentive to do so.

However, the need for more home-grown technological innovation has encouraged increasingly favourable attitudes on the part of industry to graduate school education. This change of attitude dates from the 1980s, when Japanese industry found fewer research innovations to borrow from the United States and many companies wanted to have high-quality researchers in their central laboratories. Industry has tried to maintain connections with the academic sector by donating equip-ment and recruiting the best students. Although slow to recognise the value of graduate school training, companies have increasingly moved from recruiting bachelor degree holders to master graduates, and per-haps in the future they may even recruit more from doctorate programs. At present the latter are often viewed as being overly specialised.

Why does the private sector not try to bring market forces to bear and remedy the situation? One of the reasons why Japanese firms have been slow to make engineering education more practical and directly related to their needs is that they value the flexibility of new engineering graduates more highly than any mechanical skills which they might possess prior to joining a company. It has been found that the Japanese undergraduate engineering curriculum is more general than that of the United States, with little choice in the way of course options. Assessment tends to be in the form of written exams which emphasise general theory

(Westney & Sakakibara: 1986, 26). Perhaps this is to be expected, as most academics teaching in Japanese engineering programs lack outside engineering experience (Kinmonth: 1989, 486). This may not be a major problem, as technical skills can be incorporated into the initial training of recruits and many will follow technical specialties considerably different from those they received in training at university (Kinmonth: 1986, 411). And after an initial period spent in R&D, they are likely to take up management positions (Sakakibara & Westney: 1985, 7–9).

The Japanese graduate school has not been as fully developed as its American equivalent in terms of coursework. It tends to be maintained as a laboratory-based, apprenticeship-style system, in which doctoral degree students assist master degree students. Furthermore, the graduate school system lacks mobility, with universities tending to admit their own graduates into a master's program. While this allows students to proceed quickly to research, this system does not allow students to experience a range of research environments and teaching approaches (Westney & Sakakibara: 1986, 27). While Japanese students from other universities may choose not to enter the graduate schools of alternative universities in great numbers, problems arise when foreign students represent a large number of the graduate entrants. It is not only that they have a different educational background, but it is difficult to maintain an apprenticeship-type system when the senior students are foreigners and lacking in the communication skills necessary to pass on their knowledge (Arai: 1992). It is imperative that there are Japanese doctoral candidates, for laboratories often rely on such a labour force to sustain their research programs. This is no different from universities in other parts of the world.

Even under the prewar system of science schools, doctorates were conferred early in a researcher's career. Now the degree program has been very much internationalised and has converged towards the American program in order to facilitate international exchange. This is not the case in all non-science schools, such as the social sciences and humanities. In these areas, the prewar notion of doctorates being conferred at the end of a scholar's career still prevails. Since most professors do not themselves have doctorates, they are reluctant to bestow doctoral degrees on others. Under the postwar graduate program system, a master's degree is usually given after two years of graduate schooling and the presentation of a master's thesis. Many master graduates remain in graduate school and enter the doctoral program for three years, after which they have normally completed the nominal coursework required of them. But doctorates are not conferred, and the candidates are not expected to have written a PhD thesis. PhD programs in the social sciences and humanities are nominal and candidates tend to be marking time waiting for an academic position rather than following any particular program of coursework. Such young researchers, who are denied the dream of a PhD, often become frustrated, but unless doctorates are conferred on their old professors, real PhD programs will be difficult to establish. There are some fields in which a small number of students are awarded a PhD, but these tend to be areas where international contact is frequent. So it is that after forty years of experience under the postwar graduate system, there has not yet been significant improvement in the encouragement and nurturing of doctoral study.

Universities as Places of Research

Some Japanese academics are able to devote themselves to research rather than combine it with teaching. There are research professors who have positions in university-affiliated research institutes where they enjoy academic freedom without being overwhelmed by any heavy teaching duties. They are perhaps the legacy of the 1950s and 1960s Laboratory Democracy Movement, in which young academic scientists promoted a network of common-use university-affiliated research institutes. These young researchers found it impossible, however, to conduct big academic science within the constraints of limited university budgets. Since the 1970s research institutes have been reorganised as national research institutes without university affiliation and are directly administered by the Ministry of Education. Examples are the Institute of Space and Astronautical Science and the Tokyo Astronomical Observatory. 'Public' science includes such national institutes. Not all researchers see this autonomy from universities as a positive thing.

Although there are advantages such as larger research budgets and more project-oriented research, some scientists consider the loss of university affiliation as being a loss of autonomy in research. There is also a fear that by cutting links with universities, national institutes will lose touch with the fresh ideas of young graduate students. Perhaps national institutes are the only places where Japanese can viably conduct big, academic science, but it may be too early to assess whether this is so.

Existing social arrangements in universities may not be conducive to research. A recent survey of Japanese academic scientists conducted by the Japan Science Council found that natural scientists were most critical of the existing university hierarchy. The majority (67.8 per cent) opposed the existing system. While more than half of scientists (natural science, engineering, agriculture and medicine) would like to adopt the appointment system of American universities and have more postdoctoral fellows instead of assistants, introduce associate professorships, and have more inter-collegial exchange of faculty members, less than half of non-scientists (law, economics and humanities) were in favour. This indicates that the scientific community is more open to change and internationally oriented than the non-science academic community.

Yet it would be difficult not to agree that reforms are necessary if Japanese universities are to fulfil the research function which has been expected of them. Many university laboratories are outdated and underfunded, and increasingly unable to attract young researchers. Will this impact on Japan's industrial competitiveness and what are some of the causes?

Many Japanese university appointments are, like other forms of employment, life-long. In spite of the personal advantages of the life-long employment system, many academics think that such a system has problems. More than half of junior academics (lecturer and assistant) are in favour of the introduction of a fixed-term appointment system for all academics, though less than half of senior academics (professor and assistant professor) support it. In medical departments, 55 per cent support a fixed-term appointment system, reflecting the keen competition for academic posts.

In order to promote the research function of universities, Japanese scientists generally think it important to promote interdisciplinary cooperation and international collaboration. This is particularly so in scientific disciplines, especially medicine. Economists feel that interdiscipline and an international outlook have not been developed in their research practice, reflecting the sharp party division between Marxists and modern economists.

Despite the dissatisfaction with the present state of affairs in Japanese academia and the reform-mindedness of Japanese scientists, the reform measures may not be adopted very quickly as the academic bureaucracy has stifled radical reforms in the past and will continue to do so in the future, as long as the Japanese academic is located in a part of the civil service bureaucracy which does not find research very congenial.

Existing structures within faculties tend to discourage individualism: a university faculty member is not considered to be an independent unit but a member of a team. One professor, one or two associate professors, assistants and graduate students are grouped together as an administrative unit modelled on the bureaucratic hierarchy. Though individual efforts have been made to overcome bureaucratic constraints, no one is entirely free of the barriers it places on research activity, especially interdisciplinary cooperation. Those reform-minded scientists who are inspired by the leading edge of American research, accuse the Japanese scientific community of being less supportive of individual competition, avoiding headlong competition, and disliking individual aggressiveness. As a result, only the practice of normal science prevails and there is less

chance of new paradigms emerging. Rather than conclude that the
Japanese lack creativity, one could argue strongly that the education system may not be particularly conducive to it. Where do we lay the blame?

When one looks at the history of university reform in Japan, the lack of
dynamism and deviation from the norm is striking and the same can be
said for research. Most academic research is conducted by public universities where control by the Japanese bureaucracy in the form of the
Ministry of Education, prevails. The major role of bureaucrats in public
universities is that of quality control, which tends not to tolerate deviation from the standard. Consequently, the budget structure of research
often involves so much forward-planning that a dramatic breakthrough
in research is unlikely to occur. While democratic distribution of
research funds over many areas ensures that all the academic community
is equally treated and few complaints are heard, there is only enough to
give a measure of encouragement to everyone. Mediocrity ensues. Perhaps this sort of democracy is not compatible with the nurturing of
scientific excellence. The equal distribution of resources, while 'democratic' in nature, prevents highly talented researchers from greatly
expanding their projects. The combination of a life-long employment
system and the chair system mean that the mobility of researchers is
severely hampered and fast promotion is difficult to achieve. Bright,
young researchers sometimes look overseas to further their careers
(Yamamoto: 1993, 180).

Whether universities can become more diversified and keep these
researchers in Japan is a moot point. In the past, universities have tended
to aspire to have research infrastructure similar to that of the University
of Tokyo. But Japan cannot afford to have a national research university
in each prefecture, and from the viewpoint of education, it may not be
desirable. Yet it would be difficult to introduce a two-tiered system of
teaching and research universities, as such a move would be perceived as
working against 'democratic' ideals and lead to a certain élitism in the
higher education sector (Yamamoto: 1993, 181–2).

The private enterprise approach to science seems to have finally infil-
trated even the Ministry of Education which increasingly encourages
universities and researchers to compete for funds on the basis of merit
(Yamamoto: 1993, 181). Whatever happens, Japan is unlikely to return
to the prewar structure of S&T where basic science was more con-
spicuous than it is now.

The pace of the development of private science in the postwar industrial boom only spilled over into academia in the 1990s. The postwar
American model provides no magic formula for determining the right
balance of public, academic and private science. Perhaps the Japanese
postwar privatisation model may indeed prevail in the twenty-first

century, if the trend towards privatisation of science is any indication. This trend is discernible in South Korea, where government funding of R&D dropped from 44 per cent to 16 per cent during the 1990s, a figure similar to that in Japan (Raitberger: 1994). Japanese funding for scientific research reached a record 15.1 trillion yen ($US118 billion) in the 1996 financial year. The private sector contributed 78.9 per cent (11.9 trillion yen), whereas that of local and national governments declined to 21 per cent, a drop of 4 per cent compared to the year before (*Japan Washington Watch*: 1997).

The 'Hollowing Out' of Japanese Industry

Where will R&D be conducted in future? In Japan there is no room for complacency. In the 1990s the symptoms of industrial decline became all too obvious. In the early 1990s, at the time of the so-called 'bubble economy', the Japanese establishment became concerned that the newly-graduated top scientists and engineers avoided pursuing careers in manufacturing, and opted for more lucrative careers in banking. Then, during a 'hollowing-out' phase, Japanese industries moved their manufacturing activities to other parts of Asia in order to combat the appreciation of the Japanese yen and the high cost of local production.

Just as there were American claims of Japanese free-riding, Japanese industry has also been accused by Asian countries of being reluctant to transfer technology and of being content to merely exploit their cheaper labour. In reality, however, it is inevitable that Japan's technology and even its R&D function are destined to move with the onset of the hollowing-out phenomenon. This will affect basic and applied research in Japan and it may signal the de-industrialisation of Japan and a shift in the centre of industrialised science. Japan has undergone an unprecedented economic recession in the late 1990s, and firms have reduced their intake of graduate recruits. On the other hand, Japanese-trained Asian science and technology students have returned to their respective countries and found good jobs, meeting the needs of the Japanese factories which have been relocated there. The Japanese-educated personnel provide effective liaison between local staff and Japanese management. Their salaries may be half those received by Japanese in equivalent positions back in Japan, but they are nevertheless considerably higher than salaries received by other locals.

Is this sort of de-industrialisation symptomatic of a central shift in science? The centre of academic science has moved from one place to another throughout history. In the twentieth century we experienced a shift from Germany to the United States. What will happen in the twenty-first century? As long as the language of science remains English, the centre may not move from the United States in the foreseeable future. However, the central shift of industrialised science is quite different.

The centre in industrialised science is not so precisely defined as that of academic science. In academic science, a principal role of any discipline is to produce an academic journal which sets the paradigm and standard of what scientific work in the discipline should be concerned about. Workers all over the world conform to this standard, not only when writing scientific papers but also with respect to content, by imitating the style of the existing research. That is, journals help define 'normal science'.

In the case of industrialised science, which is mainly practised in corporate research laboratories, the centre does not function properly – it is not needed. Still, there is a kind of network existing among corporations in contractual relationships, manufacturing under licence, or between transnational firms. In this sense, the centre attracts a number of researchers and engineers, when and where they are required. Thus, the United States and Japan are going to attract less people, since the sites of production are increasingly found in the newly developing nations of Asia.

However, the centre may become less meaningful when Internet networking replaces top-down cause-and-effect linear relationships between the centre and periphery. The network of less hierarchical, weak relationships among transnational enterprises may well facilitate technology transfer much more easily than we have hitherto thought. It is primarily individual-based rather than company-based information transfer. Hence, this electronic network business will serve to diminish the advantage of the strong centre of multinational companies, supplemented by networks which centre on scattered workplaces, where scientists and engineers communicate with each other using non-open, non-electronic media.

Conclusion

In summary, this suggests not only that the research function of universities is a question of the allocation of adequate resources, but it is also one of a changing role for universities. Stronger links with industry are likely to promote greater research activity, but the very structure of the Japanese education system and the Ministry of Education policies that define it require change. An investment in such research by industry and government willingness to undertake reforms means, at the very least, an investment in Japan's future workforce (Nakayama & Low: 1997).

The Japanese neglect of basic science has mainly been criticised outside Japan by American science policy-makers and journalists who are concerned about the loss of intellectual property rights. In contrast, Japanese practitioners of academic science bemoan the poor financial state of universities. Both of these charges reflect how, in postwar Japan, academic science has been overshadowed by private science, particularly in corporate laboratories. This has been a feature of technological development in Japan (see Table 7.2).

Despite the grievances of Japanese academic scientists, there is a constant though slow, upward trend in Japan's contribution to the world production of academic papers. Japan's productivity is close to the European average. Internationalisation occurred in physics and mathematics in the years shortly after Japan's wartime defeat, but now academic papers in engineering science emanating from Japan are frequently cited in international journals, indicating that other nations such as the United States are taking notice of Japan's research effort and its achievements in the commercialisation of technology.

To what extent will the trend towards the privatisation of science affect R&D in Japan? S&T activity was largely privatised in Japan's postwar period. Privatisation in this sense is not a process in which the institutional affiliation of research workers is transferred from national to private ownership. Research activities conducted in Japanese universities, and mainly public universities at that, may not be so easily privatised and moved offshore. However, one trend which can be identified is what can be called 'knowledge deregulation', that is, a lifting of government constraints on research activities. The Ministry of Education no longer needs to be concerned about controlling leftist ideology in the education sector. University sectors are now able to conduct their own reforms without the overbearing intervention of the bureaucracy. To what extent they succeed will partly depend on overcoming interministry rivalries that are outlined in later chapters.

CHAPTER 2

Cooperation versus Competition

National Projects and Japan's Science Cities

Introduction

Chalmers Johnson's classic study (1982) of Japan's Ministry of International Trade and Industry (MITI) has been of seminal importance in our understanding of the Japanese political economy. The Japan that he and other 'revisionist' thinkers, such as Clyde Prestowitz, James Fallows, Karel van Wolferen and Laura D'Andrea Tyson, describe is one which largely acts as one, under the administrative guidance of bureaucrats. Features such as close government–business ties, *keiretsu* (corporate alliances), trade barriers and industry-targeting make the Japanese economy different and renders it not comparable to other countries (Callon: 1995, 198–9). But, as Scott Callon argues convincingly, Johnson's study is now out of date and even more recent studies, such as Marie Anchordoguy's *Computers Inc.* (1989), focuses on the period up to the early 1970s. Callon's own study starts where Johnson leaves off, the year of 1975.

According to Callon, the revisionists overemphasise the positive effects of state intervention in markets, overemphasise the role of bureaucratic power, and under-recognise the pluralistic nature of the Japanese political economy. Viewed in this way, perhaps Japan's society is not so different from other societies. As other chapters in this book argue, variation and conflict can be found throughout Japanese society. Callon looks at Japanese high-tech consortia (VLSI (Very Large-Scale Integration), Supercomputer, Fifth Generation, and TRON (The Real-time Operating System Nucleus)) in detail and finds that there are extremely high levels of conflict and competition, which ultimately control the consortia and inhibit them from meeting their goals. In addition, Japan's success in the 1980s meant a change in the conditions under which MITI operated. MITI had to contend with confident firms who no longer felt they needed MITI; the firms learnt that it was easier to catch up with the research frontier than to lead it; and trade pressures limited MITI's options for action (Callon: 1995, 148).

There has been some doubt cast on the effectiveness and continuing relevance of the industrial policies of MITI, especially given the 'hollowing out' of manufacturing in Japan, and the subsequent Asian economic crisis. During the 1980s there was a rapid increase in R&D expenditure by major Japanese firms (Nakaoka: 1992), with private industry accounting for about 70 per cent of total R&D expenditure, the government being responsible for less than 20 per cent, and the academic sector making up the remainder (*Science and Technology in Japan*: 1995). The economic recession caused many companies to cut back on R&D expenditure and this was the major reason for Japan recording its first decrease in R&D expenditure in thirty years in 1993 (*STA Today*: 1995). Previously, Japanese companies tended to maintain or even increase R&D outlays during economic downturns, in the hope that profits would soon return (*Australia–Japan Economic Institute Economic Bulletin*: 1994; Peters II: 1993). The magnitude of the late 1990s recession discouraged such spending.

In response to the fall in corporate spending, the Japanese government has indicated a willingness to step in to revitalise the economy and ensure that it remains competitive in the future. This says much about the importance of government–industry relations in Japan. Does the close relationship encourage more competition, cooperation or both? Collaborative arrangements are often inspired by international competition, but does competition at the local level get in the way? How do the Japanese deal with the tension between competition and cooperation? While many ask such questions, they are yet to be answered satisfactorily (Smilor et al.: 1988).

This chapter outlines the origins of MITI's national program of large-scale R&D projects. It focuses on the Fifth Generation Computer Project, and asks whether such projects have involved more competition than cooperation. It then looks at Japanese S&T growth centres as more recent manifestations of cooperation between universities, government and the private sector. While there is a growing literature on the topic of government–industry relations, ties between universities and the private sector are a recent phenomenon in Japan, and studies of the tripartite relationship are few. We look at some of this literature, then examine a range of S&T growth centres (from science cities to S&T parks) to explore the methods and strategies which the Japanese are adopting to facilitate the strengthening of university–industry–government relations.

MITI's National R&D Projects

'Technological reform' was the slogan of the late 1950s, and scientific progress was felt to play an important role in economic progress and the improvement of the Japanese standard of living. The standard of Japan's science-based technology in the 1960s was not high, however, and most basic industrial technology was imported. In addition, the amount of GNP invested in research, while gradually increasing, was still low compared with that of other industrialised countries, and it was feared that the gap between world technological standards and those of Japan would widen even more.

Government subsidies had been part of attempts to promote technological reform in industry since before the Second World War. Soon after the war, MITI and the Science and Technology Agency (STA) resumed the practice of awarding government subsidies. MITI's program of large-scale projects was part of such technological reform. From 1951 the newly-created Industrial Technology Agency (ITA) (Kogyō Gijutsu-chō) sponsored collaborative research and also designated research. Designated research refers to the system in which the most economically urgent topics of experimental research are specified by the head of the ITA, and a budget and personnel are allocated. This system of support for private companies was gradually revised and evolved into the large-scale project system.

The 1963 report on the findings of the Industrial Technology section of the Committee for the Survey on Industry (Sangyō Kōzō Chōsakai, Sangyō Gijutsu Bukai) stated that Japan was facing a period of change from technological development that relied on the adaptation of foreign technologies to that of original development, and maintained that businesses would have to increase their efforts to assist this development. The report also pointed out that the percentage of government expenditure on research was still far behind that of other industrialised countries, and there was a need to increase government investment. As appropriate policies, the report suggested that government research and subsidies for private companies be concentrated in areas of technology where private companies were weakest, and also that a system be established to promote the efficient development of technology central to industry (Tsukahara & Kamatani: 1995). The following ways of encouraging research were recommended: (1) the expansion of tax subsidies and funding; (2) the establishment of a taxation system which facilitated the allocation of funds for the development of technology; (3) the establishment of a commissioned research system; and (4) free use of national institutions and patents when necessary.

In response to this report, the Board of Industrial Technology (Kogyō Gijutsuin) established a system in 1964 aimed at funding commissioned experimental research in industrial technology. The following areas were identified as requiring government assistance and project development: (1) MHD (magneto-hydrodynamic) electricity generation; (2) desalination of sea water; (3) coal gas transformation (*sekitan chika gasu ka*); (4) automation of coal mining; (5) direct current power transmission; (6) new materials (high pressure, high temperature technology); (7) electronic calculators and electronic translators; and (8) new processing technology.

In April 1966 the Board of Industrial Technology began the Large-Scale Industrial Technology Research and Development System (Large-Scale Project System). The planned time-scale for each project was set at approximately five years. In the first year, three projects were funded: MHD electricity generation, ultra high-performance electronic calculators, and anti-gas emission measures for the exhaust emitted from thermal power plants. It was also recommended that the project be expanded extensively to include follow-up research relating to the new projects, and that the subsidy system for experimental research in mining engineering technology be strengthened. The establishment of a system to encourage the development of new machinery was also seen to be important.

The following are features of the history of the large-scale R&D project system: (1) it promoted R&D and reinforced government initiatives; (2) it sought to develop key technologies through government–industry cooperation; (3) it was not always linked to commercial profit; (4) its *raison d'être* declined with the growth in private funding of R&D; and (5) it became increasingly difficult to find projects that offered companies the prospect of exploiting the technologies commercially.

MITI Policy in the Late 1970s

In the late 1970s, following the second shock of reduced oil supply following the Iranian Revolution and Iran–Iraq war, Japan experienced a severe recession. The computer industry nevertheless showed a relatively high rate of growth, centred around the mainframe producers of Fujitsu, Hitachi, NEC, Toshiba, and Mitsubishi Electric. Part of the reason was the support given to the industry by MITI under 1971 legislation to promote manufacture of electrical machinery, in the form of various tax reductions, loans and directed cartels. MITI also established a variety of subsidy schemes, and projects such as the VLSI Project (1977–80, with a budget of 291 million yen), the Pattern Information Processing System Project (1971–80, budget of 220 million yen), and the Next Generation Basic Technology Project (1979–83, budget of 222 million yen). However, the world mainframe market was dominated by IBM and Japanese computer manufacturers had little choice but to devote themselves to catching up with IBM.

The Fifth Generation Computer Project

As Sawada has documented (1996), the Institute for New Generation Computer Technology (ICOT) was established on 16 April 1982 with central responsibility for the Fifth Generation Computer Project. ICOT was funded by Hitachi, Fujitsu, NEC, Toshiba, Mitsubishi, Oki, Sharp and NTT, eight companies which formed the core membership of the Institute. The first chairman of the board of directors was Yamamoto Takushin, president of Fujitsu, and the first executive director was former MITI official, Yoshioka Tadashi. In June 1982 the ICOT Research Institute began operations with Fuchi Kazuhiro as director. The Institute had three sections. There were forty-one researchers, mainly from the core manufacturers, who were assigned to the project for a fixed term of three years, although there were also some personnel recruited specifically for the project by the companies. The manufacturers also stationed personnel to construct the hardware commissioned by ICOT and to install and implement the software. The Fifth Generation Computer Project, with a time-scale of ten years, aimed at the development of a revolutionary computer system using large-scale parallel processing. Fuchi later stated that 'the project was planned to develop general-use computers for the 1990s'.

The ICOT machine was established as a functioning example of parallel inference architecture, but it was destined not to be evaluated particularly highly outside the Institute. Why was this so? From the mid-1980s the processing speed and memory capacity of personal computers increased rapidly, and workstations were popularised that possessed unbeatable cost-performance advantages when compared with mainframes. Various intelligent processing techniques that had been seen as only possible with parallel inference were realised with the advent of these mini-computers and user interfaces like the Internet. In addition, so-called 'soft computing', such as fuzzy inference and neural networks, appeared in the computer engineering field. The Fifth Generation Computer Project did not possess the flexibility to encompass these changes. In spite of these developments, artificial intelligence has not performed as well as originally expected. Since the latter half of the 1980s people became increasingly aware of the difficulty of implementing common rules in artificial intelligence.

Furthermore, it could be argued that the expectations for the project were too high. MITI conducted an extensive media campaign in an attempt to win public approval in its negotiations with the Ministry of

Finance, and this stimulated both public opinion, foreign computer scientists, and also influenced the researchers themselves. The 'dream' began to lose its appeal about 1985 and, in fact, J. Marshall Unger (1987) records the existence of rumours regarding the project's cancellation. Troubled by the gap between technological prospects and the policy framework, in addition to a fall in public support, the researchers faced growing isolation. There was also the declining enthusiasm of private companies and cuts in public funding, lack of personnel due to the unusual growth in the computer industry, and a lower private sector profile when this growth slowed. Fuchi and Uchida reduced the scale of the project.

The project formally came to an end in March 1995. Despite being the subject of much criticism centring on the lack of commercial results, some participants have argued that the primary goal was to carry out government-funded basic research aimed at making a significant contribution to international science, rather than a narrower desire to improve Japan's industrial competitiveness (Nakamura & Shibuya: 1996).

Cooperation or Competition?

Despite the problems of the Fifth Generation Computer Project, industry–government cooperation in Japan has been hailed as providing useful models for the rest of the world. This can be traced to the announcement by MITI in 1981 of its Fifth Generation Computing Systems' ten-year program. Like many of Japan's national research projects, the Fifth Generation Computing Systems Project (later known as the Fifth Generation Computer Project) has tended to focus on basic, pre-commercial technologies. This emphasis, combined with long gestation periods, high risks, heavy capital outlays, economies of scale, large leaps in learning and potential commercial spin-offs, seem to make good sense of inter-firm cooperation. Government steps in where market incentives are insufficient to inspire collective action (Okimoto: 1989, 68–9). Okimoto tentatively concludes that Japan's national research projects contribute most by: identifying potential technologies for R&D cooperation; promoting information generation and exchange; providing R&D funds to the private sector; encouraging long-term development of pre-commercial technologies; diffusing those technologies; and equalising technological capabilities. Their value might therefore lie as much in their secondary effects as the ostensible primary goal of advancing cutting-edge technology (Okimoto: 1989, 72).

Okimoto's findings are echoed by Ray & Buisseret, who suggest that the West misunderstood what the Japanese meant by collaboration (Ray & Buisseret: 1995). Hane has argued convincingly that R&D consortia in

Japan are aimed at enhancing incentives for competition, rather than imposing cooperation. In his words, 'procompetitive coordination rather than precompetitive cooperation is the dominant strategy' (Hane: 1995, 85). Duplication in research by members of consortia is, in this view of things, desirable since it promotes competition.

Nurturing Creativity and New Industries

The Japanese government has been concerned by the declining rate of growth of new businesses in the small and medium enterprise category. Whereas it had been about 7 per cent in the 1960s and 1970s, it fell to 4 per cent by the early 1990s. This contrasts with the United States, where bright young engineers working in large corporations start up their own spin-off venture businesses. In the absence of such entrepreneurial spirit among the Japanese (Moritani: 1995), the government hopes that technology from both domestic and foreign sources will stimulate the creation of new industries.

The government has also encouraged cooperation between universities, government research institutes and private industry, in order to stimulate innovation and pool its resources. This has been against the backdrop of reduced domestic production, expanded overseas production, and the growth of low-productivity, non-manufacturing industry within Japan.

As mentioned earlier, Ray & Buisseret suggest that Japan's use of collaboration has been misunderstood by the West. The widespread view that MITI's use of Engineering Research Associations (ERAs) during the 1960s and 1970s to catch up with American and European computer technology requires more careful analysis. ERAs were more motivated by the desire to close the gap with the West and to fight off foreign threats such as that posed by IBM, rather than by any strong desire to cooperate with fellow Japanese researchers. In the absence of such fears, the will to cooperate disappeared. Ray & Buisseret point to the importance of informal networks of communication among Japanese firms (Schaede: 1995), which are, in turn, 'energised' by strong rivalry between firms and different ministries (Ray & Buisseret: 1995). It is perhaps these informal networks rather than any formal arrangements that may hold the key to understanding Japanese R&D collaboration. Unfortunately, it is the formal arrangements in the form of cooperative R&D projects which have tended to attract so much attention in the West.

Itō argues that the effectiveness of ERAs lay in their use by MITI to reinforce its regulation of industry, rather than in their ability to promote technological development. While the ERAs were ostensibly associations consisting of companies interested in carrying out joint research, they also served to organise major industrial sectors, effectively mobilising, under the control of MITI, the resources of companies in each sector for their common good. ERAs facilitated the policy process, helped circulate information, and at the same time encouraged competition (Itō: 1991).

Forms of Cooperative Research in Japan

As elsewhere, cooperative arrangements are formed for basic research, generic technology research, and applied R&D. Multiple-firm consortia are often used to pursue early research though the actual benefits of such consortia are not clear (Smilor & Gibson: 1991). Joint ventures between a Japanese firm and an overseas firm occur when it comes to applied R&D, and non-research activities such as technology sharing and production. It is not surprising that universities tend to participate in basic rather than applied research. Why have such arrangements occurred? Japan is strong in the 'private' science of company laboratories, and much weaker in academic science, as practised in the academic sector of universities and affiliated institutes.

The 1990s economic recession has forced companies to re-evaluate their corporate R&D strategies. More than ever before, product development is being tailored to consumer needs, and companies are focusing on core activities. But the dramatic increases in the cost of developing innovative products and the short life of consumer products has pressured managers to place time limits on research and the evaluation of research results (*Australia–Japan Economic Institute Economic Bulletin*: 1994). Basic research has declined in importance compared to applied research, and many companies have been in the process of restructuring the organisation of corporate R&D. While many companies see the downturn in investment in R&D as a temporary phenomenon, it is clear that there will be a move away from basic research and an emphasis on product development (Japanese Government, Science and International Affairs Bureau: 1994). The Japanese government's proposed increase in R&D funding for the early years of the new millennium may assist basic research conducted in Japanese universities, but Japan is unlikely to return to the pre-Second World War situation of a S&T heavily focused on basic R&D.

The Role of Government

MITI has played a major role in facilitating generic-technology research, such as in the areas of semiconductors and optoelectronics. It has done so by coordinating cooperative research projects, and providing seed

money for emerging technologies. It is significant that the Ministry of
Education has made moves to encourage links between academic institutions and the private sector. This change in attitude on the part of the
ministry is contributing to a blurring of public and private funding and
an increase in research funds to universities. It is also reflected in the
ministry's attempt in 1993 to create a system for joint R&D projects
between national universities and private industry. The system involved
research grants similar to those granted under a program run by the
United States National Science Foundation (NSF) during the period
1978–86. Whereas the NSF Industry/University Cooperative Research
Projects Program supported 100 to 140 projects per year at an annual
cost of $US10 million to $14 million, the Japanese program, in its first
year, involved ninety universities conducting 1392 joint research projects
with 823 firms; 1527 people participated in the projects. In 1993 this was
at a cost of 5.03 billion yen or approximately $US50 million. Research
was mainly in the following areas: materials development (for example,
ceramics) (22.8 per cent), equipment development (for example, micro-
scopes) (19.7 per cent), civil engineering and architecture (14.9 per
cent), software (12.3 per cent), energy development (11.1 per cent),
biotechnology (10.4 per cent), and electronics (8.8 per cent). In terms
of immediate benefits, patent applications were lodged for thirty-
three projects (Japanese Government, Science and International Affairs
Bureau: 1994).

Benefits and Costs

Many academics have resisted ties with private industry lest their quest
for curiosity-driven knowledge become muddied by economic considerations. However, in reality, limited university budgets and obsolete
equipment have probably served to constrain scientists and engineers
more than any association with the private sector ever could. Admittedly,
there are other considerations, such as differences in organisational
structure, policies, and interests of researchers, which create boundaries
between different sectors (Geisler & Rubenstein: 1989).

In an anthropological study of industry–university cooperation in
Japan, Coleman found there were many impediments to cooperation.
Academics sometimes differ from industry researchers in their approaches to communication, which in turn is related to different ideas of
what constitutes research. The motivation to pursue research is also
varied, with industry researchers viewing participation in cooperative
ventures as being of little benefit to their research careers. In their eyes,
basic research would not contribute to corporate profits, and is unlikely
to be of credit to them or their companies. As these findings suggest,

there are very real problems in attempting to bring together industry and academia, given their different goals and orientations (Coleman: 1995).

The next section looks at collaborative relationships in scientific and technical growth centres, ranging from science cities to science and technology parks. The Japanese are determined to encourage cooperation between universities, government research institutes and private industry via these spaces. Is this a desirable way for this cooperation to occur? What factors affect the success of these centres? While it is probably still too early to cast the final word on Tsukuba Science City, and far too early to judge Kansai Science City, we can at least examine the methods and strategies the Japanese adopt to facilitate these cities. It must be remembered, however, that this examination is done against the backdrop of the 'hollowing out' of Japan, which is causing reduction of domestic production, expanded overseas production and the further growth of low-productivity, non-manufacturing industry within Japan.

S&T Growth Centres

There are over a hundred science cities/technopolises/research cores/ industrial brain areas/strategic development areas in Japan at various stages of development, in addition to over a hundred science and technology parks operating in the late 1990s or being planned (see Figure 2.1). This section focuses on attempts by these S&T growth centres to link universities with industry and government research institutes.

In the past, such attempts have been difficult to accomplish. The technopolis strategy was specifically augmented by additional laws to facilitate this in regional areas. Under the *Private Participation Promotion Law* (1986), interest-free bank loans and other funds were provided to encourage the construction of 'research cores', incubators and facilities for telecommunications, conventions and fairs. Research cores are either located in designated technopolises (twenty-six in 1993) or in big cities and they usually consist of facilities for experimental research, research training, information and communications, and venture business incubators. Private firms become tenants in research cores (Hayashi: 1991).

Tsukuba Science City

A major goal of Tsukuba Science City has been to encourage cross-fertilisation of ideas and exchange of information. The KEK National Laboratory for High Energy Physics is one example of large-scale facilities used by researchers from many different organisations. While KEK's facilities have attracted research groups from throughout the

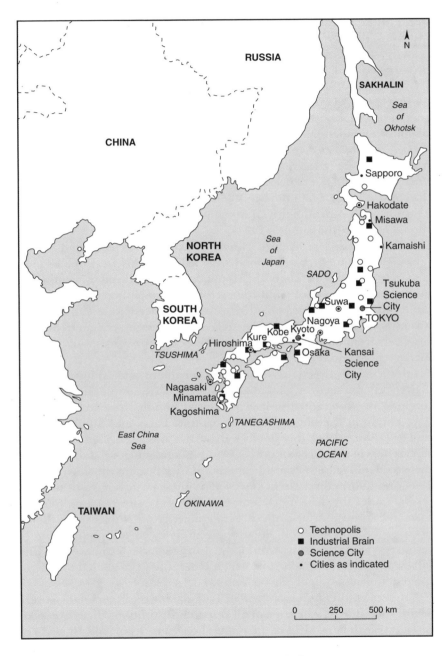

Figure 2.1 Science and technology growth centres in Japan

world, there has been a lack of synergy among other Tsukuba research institutes, despite so many being located in the one place. In order to remedy the situation, since 1976 regular conferences have been held to promote better liaison and encourage research exchange.

The Tsukuba Research Consortium was also established to encourage more interaction with the private sector. Supported by eight core-member companies, the consortium provides facilities and funds for meetings and seminars attended by researchers from government institutes, academia and the private sector. In the late 1980s twenty researchers in their thirties from university, government and industry laboratories first became involved in a number of five-year-long joint projects under the auspices of the consortium. Even in the late 1990s, five such projects were still active. This sort of consortium-driven initiative is likely to become more widespread in Japan (Kawamoto: 1994).

In 1988 Ibaraki prefecture (where Tsukuba is located) and MITI's Japan Development Bank joined with private firms to promote joint research activities through the Tsukuba Research and Development Support Centre, one of eight research cores established by the government. In 1994 the Tsukuba University Advanced Research Alliance was established to promote joint research between academics and researchers from outside the university. These are new systems of research management and organisation.

Interaction between universities, government and industry is now actively encouraged by Tsukuba University, for example, in the actual teaching of postgraduates. Researchers at national research institutes have taught at the university on a part-time basis, and numbered fifty in 1990. Since 1992 this pool of expertise was expanded to include researchers in private laboratories, who supervise doctoral students using the excellent facilities available at laboratories outside the university. In 1994 one hundred researchers served as guest professor/associate professors under this scheme (Kawamoto: 1994). As with research funding from the private sector, these arrangements are increasingly being encouraged. These are all creative attempts to make optimum use of resources while working within the bureaucratic framework of the Japanese education system, one which is definitely not geared to nurturing the individualism of Silicon Valley.

A survey of foreign researchers in Tsukuba for the 1996 financial year found that at least a quarter of all research institutions there accepted foreign researchers. Most of the researchers came from Asia. In terms of nationality Chinese visitors were largest in number, followed by Koreans, Americans, and then researchers from Thailand and the Philippines. The Japanese government is eager to further increase the number of foreign researchers, but much depends on the research environment.

Kansai Science City

Kansai Science City owes more to 'bottom-up' consultation between academic researchers, business leaders and local bureaucrats who have ultimately influenced national planning and policies, than the 'top-down' style which characterises the development of Tsukuba Science City (Shimoda: 1994). The concept of the Kansai Science City was first raised in 1970 by Professor Okuda Azuma, who had previously been president of Kyoto University. The Tsukuba experience made it clear that the private sector needed to be involved with planning at an early stage if the Kansai project was to be a success, as would universities and government institutions. This emphasis on the private sector makes Kansai Science City an interesting example of a privatised science city. Given this momentum, it was fortuitous that the project dovetailed well with plans to build a new $US6 billion Kansai International Airport to service Osaka and beyond. An initial plan for the City was proposed in 1978, with a more detailed pilot plan drawn up by Kyoto, Osaka and Nara prefectures in 1981. To facilitate construction, the Kansai Research Institute Foundation was established to oversee it in June 1986. The *Kansai Science City Construction Promotion Act* was promulgated one year later and, in March 1988, the Prime Minister approved construction plans. By December 1991 thirty-five private firms had, or were in the process of, establishing laboratories there.

The science city has made slower-than-expected progress due to the 1990s recession. At the very centre of the City is the Seika-Nishikizu District. Research facilities which have opened there in the late 1990s are mainly located in the Hikaridai part of the district and include the Keihanna Plaza, Advanced Telecommunications Research Institute International (ATR), Association for Promotion of New-Generation Network Services Pilot Project Key Station, Communications Research Laboratory and Seika Communications Research Centre, Shimadzu Keihanna Research Laboratory, Sumitomo Metal Industries High-Quality Life Research Laboratories, NTT Communication Science Laboratories, Matsushita Electric Laboratories, and the Kyōcera Keihanna Laboratory.

Many small- to medium-sized enterprises have established research facilities in the Hi-Touch Research Park in the Heijo-Soraku District. The research park was established in March 1987, and the first stage with facilities for ten companies was opened in September 1990. Another three facilities opened in 1992. Most conduct lifestyle-related research in areas such as housing, fine arts, home furnishings and other areas of design.

Private firms in the Kansai region are strong in biotechnological and chemical research. Suntory, a brewing company, and the pharmaceutical firm Tanabe Seiyaku have made plans to locate research institutes in the science city. The major electronic firms of Hitachi, NEC, Toshiba and Oki are considering establishing facilities there as well, especially as it enables them to draw on the scientific talent of the region. Another attraction is the important institute which is already constructed there, the Advanced Telecommunications Research Institute International (ATR).

One form of cooperation in the private sector-driven Kansai Science City has been the secondment of personnel from firms such as Kansai Power to administrative positions. Hicks has suggested that the use of secondments in forming research links may be more prevalent in Japan than in the West (Hicks: 1993). In this way, seconded employees contribute to the greater mission of the science city and at the same time expand their networks.

Science and Technology Parks

By March 1994 there were seventy science and technology parks actually operating and forty-one being planned. The Japanese divide these into three categories: innovation centres (about 26 per cent), science parks (about 32 per cent), and R&D parks (42 per cent). Innovation centres possess incubators – special environments to increase the rate of innovation and proliferation of high-tech industries – to facilitate the establishment of industries, and other facilities to encourage research and information exchange. Science parks tend to be larger in scale, and are able to accommodate industries which have outgrown the incubator stage. R&D parks do not have incubators, but nevertheless attract corporate laboratories and university and government research institutes as their tenants.

Incubators are a common feature of both innovation centres and science parks, growing in popularity since 1988. There were forty-five in existence in 1993, with a further twenty being planned. It is difficult to judge whether incubators are effective in nurturing new industries: there does appear to be a trend away from them. Whereas 64 per cent of the seventy science and technology parks have incubators, only 49 per cent of the forty-one parks still being planned feature them. This reflects some of the doubts expressed in the research on R&D consortia mentioned above (Yoshizawa et al.: 1995).

What has led to some of the doubts about the value of incubators? Apart from the lack of actual examples of incubators which have success-fully nurtured new industries, there has also been uncertainty over how best to manage incubators. In addition, the lack of entrepreneurs mentioned earlier is seen as a major handicap, especially in comparison with the United States, and the cutback in R&D spending by the private sector has discouraged the establishment of facilities for which the economic benefits are uncertain (Yoshizawa et al.: 1995).

Science and technology parks tend to emphasise regional development and are often lacking in the universities and government research institutes which ideally should be at their core. The public research institutes which do exist have mainly been established by public corporations, rather than by universities. Despite a recent change in attitude by the Ministry of Education, the red tape involved makes it institutionally difficult for national universities to conduct joint research with private firms (Asano: 1994). Tenants of these parks tend to be large- or medium-sized enterprises. Their size and company culture may work against the fostering of new firms, but most make an effort to facilitate research exchange between university, industry and government. Indeed, most parks are public-sector projects managed by government, local authorities or public corporations intent on attracting private firms to their location (Asano: 1994).

Conclusion

Initiatives of the type described in this chapter may eventually lead to new industries which will go some way in shifting production to higher value-added goods and into new fields. However, creating synergies of the type suggested requires much effort. MITI has previously sought to do so via national R&D projects, but has met with mixed success. Cooperation between competitors is difficult to achieve in Japan, as elsewhere.

MITI has been reconsidering the direction of its technopolis strategy and industrial 'brain areas' policy. The 'hollowing out' of Japan has led to a change of environment, one that will have to be adapted to. The Asian economic crisis of the late 1990s has further complicated the situation.

PART II

Science and Technology for Economic Growth

CHAPTER 3

Quality versus Quantity

Quality Control and the Automobile Industry

Introduction

In November 1997 Honda Motor Company pushed Nissan Motor Company from the no. 2 spot in domestic auto sales in Japan for the very first time. Honda attributed the growth in domestic sales to popular demand for minicars (*Japan Times*: 1997c). In the Japanese automarket there is no room for complacency. In December 1997 Toyota Motor Corporation's 'hybrid' car Prius went on sale in Japan for $US17 000, part of Toyota president Okuda Hiroshi's plan to compete with United States automakers for the global market. Reports were that orders were double those envisaged, little wonder given that Toyota was said to be losing US$10 000 on each car sold. It is clear from this that in the late 1990s market share was more important than the bottom line for Toyota, which was still the leading automaker in Japan (*Japan Washington Watch*: 1997b). Advertisements for the Prius car boasted of 'The Toyota hybrid system: a breath of fresh air for the environment' (*Japan Times*, 17 December 1997, p. 5), and were undoubtedly timed to capitalise on concerns about global warming, and the Japanese government's decision to cut down on carbon dioxide emissions. The Prius is truly a hybrid car, a vehicle designed to respond to various concerns of not only the auto company but also Japanese citizens, as well as the international market. How can we account for Japanese success in auto-manufacturing? There is a considerable literature on the Japanese automobile industry (Chao: 1994) and a useful survey of companies can be found in Shimokawa (1994). Many people suggest that the Japanese industrial sector has derived much of its comparative advantage through a new approach to production organisation rather than through the use of flexible automation technologies. This chapter will focus on the significance of quality control in the shift of emphasis from mass production (quantity) to more flexible specialisation in manufacturing. Standards have been important in maintaining quality and protecting consumers from faulty products, but they have also served as trade barriers. Japanese Industrial Standards (JIS) have been pitted against those developed by the International Organisation for Standardisation (ISO).

In the 1980s quality control received considerable attention in the West's search for the secret of Japan's technological success, and a large number of books offered advice on how the West might use the same method: this can be viewed as a feature of technological development in Japan (see Table 7.2). But in the same way that the highly praised quality control is not a Japanese invention but a Japanised concept, Japanese automobiles are increasingly hybrid products drawing on Japanese expertise but made elsewhere. They are global products. Globalisation of production has meant that some of the human costs of Japanese work practices have been exported as well. In both Japan and the United States, these practices have attracted considerable criticism.

Quality Control in Japan

In the postwar period Japanese firms have been highly successful innovators, supporting the utilisation of the results of R&D. Often, Japanese firms have commercialised new products which have been partly or wholly invented elsewhere. Some examples are the transistor and integrated circuit, which both originated in the United States. Despite their American origin, the Japanese led the world in the commercialisation of transistors for radios and outstripped the United States in the production of high-quality colour television sets. Again, although the United States took an early lead in the introduction of robotics, by 1984 Japan was using four times as many industrial robots as the United States (Mowery & Rosenberg: 1989, 219).

Japanese products are well-known for their quality and design. The postwar drive for quality by Japan's manufacturers made use of personnel involved in the war effort. The designer of the Zero fighter engine, for example, became an engineer for Nissan and used his aircraft design skills to give Nissan cars features such as reliable door latches and effective noise control. But apart from good design, some of the success of Japanese products can be traced to strict quality control. The term 'QC circles' (QCC) refers to a management tool for the upgrading of worker productivity and the quality of a product. Its origins can be traced to the West, where the quality control concept was introduced and adapted. Problems occurred with the quality of goods that were mass-produced by untrained workers in American factories before the Second

World War, and the concept of quality control evolved to address these problems by means of sampling inspections during the production process. This grew into the system of Total Quality Control (TQC) used in military production, where statistical methods were developed to ensure goods met the military's strict standards of quality (Nakayama: 1995a, 269–74).

Tsutsui (1996) has argued that the 'discovery' of quality control in Japan can be traced to a management expert, Kiribuchi Kanzō, and a monograph he published in 1934. He also argues that a few firms experimented with managerial statistics even before this time, and that during the Second World War Kitagawa Toshio published a translation of E. S. Pearson's book *The Application of Statistical Methods to Industrial Standardisation and Quality Control.* In Japan, the Mathematical Statistics Society (Sūri Tōkei Gakkai) was formed in 1941 and attempted, with little success, to persuade industry and the military to apply its method of 'statistical sampling'. The Japan Standards Association (JSA) was established in December 1945, and began publication of its magazine *Standards and Measures* (now *Standardisation and Quality Control*) the following year.

The main impetus behind the spread of quality control in Japan was the private organisation, the Japanese Union of Scientists and Engineers (JUSE), which formed a Quality Control Research Group in 1948 to investigate foreign writing and application of quality control and realised the importance of immediately implementing the practice. From 1949 a basic course in quality control was introduced as a regular lecture within the JUSE, and members of the Nihon Nōritsu Kyōkai (Japan Efficiency Society) began advising businesses on quality control methods.

In 1946 the Allied Occupation Forces, plagued by frequent breakdowns in telephone communications, recommended the implementation of new quality control methods to the Japanese telecommunications industry. John W. O'Brien warned in a lecture to the JSA that Japanese exports would not be competitive in world markets without quality control. As a result of the movement toward industrial rationalisation, the *Industrial Standardisation Act* (*Kōgyō Hyōjunkahō*) was implemented in July 1949. In the period between 1946 and 1949, however, Asia continued to be the main market for Japanese exports and because the quality of products was less of a problem in this market, Japanese manufacturers were slow to begin implementing quality control.

Japan's quality control is linked to the American business economist, W. Edwards Deming, though the reason for this is not clear. A professor of statistics at New York University, Deming first visited Japan in December 1946 as a member of the American observation group on statistics. In 1948 he implemented quality control at the Tamagawa branch of Nippon Electric Company (NEC or Nihon Denki) under instruction from General Headquarters. This attempt, while fairly successful, applied unchanged American methods, and its influence was limited to the telecommunications industry. With the beginning of the Korean War, the necessity for strict quality control for military supplies brought quality control out of the realms of theory and into practice across a broad range of industries. At this time, Deming, who had advised the military industry on quality control during the Second World War in the United States, was in Japan to give lectures. Deming's ideas were not generally accepted in the United States, where quality control in the 1950s and 1960s was limited to military production. Civilian companies tended to consider quality and productivity to be mutually opposed concepts, and to accept that some quality must be sacrificed to achieve high productivity. In Japan, however, circumstances surrounding the Korean conflict changed the direction of Japan's exports from the Asian market to the quality-conscious American market, and encouraged the early application of quality control.

The economic boom caused by the Korean conflict receded in early 1951, but in April of that year W. F. Marquat (Head of the Economic and Scientific Section at General Headquarters) recommended that Japan's industrial power be given greater consideration in America's Far Eastern economic policy. Japanese industry began to demand more regular, better planned and stricter quality controls. Deming's lectures in Japan were published and became an immediate best-seller. He also visited Japan in 1951 to promote his quality control methods to senior management. The Deming Prize was established in September of that year from the proceeds of the book's sale, and offered an award for outstanding application of quality control in a company as well as the main prize for an individual. This award for the practice of quality control contributed greatly to its adoption by Japanese industry.

The Korean War provided the impetus for the recovery of the Japanese economy, but quality control was one of the technological conditions of this recovery. Japanese industry welcomed quality control as a way to rationalise management without investing scarce resources in imported machinery or facilities. Deming is therefore better known in Japan than in the United States, where it took longer for his ideas to be accepted.

Statistical quality control developed further in the early 1950s, and the following points were seen as problems: overreliance on statistical methods; overreliance on the formal aspects of planning; and a lack of understanding by higher management. In 1954 Joseph M. Juran emphasised the need to include quality control as a principle of management, not merely a technical solution. In the late 1950s the

Company-Wide Quality Control movement (also called Total Quality Control: TQC) began to replace the statistical quality control of previous years. While SQC was based on product checks in the final stages of production, TQC involved supervision of each stage in the production process. Quality was not the sole responsibility of a small group of specialised workers but a matter of concern for all workers.

In 1962 JUSE first published the magazine *Quality Control on the Factory Floor*, and quality control circles began to appear in companies throughout the country. Quality control circles involve five to ten workers and are a method of communicating ideas by suggestions to the higher levels of management. Japanese quality control circles were formed in all areas of production, bringing quality control into the entire production process, rather than just in supervision of the final product, and involving both management and workers. The main promoters of quality control were JUSE and the Japan Efficiency Society. With the patronage of MITI they sponsored a number of events on an international scale.

There was some opposition to TQC from workers' unions on the grounds that it was a system imposed from above and involved unpaid overtime, but their main efforts were directed at improving working conditions in general. The OTCA (Kaigai Gijutsu Kyōryoku Jigyōdan; later the Japan International Cooperation Agency) was formed in 1968 to promote training in industrial standardisation and quality control in the industrialising countries, spreading quality control to, for example, sub-contractors in Taiwan and South Korea. Quality control has become firmly established in these countries.

Cusumano (1985, 372–3) has argued that Nissan Motor Company's reliance on United States and British technology, and its relative lack of enthusiasm for a broad quality control program in the 1960s and 1970s, relegated the company to the no. 2 spot, after Toyota Motor Corporation. Kaplinsky (1994, 309) suggests that Nissan has been more interested in achieving flexibility through automation rather than developing new forms of work organisation.

In the early 1970s factory automation led to widespread labour alienation. Japanese management dealt with this by devising strategies such as hourly job rotation and the replacement of the belt-conveyor system with a more humane method of production-line work. Another strategy was the creation of quality control circles (QCC) on the shop floor. In reality, this was not a spontaneous movement but a labour management strategy devised by quality control specialists hired by management. Labour unions entertained doubts about the QCC movement. Unlike European and American unions, Japanese unions are company-based and cooperate more with management but there appeared to be no substantial opposition to the QCC movement on the part of unions;

indeed, quality control serves to relieve the tedium of the workplace. The QCC approach is not more humane than others but it can only be fully applied in a work culture which guarantees lifelong job security. The quality control movement was an attempt to raise the consciousness of workers and increase their desire to participate.

The journalist Kamata Satoshi joined an auto factory in the early 1970s as a temporary assembly-line worker to see what Japanese management procedures were like in practice. The account of his experiences was translated and published in English as *Japan in the Passing Lane* (1983). While it has been more than twenty-five years since Kamata worked at that factory and work conditions have improved considerably, the human cost of such work is still a concern.

Whereas the responsibility for quality control in Western countries has tended to lie with managers and engineers, the Japanese have involved blue-collar workers on the production lines, product designers, marketing staff, sales people and R&D personnel. The concept of quality control is thereby broadened to one of TQC or QCC. By obtaining input from blue-collar workers, the company is able, as a whole unit, to discuss and work together in the upgrading and improvement of the quality of a product. Manufacturing costs can sometimes be reduced and ways of improving customer service can also be found (Kotler et al.: 1985, 37, 51).

Various types of quality control have been used in Japanese companies. The 'zero-defect' concept aimed at error-free production and the goal of QCC provided a channel of communication whereby workers could suggest creative ideas and improve the manufacturing process. Workers would inspect the tasks performed at the previous stage of a production line, and quality control inspectors at the end of the line would look for possible defects in the finished product (Kotler et al.: 1985). This emphasis on improving product quality and high productivity often involves the Japanese in having daily meetings to review quality performance. Close attention to the overall manufacturing process in some ways makes up for the lack of Japanese innovation (Kotler et al.: 1985, 109).

Academic research on quality control was delayed for some years, as quality control was considered to be part of the management strategy of each particular company. In the 1970s the magazine *Quality* (*Hinshitsu*) investigated quality control from the viewpoint of the consumer, and quality control came to be seen as part of the discipline of management engineering, in itself a division of business management. The majority of the researchers involved in this subject, however, have a background in the sciences.

Public policies in S&T in Japan have been highly compatible with the aims of private firms. Firms have tended to adopt what can be called an 'incrementalist' strategy of careful analysis of a product, consumer taste, and manufacturing technology. QCC are one means by which the processes of manufacturing and development have been brought together. They are, however, also careful to monitor advances which might be incorporated into their products or lead to new products (Mowery & Rosenberg: 1989, 229–30).

The management of innovation within Japanese firms necessarily reflects some basic characteristics of Japanese organisations:

- heavy reliance on on-site information rather than hierarchical control of specialised knowledge;
- *kanban* system in manufacturing and *ringi* system in administration which emphasise reliance on horizontal communications; and
- promotion on the basis of contribution to collective problem-solving and intra-organisational transfer of personnel (Mowery & Rosenberg: 1989, 230).

It is within this context that R&D and innovation (the production of new technological knowledge) are organised, though these practices are not necessarily the reasons for Japanese success. Kamata (1983, 201) argues that it has been the production allowances and work-quota system which have been responsible for Toyota's growth in production. The wages of workers increase depending on their ability to reach their production goals.

The following features are common to many Japanese organisations:

- the importance of the engineering department of manufacturing divisions in R&D process;
- the close connection between central research laboratories and engineering departments via transfer of researchers and engineers; and
- the promotion of researchers and engineers according to contributions to company-specific R&D projects and leadership in commercialisation of products rather than according to individual research skills (Mowery & Rosenberg: 1989, 231–4).

Thanks to these characteristics Japanese firms are arguably more efficient in exploiting foreign technology than the United States. Indeed, Kenney & Florida (1993, 65) have characterised Japanese factories as laboratories where ideas and concepts are tested and brought into being. The factories provide a rich source of innovation and constant improvement.

Public policy and management of innovation have emphasised the utilisation of foreign technology rather than the creation of internal technology. Given that technological borrowing will be more difficult in the future, and increasing competition from newly industrialised economies threatens Japan's export success, Japanese firms will need to respond to the challenges posed by the need for innovation. One way may be for the Japanese to make better use of universities (the source of engineers and scientists) as research institutions; more military research may be an option, as might be a more concerted push for basic research in government and corporate laboratories.

Quality Control Overseas

There have been attempts to introduce Japanese quality control methods and other technology management techniques to other parts of Asia, the United States and Europe. There were particularly strong moves to do so in the 1980s, and similar techniques had been adopted in Taiwan in the 1960s, with Korea following suit soon after, and the Philippines, China and Thailand attempted to do so in the second half of the 1970s. There have been doubts expressed about the extent to which Japanese management techniques can be transferred to other countries because of the specific cultural context in which they were first implemented. Raphael Kaplinsky (1994, 269) argues that this 'Easternisation' is not so much an attempt to reproduce 'traditional' Japanese social relations, but one aimed at diffusing the 'technics' of Japanese management techniques. Transfer requires that the social relations of domination, which were an important part of the Taylorist paradigm of mass production and control, be overturned and labour treated more as a resource. Under Taylorism, government attempted to control production tasks according to scientific principles. In this new scheme of things, workers participate in process and product improvements.

Kenney & Florida (1993, 263, 281–2) point out that there is an underside to the transfer of Japanese work practices to the United States. The QCC discussed above are only effective if workers have a strong sense of belonging to the firm. Attempts to transfer overseas the strict discipline imposed on workers, methods of intimidation and surveillance, and the emphasis on company loyalty which Kamata wrote about (1983) have attracted criticism. The use of temporary workers is a way of rendering workers powerless and vulnerable and the siting of automotive plants in rural, greenfield areas is said to discriminate against African-Americans and other minorities.

The Japanese seem to have had more success in transferring what could be described as cultural practices, rather than, for example, just-in-time inventory measures. The UN World Investment Report (1995, cited in *Education About Asia*: 1997) found the following percentages of foreign manufacturing affiliates to whom Japanese parent companies transferred management practices: common dining room (69 per cent); open-concept offices (65 per cent); uniforms (41 per cent); morning meetings (35 per cent); bonus system (25 per cent); just-in-time inventory (14 per cent); enterprise-based trade union (12 per cent); lifelong employment (11 per cent); seniority-based wage system (2 per cent) (*Education About Asia*: 1997).

The expansion of Japanese production in the late 1980s was made possible by capital raised by asset inflation in securities, banking and property; a process referred to as the 'bubble economy'. Fears grew that the land values and stock prices had expanded beyond the capacity of the real economy to sustain them. Since the Japanese 'bubble' economy burst in the early 1990s, the enthusiasm for Japanese management strategies has waned. In Japan, the peculiarly Japanese consciousness-raising aspect of QCC is becoming weaker, but the Western enthusiasm for Japanese cars has not abated. Despite the stagnating economy in Japan, the weaker yen in 1998 had many people predicting that there would be an increase in auto exports to the United States, and greater competition in price. In 1998 the eight Japanese automakers accounted for about 23.5 per cent of the market, an increase from the previous year (*Japan Washington Watch*: 1998). Quality control is but one factor affecting the competitiveness of Japanese cars.

Quality Control versus ISO

Quality control and standards often ensure that goods and services we use are reliable and effective; they can provide protection for consumers. At the same time, however, the use of different standards can act as a technical barrier to trade. Export-oriented industries are particularly attuned to the need for international standardisation which provides common reference points for all countries, facilitates trade liberalisation, and enables use of components and products from one industrial sector in another (ISO: 1999).

ISO was established in 1947 and was active throughout the postwar period, working from its main office in Geneva. It is a non-governmental organisation and acts as a world-wide federation of national standards bodies from about 130 countries. Apart from a small number of stand-ards specialists, the average Japanese person was not aware of its exist-ence and function. In 1987 ISO standards were created which have come to be accepted by countries throughout the world. Only since 1996 have ISO standards come to the attention of the mass media and become widely known among industrialists and, in turn, local governments. Of primary concern was the first ISO 9000 (quality control) series, and later the ISO 14000 (environment) series.

Japanese S&T attracted world attention in the 1980s, as a result of heavy exports of Japanese industrial products, especially automobiles and semiconductors. Many saw the secrets of Japan's success in terms of its management strategies, particularly the use of QCC at the shop-floor level. The 1980s saw the establishment of Japanese manufacturing plants overseas where QCC was introduced. European and American factories adopted it under various names, often using the abbreviation 'QC' to stand for 'quality circle', and dropping the word 'control' lest it be construed as an attempt to control labour. In this book it has been referred to as QCC. QCC has been favourably received among blue-collar workers whereas white-collar workers have often been reluctant to lose their authority. This reflects how QC (quality control) strategies are more suited to the production line rather than the office.

In 1987 the ISO 9000 series (quality control) was formulated, primarily based on BS (British Standard) 5750. It was one of the important steps towards unification by the European Community. Japanese industry did not take it so seriously, confident of the quality of its own products. Europeans, however, tried to apply the standards as a way of fighting imports from Japan (as well as the United States), by demanding ISO 9000 series certification from Japanese export companies. European governmental procurement requires this certification from all contractors. Japanese standards differed from European standards and exporters had to make adjustments accordingly. The Japanese government tried to coordinate this process of negotiating between Japanese Industrial Standards (JIS) and ISO standards. JIS were established as voluntary, national standards in 1949, and cover over 8000 industrial and mining standards. The Japan Industrial Standards Committee (JISC) is the national standards body and is a member of ISO (Tanabe: 1997, 67).

ISO 9000 was started by British corporations in 1987, and adopted by other European countries. The British share of total certification peaked in 1993, accounting for two-thirds of the total number of certificates issued. The British were then gradually overtaken by other European countries, with the United States and Japan lagging behind (Ho: 1995, 176). Rather belatedly, Japanese industry began to realise the importance of certification. The delay caused a loss of European market share. The export-oriented manufacturers of consumer appliances took the initiative in obtaining certification and this then spread to other industries. The chemical industry which suffered setbacks due to the anti-pollution movement in the 1970s, was most responsive.

Some Japanese regard QCC and the ISO 9000 series as being dia-metrically opposed in philosophy. While the QCC has the appearance of promoting democratic initiatives from lower levels, the ISO 9000 series introduces top-down, authoritarian control measures, from white- to blue-collar workers. Some Japanese suspect that because ISO 9000 is based on the British Standard it is better suited to sharp British class differentiation between workers. MITI warned the ISO that it constituted a kind of non-tariff barrier that infringed the General Agreement on Tariffs and Trade. Whatever the initial motivation behind the intro-duction of ISO 9000, it is a welcome measure in terms of setting international quality standards which complement quality control.

The decline of Cold War institutional structures in the late 1980s saw the rise of global environmental issues on the international political agenda. Since 1992, when the Brazil environment summit took place, the ISO 14000 series of standards for environmental control and auditing have been discussed. Deeply concerned about the delay of debate regarding ISO issues in the case of ISO 9000, the Japanese acted promptly by sending Japanese members to the ISO commission and advanced in accordance with the ISO the promulgation of the domestic JIS standardisation (Hirabayashi & Sasa: 1996, 23).

While quality control (ISO 9000) directly addresses the concerns of consumers, the response of manufacturers is quite understandable. Environmental control (ISO 14000) is more the concern of local resi-dents and environmental non-government organisations, rather than the concern of corporations, stockholders and customers. Even in the 1970s when corporations were attacked for irresponsible environmental behaviour, they generally thought that a large allocation of resources to anti-pollution measures would endanger corporate survival in a cut-throat, competitive world. Despite such concerns, a corporate culture emerged in the 1980s and 1990s which placed higher priority on environ-mental issues. This was especially true in environmentally advanced European countries, where industrialisation has a longer history and de-industrialisation has occurred. In Europe, enterprises that neglected environmental issues saw the value of their shares decline.

The Eco-Management and Audit Scheme (EMAS) was drafted in the 1980s and accepted by twelve member nations of the European Community. EMAS adopted ISO 14000 (Hirabayashi & Sasa: 1996, 148). It came into effect in April 1995 in Europe and its legal enforcement was agreed to by signatory nations. It was very strict, exposing industrial waste and publishing the results of audits. It was resisted by the American industrial world and its legal enforcement was not adopted. Instead, an 'outsider's audit' by an expert organisation rather than an 'internal audit' by the enterprise concerned became the norm.

In the process of formulating ISO 14000, European Community countries were more strict than the ISO, and American industry opposed it. In the beginning the Japanese were closer to Americans but later switched to the European standard. Japanese enterprises have never been legally forced to obtain ISO 14000 certification but in the actual practice of competing in the world market, those who obtain certification have a definite advantage. Thus, Japanese corporations send staff to Geneva and Brussels (the capital of the European Community) to catch up with trends in ISO standardisation, so that they are at no disadvantage *vis-à-vis* European corporations.

Japanese corporations, when establishing an overseas plant, tend to choose a location in Asia where no strict environmental controls are in force. Their attitude and behaviour were tolerated in the recipient countries when foreign capital investment was wanted. However, the *Keidanren* (Federation of Economic Organisations), which has an influential role in Japanese big business, was concerned that such a state of affairs would cause international conflict in the long run. In April 1991 the *Keidanren* advised that each company should have a director devoted to the environment and each year the company should undergo an internal audit. Companies were not compelled to heed such advice, however, Japanese corporations responded surprisingly quickly in preparing for ISO 14000 certification, mainly because no corporation wished to deviate from what other Japanese corporations were doing. This was a typical Japanese conformist approach, despite the fact that the alleviation of global warming does not lead to immediate profits.

ISO 14000 was promulgated in 1996. This time Japanese corporations were not slow in obtaining information about ISO 14000 and a sort of ISO 14000 boom ensued among Japanese corporations. Corporations put banners in front of the entrance to company buildings bearing slogans such as 'Let's obtain ISO 14000'. At the end of October 1998 Japanese corporations recorded 1320 certifications, far outnumbering that of British companies which ranked second.

Conclusion

Despite Japanese success in innovation and careful attention to quality control, in the late 1990s Japanese auto manufacturers were experiencing difficult times. In October 1998 Nissan Motor Company reported $US562.7 million in unrealised losses on its stockholdings for the first half of 1998FY (Daimon: 1998). A couple of months later, it was reported that Toyota might close some production lines in order to reduce domestic automaking capacity by 8 per cent over three years, given the stagnation of the market and fall in exports (Bloomberg: 1998). In 1999

Nissan signalled that it was prepared to allow a foreign car maker to buy a controlling stake in the company. Ford Motor Company already held a controlling stake in the Japanese car maker, Mazda Motor Company. Heavy debts and declining sales have encouraged Japanese companies to seriously consider joining forces with foreign corporations (*Australian*: 1999a).

Innovation and standardisation are intimately related. However as we saw with ISO standards, they can be used as a political tool, and effectively inhibit development of alternatives. ISO prides itself on a consensus approach to the development of standards, using procedures that are open and transparent. We are still not clear about the impact of standards on innovation and vice versa. Japan's experience shows how standards-setting can isolate one country from others. Superior technology alone will not ensure markets. Japan has learnt that being part of the international standards-setting process is essential.

CHAPTER 4

Technology versus Commercial Feasibility

Nuclear Power and Electric Utilities

Introduction

The Japanese are strong in technological development carried out in industrial laboratories rather than the basic research of universities and national laboratories. This type of knowledge lends itself more readily to 'capture' by its creators and contributes more to private rather than public good. This refers to the tendency for economic returns to flow to a single firm rather than to the Japanese people. But as Mowery (1993, 172) has pointed out, the true picture is not so simple, with applied research being able to contribute to the public good just as firm-specific benefits can be generated by basic research.

This chapter looks at the history of power generation in Japan, beginning with the development of electric power. For much of its history in Japan, the power generation industry has been dominated by the private sector. We then discuss the development of nuclear power and how it has involved many of the same players. Public good and private good becomes blurred in Japan, and when it comes to nuclear power it is not always clear whose interests are being pursued. The final section looks at recent developments, and suggests that the future for nuclear power in Japan has become clouded, with the Science and Technology Agency (STA) seeming to pursue the development of technology for its own sake, and electric utilities more concerned with commercial feasibility.

The Electric Power Industry in Japan

The hundred-year history of electric power in Japan can be divided into at least seven periods or stages: (1) period of introduction (1882–95); (2) period of growth (1896–1906); (3) period of expansion

66

(1907–22); (4) period of competition (1923–31); (5) period of monopolisation (1932–37); (6) period of wartime control (1938–45); and (7) the postwar period (*Far Eastern Economic Review.* 1950; Samuels: 1987, 135–67).

For most of its history, the Japanese electric power industry has been completely private, something quite unusual when compared with electric utilities throughout the world, and unusual when compared with other industrial sectors in Japan. Unlike areas such as mining, transportation (railways), steel or munitions, the utilities were developed by entrepreneurs using private capital. These entrepreneurs were often *daimyō* (feudal lords) or their retainers. The entrepreneurs invested in the private development of electric power as early as 1882, without state guarantees, only three years after Thomas Edison had invented the incandescent electric lamp. Thomas A. Edison sold the Japanese their first electric light plant which was installed in the Imperial Palace in 1887. The first electric street car was running in Ueno Park in Tokyo by 1890, as was the first electric elevator (in Asakusa). Due to the high rates charged for electric power, use of electric power tended to be confined to industry and the bureaucracy.

Japan's first electric utility was Tokyo Dentō (Tokyo Electric Light Company), which was established in 1886; by 1897 there were forty-one utilities. There was increasing competition between utilities, with four different, unregulated electric utilities operating in Tokyo by 1889. In 1890, however, an electrical fire destroyed the Imperial Diet building which housed the national parliament. In 1891 the Ministry of Communications (Teishinshō) was given the supervisory responsibility for electric power. With an increase in the number of firms and consumers, the ministry took the authority to issue permits (licences for private electric utilities) away from prefectural governors. In 1896 regulations were put in place which required safety precautions for generators and electric railways. Transmission voltages were standardised and the permit authority was centralised as well. The Japanese victory in the Sino–Japanese War (1894–95) brought a windfall of indemnity payments totalling 360 million yen. This provided investment capital, and the electric power industry again expanded to meet industrial demand for electricity. The next ten years would see a trebling in the number of utilities. The defeat of Russia in the Russo–Japanese War in 1905 provided a further stimulus to the growth in the number of electric utilities.

With the development of hydro-electric power under the government's policy of promoting the electric power industry, the supply of electric power increased sharply during this period. Demand for electric power from industry also stimulated great development of the electric power industry (*Far Eastern Economic Review.* 1950, 760). During the period 1903 to 1914, mechanised factories increased from less than 4000 to more than 10 000. Mechanisation increased particularly in industries involved with chemicals and machinery. Safety problems were largely solved and long-distance transmission facilities were introduced. There was an increasing move away from small steam generators to larger hydroelectric facilities. The spread of the electric railway system also stimulated further demand for electric power.

The Japanese electric power industry was stimulated by the First World War. Light industry still accounted for 80 per cent of mechanised factories in 1914, and 80 per cent of the workforce was involved in light industry. The next four years, however, would see investments in chemicals, shipbuilding, metals and machinery production expand enormously. As a result of increasing demands made by heavy industries, the utilities increased investment in new power generation by 500 per cent. Five electricity wholesalers dominated the industry, providing one-quarter of all power which was generated in Japan. The bureaucracy had considered state control of the electric power industry but its efforts to bring this about were unsuccessful. The use of electrical power in industrial operations increased from 9.4 per cent in 1906 to 24.8 per cent in 1916, surpassing that of steam power. Owing to the depressed state of business after the First World War the supply of electric power became excessive and competition among the electric utilities became very keen. By 1929 the use of electrical power in industry reached 88.9 per cent. In the machinery and tools industry it reached 97.9 per cent, and 92.8 per cent in the chemical industry (*Far Eastern Economic Review*. 1950, 760). In order to resolve the problem of an oversupply of electricity in the depression of the early 1930s, and in order to avoid the problems of excessive competition, a cartel called the 'Electric Power League' was formed in 1932 between the five dominant electric utilities, but after the Manchurian Incident in 1931 Japan put more effort into preparing for war. The increased demand for heavy machinery and plant construction required cheap and stable sources of electric power. The Manchurian Incident also served to intensify calls for control of the electric power industry.

It has been estimated that at the peak of the electric power industry during the pre-Second World War period, the electric power companies numbered 818 (Kakinuma: 1986, 46). The Second World War saw the reorganisation of the electric power industry under government pressure, imposing greater state control over electric power. The *Electric Power State Control Act* was passed in April 1938. Support of the nationalisation of the electric utilities was widespread as industrial consumption of electric power had trebled between 1926 and 1936. On the eve of the Pacific War, industry was consuming two-thirds of all electric power generated in Japan. With the implementation of the *National Mobilisation Law* in April 1942, the several hundred electric power distribution firms were merged into nine regional companies. This structure enabled the Japanese government to regulate the demand for electricity and to concentrate its use for munitions production. The system during the Second World War was one of one giant state-controlled utility, Nippatsu, that delivered power through nine regional companies. This structure later provided the basis for the privatisation of the industry after the war. On 1 May 1951 Nippatsu was abolished and nine private utilities were formally established: Tokyo (Electric) Power, Kansai Power, Chūbu Power, Hokkaido Power, Tōhoku Power, Hokuriku Power, Chūgoku Power, Shikoku Power and Kyūshū Power. These utilities had responsibility for power generation, transmission and distribution.

Electricity generation has changed from being mainly hydroelectric before the Second World War, to coal generated, and then to oil generated after the war (Kakinuma: 1986, 46). Japan's rapid economic growth (before the oil crisis of 1973 and 1974) was achieved by taking advantage of cheap oil supplied by United States-based oil companies (Fukai: 1988, 169).

The history of electric power in Japan shows that private control of the industry has been mostly maintained. It was only during the Pacific War that the Japanese state and its allies in the private sector were able to bring about a partial nationalisation. This results in a situation where Japan has the most fully privately controlled electric power sector in the world.

The Development of Nuclear Power in Japan

A feature of the nuclear power program in Japan is the fact that responsibility for the electricity supply, ownership of nuclear fuel and commercial power reactors is concentrated in the hands of private industry. Some scientists and members of the public have long felt this tends to make questions of public safety secondary to questions of self-interest. This next section examines the history of nuclear power in Japan, focusing on the dual structure that has inhibited its development.

The determination of the government and industry to promote the commercialisation of nuclear power, in the face of opposition from some scientists and more recently the general public, has been a feature of the development of the nuclear power industry since its very beginning. By looking at its history, answers can be found to explain why the Japanese nuclear power industry has been so stubbornly resilient. The example of nuclear power will show that Japan's rapid postwar development was, more than anything else, due to the close collaboration between organised business, government and the scientific establishment. It is argued that if the industry had followed the normal pattern of technological borrowing and later improvement, the nuclear power industry would have met with greater 'success' in terms of technological development. Instead, the 'scientification' of nuclear power brought about by some scientist-critics and promoted by the STA has meant that the industry has been promoted separately by two groups with different interests, one more concerned with the domestic development of technology, and the other with commercial practicalities.

We can divide the history of nuclear development in Japan into the following six periods (Yoshioka: 1996b): (1) military development (1939–45); (2) prohibition (1945–53); (3) institutionalisation (1954–65); (4) take-off (1966–79); (5) steady expansion and privatisation (1980–94); and (6) general stagnation and decline of plutonium breeding (1995–). The key events that divide each of the periods are: the defeat of Japan in 1945; the approval of the first national budget plan for nuclear power research in 1954; the agreement to introduce the first American light water reactor (LWR) and the decision to establish the Power Reactor and Nuclear Fuel Development Corporation (PNC) in 1966; the recovery of the technological reliability of the LWR and the start of privatisation of major STA-group national projects in 1980; and finally, the end of the steady growth in the number of commercial nuclear power reactors, the termination of the advanced thermal reactor (ATR) and the 'Monju' accident in 1995 (discussed later in this chapter).

Post-Second World War Developments

The development of nuclear power in Japan bears similarities to that in the Federal Republic of Germany (FRG). Due to the terms drawn up at the end of the Second World War and the Cold War politics that followed, Japan and FRG initiated programs a decade after those of the USSR, the United States, the United Kingdom and Canada. Furthermore, when programs did commence in Japan and FRG, most of the technology was imported and materials such as enriched uranium were obtained via the United States Atoms for Peace Plan.

In 1946 the *Atomic Energy Act* was passed by the United States Congress. In effect, this created the Atomic Energy Commission (AEC) and placed severe restrictions on the dissemination of nuclear research. As a result, the prohibitions effectively provided the United States with a ready customer for nuclear power since they prevented Japan from catching up in nuclear research work and thereby made it reliant on American nuclear power. The prohibitions on research related to nuclear energy did not prevent growing interest on the part of physicists and industrialists in the scientific and commercial possibilities offered by this new energy source. Fushimi Kōji, professor at Osaka University and one of the enthusiastic scientist-proponents of nuclear power, argued at a 1951 general assembly of the Science Council of Japan that the soon-to-be-signed peace treaty should not contain any clauses prohibiting nuclear energy (Yanaga: 1968, 178).

The Allied Occupation enabled ties to be formed between American industry and Japanese utilities and equipment manufacturers, often with militaristic overtones. The decision of the United States Atomic Energy Commission, on 11 November 1949, to allow Japanese participation in the program for the distribution of radio-isotopes came shortly after the Communists had taken power in China. Technological ties were substantially strengthened during the Korean War, when Japan imported American industrial technology under the auspices of a special procurements program.

The 'Peaceful Atom'

In order to make use of atomic energy in industry, it became necessary to make a distinction between atoms for war and civilian uses of nuclear technology. The concept of 'atoms for peace' provided the Japanese and the rest of the world with an ideal of a prosperous future courtesy of science. The Japanese were able to reconcile the establishment of a nuclear industry in their own country with the devastation which had been wrought in Hiroshima and Nagasaki less than a decade earlier. An atom which had been 'tamed' would work for the benefit of 'mankind'.

The first academic to push for the peaceful use of nuclear power in Japan was the physicist, Taketani Mituo. In 1950 Taketani published a volume on the topic through the newspaper publishing company Mainichi Shinbun. This book, *Genshi-ryoku (Atomic Energy)*, explored the possibility of the use of the atom as a peaceful way of obtaining electrical power. Elsewhere, Taketani wrote that while he felt that Japan should pursue atomic energy, there were two problems: (1) insufficient domestic supply of uranium; and (2) the danger of ending up as a 'sub-contractor' for the United States atomic bomb program. Taketani felt that as the world's first victims of the atomic bomb, the Japanese had a right to conduct research on the peaceful uses of atomic energy with the assistance of overseas countries. He felt that such countries should unconditionally supply Japan with the necessary quantities of uranium, and that atomic energy research should not be of a secretive nature (JAIF: 1971, 12–14). On 8 December 1953 President Eisenhower presented his plan of 'Atoms for Peace' to the General Assembly of the United Nations, which set the stage for international cooperation in atomic energy and the creation of the International Atomic Energy Agency (IAEA). In the initial stages of interest in atomic energy, those in government and industry first turned to technocratic physicists such as Sagane Ryōkichi, Fujioka Yoshio and Fushimi Kōji for advice. Kaya Seiji, professor at Tokyo University, and Fushimi both felt that an Atomic Energy Commission was needed in Japan. One of the first public pronouncements regarding the need to pursue atomic energy research was uttered by Kaya, at the opening of Yukawa Hall, also known as the Research Institute for Fundamental Physics, at Kyoto University on 20 July 1952. He suggested that a fact-finding mission be sent overseas and that an atomic energy commission be formed in Japan which would be responsible to the government. Kaya believed it would be difficult to establish such a body within the framework of the Science Council of Japan. Fushimi also believed that such a commission was needed (JAIF: 1971, 10–11). In 1953 the United Kingdom Atomic Energy Authority (AEA) was established and plans were approved for the construction of the first large nuclear power reactor in the world: a 138 MWe gas-cooled graphite-moderated Calder Hall reactor. By the end of 1956 the facility was successfully generating electricity.

Some physicists were cautious and suggested that atomic energy policy be based on the results of sound scientific research carried out in Japan, whereas the industrialists who became involved tended to see it as another moneymaking venture. This was one of the fundamental reasons for the long conflict between scientists critical of nuclear power and the government–industrial complex, which included their more technocratically-minded scientist-colleagues. The more critical scientists were committed to the importance of a domestic research base whereas economic and industrial activities in Japan from the 1950s tended to be based on imported technology. The physicists consequently found themselves as advisers to the government on questions of nuclear safety rather than questions about the technology itself.

Nakasone Yasuhiro was the first Japanese politician to show serious interest in atomic energy. As early as 1951 he visited Kaya, making inquiries about nuclear power. In March 1954 Nakasone made a budget request for an additional 250 million yen for S&T, 235 million of which would be allocated for the construction of a nuclear reactor. This was approved by the House of Representatives against the wishes of the scientist representative organisation, the Science Council of Japan (JSC). That first atomic energy budget set the tone for the estranged relationship between government–industry circles and their scientist-critics.

On 1 March 1954 the United States conducted a hydrogen bomb test at Bikini Atoll. On 16 March 1954 the *Yomiuri Shinbun* reported that twenty-three Japanese on a tuna fishing boat called *The Lucky Dragon* had been contaminated by radioactive fallout near the atoll. This had occurred inauspiciously on about the same day that it was decided to present Japan's first reactor budget before parliament. The incident served to discourage the attempts to begin a Japanese nuclear power program (JAIF: 1971, 16; Lapp: 1958). On 9 June the Federation of Economic Organisations made a submission to the government urging the establishment of an S&T agency, this time not for defence purposes but for the 'promotion' of S&T, and to help formulate and administer government policy, especially nuclear power (Yanaga: 1968, 181).

The JSC, formed in 1949 during the Allied Occupation to provide democratic scientific opinion, was often in conflict with the government over the importance of basic research. The nuclear physicist critics in the JSC expressed their displeasure at the large budget appropriation for atomic energy, particularly since it had been done in the absence of a properly formulated policy and without consultation. At the autumn JSC meeting, a statement was made that set out three basic principles or conditions necessary for nuclear research: (1) non-secrecy; (2) democratic control; and (3) autonomy. Despite the concern of some scientists for the peaceful use of nuclear power, the close collaboration between government and industry effectively excluded much input from the more critical scientists.

Formation of an Atomic Energy Program

The Japanese rush to establish an atomic energy program was partly a result of a desire to take full advantage of the possibilities of transfer of nuclear technology from the United States under the Atoms for Peace plan. The beginning of the program was, like many of Japan's postwar industries, characterised by a great reliance on scientific and technical information from abroad. This was reflected in the early strategy of Japan's nuclear program which was, simply, to have a commercial facility in operation as quickly as possible. This was most easily achieved by importing the appropriate technology.

In May 1955 the Federation of Economic Organisations (FEO) set up a permanent Committee for the Peaceful Use of Atomic Energy, chaired by Yasukawa Daigoro. Fushimi continued to push for the peaceful use of atomic energy, stating his case in the June issue of the periodical *Chūō Kōron* (Fushimi: 1955, 34–42). The enthusiasm of the government and industry for nuclear energy was boosted when the first United Nations International Conference on the Peaceful Uses of Atomic Energy was held in Geneva in August 1955, a meeting which showed to the world the wonders of nuclear technology. (The Geneva Conferences of 1955 and 1958 are generally considered to have opened up the subjects of nuclear fission and fusion for energy purposes.) Japanese participants included scientists and representatives from business and government.

The conference had a major impact on those who attended and recommendations were made by four Diet members to enact a basic atomic energy law and set up an S&T agency, as well as two public corporations to administer and conduct R&D for atomic energy. Among the four Diet members who attended the Geneva conference was Nakasone. A Joint Diet Atomic Energy Committee was set up which included four politicians among its twelve members. The chairman was the young and promising Nakasone, later to become Prime Minister and to become known for his right-wing views. The committee was active in pushing for an atomic energy program. On 14 November 1955 a US–Japan Atomic Energy Agreement was signed in Washington and, as a result, there was a great upsurge of interest among Japanese industrial circles in the commercialisation of atomic energy (JAIF: 1971, 187–91).

On 26 November 1955 Nakasone and the Joint Diet Atomic Energy Committee made representations to the Cabinet Preparatory Council for the Use of Atomic Energy. It was argued that there was an urgent need for a national policy for atomic energy. Nakasone was supported by three scientists who were present: Kaya, Fujioka and Tomonaga Sin-itirō. Formal government authority came to rest in the Prime Minister's Office in the form of the Japan Atomic Energy Commission (JAEC), which was established under a special law on 19 December 1955. The first meeting of JAEC was held on 4 January 1956 and included scientist-members Yukawa Hideki and Fujioka. The Radiation Council was established in 1956 to help determine standards for radiation protection and the Japan Atomic Energy Research Institute (JAERI) was created that same year. R&D was to be conducted by the Institute, which would be located at Tōkai-mura, about 112km north of Tokyo. Coincidentally, the area was the homeground of commission head Shōriki (JAIF: 1971, 193–4, 222). In May 1956 the Science and Technology Agency (STA) was launched and given the task of managing Japanese nuclear R&D and of providing staff and other support for the commission.

The 1960s in Japan saw the consolidation of policies to promote S&T. Against the background of rapid economic growth research in the private sector flourished, raising the new question of the roles that industry, government and academic institutions were to play in research and development. One of the main characteristics of this decade was that the STA began activities on a national scale to promote S&T to contribute to the economic development of the nation. The Science and Technology Council (STC), established in February 1959, was an advisory body to the Prime Minister and was considerably more powerful than previous councils. It was effectively the highest government advisory body on S&T policy and would act as a type of buffer between the government and the sometimes hostile JSC. At the same time, improvement and expansion of national experimental research institutes was progressing (Tsukahara: 1995, 51–60).

In June 1961 Nakasone assumed his new position of director of the STA and head of the JAEC. The Japan Atomic Industrial Forum (JAIF) was formed in 1956 and the Japan Atomic Fuel Corporation (JAFC) in 1957. The latter became the Power Reactor and Nuclear Fuel Development Corporation (PNC) in 1967. MITI took on the responsibility for actual nuclear power generation. The Japan Nuclear Ship Development Agency (JNSDA) was established in 1963 to construct *Mutsu*, Japan's first nuclear-powered commercial vessel. Mitsubishi Atomic Power Industries were contracted to build the reactor.

There was a considerable struggle inside the government–industrial complex over who would control nuclear power. The establishment of the Japan Atomic Power Company (JAPCO) to facilitate the technology transfer of a British gas-graphite reactor represented the compromise that was reached. The company was established as a joint concern by government and industry, funded 40 per cent by private utilities, 20 per cent by government utilities and the remainder from private sources (Imai: 1970). The government's policy tended to encourage JAPCO and other electric power companies to use their own funds to build nuclear power stations with what were known to be proven types of reactors, such as LWR. Government funds were intended to be used to promote R&D for advanced technology.

Importation of Commercial Reactors

Despite protests from the scientist-critics, it was decided that JAPCO would purchase two commercial nuclear power plants of around 200 MWe, one from the United Kingdom and one from the United States. The UK Magnox-type reactor was chosen for Japan's first project in 1956 and was to be situated at Tōkai-mura. At Tōkai-mura, a small research reactor (JRR-1) of American origin (50 kW) began operation in 1957, but it was not until 1962 that the first Japanese-made research reactor would become critical.

The Japanese initially opted for British technology for Japan's first nuclear power station when it committed itself, in 1959, to the purchase of an improved Calder-Hall type power reactor of 150 MWe, amid negotiations for the importation from the United States of an enriched uranium-type power reactor. The British natural uranium gas-cooled reactor of JAPCO operated at full power in 1966, but was beset by problems. In time, however, Japanese industry turned to the importation of American LWR.

With the installation of the Calder-Hall reactor at Tōkai-mura and the establishment of an American experimental power reactor, it was felt that the nuclear power industry was establishing a firm footing. However, given the various developmental problems which were being experienced overseas, the initial excitement gave way to a more sober, realistic view of the difficulties which would have to be faced. Almost as soon as the safety checks of the plans for the JAPCO Tōkai-mura power plant had been completed and it was certain to proceed, there was an announcement made by the then head of the JAEC, Nakasone, that the long-term atomic energy generation plan would have to be revised in view of the changes in the enthusiasm for nuclear power (JAIF: 1971, 135). It was generally felt that pressurised or boiling LWRs would be a 'better choice'. Since the Meiji period, there had been good relations between General Electric and Tokyo Electric Power Company, and Westinghouse and Kansai Electric Power Company. A 12 MWe General Electric boiling water reactor had been the first reactor to generate electrical power at Tōkai-mura. JAPCO's first large-scale LWR started operation at Tsuruga in 1970, and by March 1971 Tokyo Electric had started a station using General Electric boiling water reactor technology in Fukushima. Kansai Electric had an operation in Mihama working four months earlier using Westinghouse pressurised water reactor technology. The rush to commercialise nuclear power (especially LWRs) meant that a strong R&D base was not able to be established first and an over-reliance on American expertise was the result.

Some of Japan's most powerful corporations thus came to have a stake in the continued existence of the nuclear industry (Suttmeier: 1981, 110). Five consortia have been involved in providing nuclear technology in Japan: Mitsubishi Atomic Power Industries; Tokyo Atomic Industrial Consortium (Hitachi-Fuyokai Group); Nippon Atomic Industry Group Company (Mitsui, including Toshiba); Sumitomo Atomic Energy Industries; and Daiichi Atomic Power Industry Group (Furukawa and Kawasaki) (Endicott: 1975, 87). The first three of this group of five have been major contractors of nuclear facilities.

In October 1963 a JAERI experimental power reactor at Tōkai-mura generated electricity and, in November 1965, commercial nuclear-powered electricity was generated in Japan for the first time. In 1967 JNSDA commenced construction of *Mutsu* at the dockyard of Ishikawajima-Harima Heavy Industry Company. While it was hoped that the vessel of 8300 gross tons (8433 gross tonnes) would be used partly as a cargo ship, rising costs and technical problems have continued to plague its development and have effectively ruled out its use for commercial purposes. From the time of its first voyage, the ship began to leak radioactive materials (Murata: 1967, supplement 3–4).

Dualistic Structure

The main promoters of nuclear power have been the government and industry, their close relationship resulting in the formation of a government–industry complex. There are six elements to this government–industry complex: MITI; STA; nuclear power industry; electric power companies; public corporations (Japan Atomic Energy Research Institute (JAERI), PNC, etc.); and government–industry cooperative enterprises (for example, JAPCO).

The motivating force behind the development of power reactors can be roughly divided into the two groups: the atomic power industry and electric power companies (MITI–industrial complex); and the STA and public corporations for research. This dualistic structure began in 1957 with the decision to introduce the British Calder-Hall reactor. This marked the beginning of a split between groups arguing for domestic R&D, and those urging the introduction of foreign technology. The establishment of STA in 1956 could be considered as one of the origins of this dualistic structure. Due to the very nature of STA, its absence of ties with the industrial world meant that the agency did not have the option to introduce a commercial power plant reactor. This dualistic system was further nurtured in the mid-1960s, with the beginning of the introduction of LWRs and the start of advanced thermal reactor (ATR) and fast breeder reactor (FBR) projects.

The history of the beginnings of the Japanese atomic energy program reflects strong ties between the government and business, the United States and Japan. This strong nuclear alliance between the United States and Japan has essentially continued to the present day, despite internal conflict within the US–Japan atomic complex. Indeed, the path of development of nuclear power followed by Japan can be said to have been a result of the dynamics of internal cooperation and conflict. Out of this conflict has re-emerged a dualistic structure which is reminiscent of the multi-layered wartime organisation of Japanese S&T (Low & Yoshioka: 1989).

Nuclear power generation is one of the main means of electricity production in Japan. The overall fraction of the electric power supply obtained from atomic energy in Japan has been rising steadily. About one-third of the country's electricity is now produced by nuclear power stations. But the development of nuclear power has had limited success for at least two reasons. First, nuclear power reactors in Japan are still constructed under the licences of United States corporations such as General Electric Company and Westinghouse, and consequently the local Japanese nuclear industry is still unable to develop as an export industry. Secondly, most enriched uranium for use in light water LWRs – all commercial reactors except one small Calder-Hall type reactor are LWRs in Japan – is imported from the United States and European countries.

The main task of the MITI-group is the gradual expansion of the commercial nuclear enterprise, whereas the STA-group's mission is the research and development of commercially unproven technology. The typical strategy of the MITI-group has been that of three-stage development: (1) introduction of foreign commercial plants; (2) domestic production under foreign licences; and (3) attainment of technological independence. The ordinary strategy of the STA-group has been that of another type of three-stage development: (1) domestic R&D effort independent of foreign licences; (2) technology transfer from public corporations to private companies; and (3) construction of commercial facilities based on domestic technology. The final stage of development of each group is, of course, identical with each other.

Fast Breeder Development

For more than thirty years, the JAEC and other major promoters of atomic energy have declared that the ultimate technical goal (that is, political goal) of nuclear development is to establish a domestic nuclear fuel cycle which would include domestically produced breeder reactors, and to expand it into one of the principal energy sources in Japan. If this technical goal were attained, the domestic content of atomic energy production and, ultimately, that of overall production would increase substantially, strengthening Japanese economic (and national) security by means of stability of energy supply. This has, superficially at least, been the most influential political goal (and stated technical goal) of nuclear development in Japan. An accident at the prototype FBR 'Monju' on 8 December 1995 has put into question the future of plutonium as nuclear fuel in Japan.

The accident effectively brought to an end the development of FBRs in advanced industrial nations, for Japan is the last nation to oppose the world-wide tendency to stop such programs. Americans abandoned FBR development in the mid-1970s, and all European nations which had committed themselves to plutonium breeding programs (that is, France, the United Kingdom and the FRG) abandoned them in the early 1990s. The question must be asked: why did Japan continue with FBR programs in the face of such little likelihood of technical success?

As we saw earlier, the nuclear development community can be divided into two groups: MITI and electric power companies; and the STA-group, of which STA and two public corporations – the Power Reactor and Nuclear Fuel Development Corporation (PNC) and the Japan Atomic Energy Research Institute (JAERI) – constitute the leading members. The MITI group can be said to have achieved satisfactory success, having constructed forty-nine commercial power reactors (of which forty-eight are LWRs) by the end of 1995 (JAEC: 1996). The STA group has met with little success and long delays. Not until after the mid-1970s did the STA national projects begin to come near to a nominally 'commercial' stage. Unable to purchase expensive facilities with funds from the national budget, the only way to overcome the financial difficulty was to transfer those projects to the electric power industry through privatisation.

The main promoter of FBR development in Japan has been the PNC. As the central nuclear R&D laboratory under the control of the STA, PNC had been promoting four major national R&D projects: the FBR; the ATR; nuclear fuel reprocessing; and uranium enrichment. Although these projects, except for the FBR development, had already been transferred to the electric power utilities or related corporations after the 1980s, the historical role of the PNC has been prominent. Moreover, the greater part of present PNC R&D activity is related to the four mainstream projects mentioned above, and the present role of PNC is, in turn, also maintained by those projects. In August 1995 the JAEC decided to discontinue the ATR project, but the other three major projects have yet to be terminated.

In Japan, as with every other advanced industrial nation, the final goal of nuclear development has been the completion of the 'plutonium economy', that is, a self-sustaining plutonium breeding system that supplies all the nuclear electricity. To fulfil the goal of the completion of the 'plutonium economy' it is essential to make economically viable FBRs. The JAERI began work on an experimental FBR, 'Jōyō', in 1965, later transferring the project to the PNC. Since then, the PNC has promoted the project but there were two major problems. One problem was the lack of technological information about the design and specifications of the FBR. Another obstacle was the difficulty in acquiring plutonium for the experimental reactor. Due to these difficulties, the FBR development in Japan started in the late 1960s. The construction program for the experimental reactor 'Jōyō' ('eternal sunshine') started in March 1970, and became critical in April 1977. The next stage of FBR development was to construct the prototype reactor 'Monju' (280 MWe). Work began in October 1985 and finished in April 1991. After various tests 'Monju' succeeded in becoming critical in April 1994. While 'Monju' succeeded in generating electricity in August 1995, after three months a sodium-leakage and fire occurred and it is not certain whether the PNC will be able to operate 'Monju' again. Even if the PNC is able to do so, it will take at least several years of investigations, inspections, and repairs. Another problem is that the projected cost of FBR power generation has risen rapidly, with the unit construction cost of the FBR being about 7.6 times higher than that of an LWR. When fuel considerations are included, the cost of FBR power generation is about ten times higher than that of LWR.

Two other difficulties emerged in the early 1990s. Every advanced industrial nation other than Japan abandoned plutonium breeding development programs. It was the beginning of an era when electric power utilities in Japan would increasingly refuse to cooperate in national projects on the grounds of lack of economic viability. Although the utilities had agreed to take over all the projects of the STA group in the 1980s, they have had the potential to veto participation in national projects originated by the STA. On 11 July 1995 the Electric Power Utilities Union (Denjiren) exercised the power of veto for the first time in the history of nuclear development in Japan. It declared that it had decided to decline from contributing to the construction program of the ATR demonstration reactor promoted by the Electric Power Supply Development (Dengen Kaihatsu) Inc. under the control of MITI. With the withdrawal of electric power utilities, the JAEC decided to discontinue the construction program on 25 August 1995. The reason for this action by the electric power utilities was the poor likelihood of commercialisation of the ATR. As the estimated cost of construction and fuel for a demonstration FBR will be far higher than that of a demonstration ATR, electric power utilities will almost certainly withdraw.

The widespread knowledge among Japanese that FBRs lack reliability and safety when compared with conventional LWRs, and attempts to conceal the seriousness of the 'Monju' accident, have resulted in a loss of trust in the PNC and PNC-like organisations which promote national projects. The JAEC has frozen FBR development. It is likely that the STA will strongly oppose any decision to discontinue, partly due to a desire to guard its own territory, and it would be impossible for the JAEC to force the STA to give up FBR development as the executive office of the JAEC is located in the STA itself!

Let us return to our earlier question: why does the Japanese government encourage the use of plutonium in power production? It is unlikely that Japan is attempting to become a nuclear power. Rather, it can be better explained by the dual structure of nuclear development, the decentralised structure of political power in which each agency looks after its own interests, and characteristics of political decision-making in Japan. If the Japanese government discontinues FBR development, the past and present role of the PNC will be completely denied, and the dissolution or radical restructuring of the PNC will be inevitable. For the STA which controls the PNC, the impact of termination of FBR development will also be very serious. The STA will lose the major part of its largest policy domain: nuclear development. The scale of nuclear development under the control of STA would be reduced at least by half. Considering the uncertain future of the space development program, STA's second largest policy domain, in the twenty-first century STA may have to change into an agency mainly concerned with planning and regulating.

Conclusion

Since the 1973 to 1974 oil crisis, the Japanese people have entertained fears of energy starvation, but the Japanese have come to realise that too much dependence on atomic energy is risky because almost all natural uranium and enriched uranium is imported from abroad, and nuclear power is, by nature, not a stable energy source. The magnitude of environmental damage caused by an accident at a reprocessing plant or FBR would be far more serious than that at an LWR. If a major accident were to occur in the future, the Japanese government would have no choice but to abandon the production of nuclear power.

Broadbent (1998, xiii) describes this sort of situation as the 'Growth/Environment dilemma'. The pursuit of development (in the case of this chapter, nuclear power) held out the prospect of greater self-sufficiency in energy. At the same time, however, there has been the potential for major harm to the environment. In the 1980s there was a certain complacency about the environment (see Chapter 5), and there was no nation-wide resistance to nuclear power. This perhaps reflects the belief that Japanese technology would fix any problems that emerged. It is also evidence of certain patterns of power and influence at work in Japan, patterns which will emerge in later chapters. It is no coincidence that greater affluence has meant the Japanese people are today more concerned with quality-of-life issues than with the issues that dominated during the period of reconstruction and high economic growth following the end of the Second World War. A major accident at a Japanese reactor would see the end of Japan's nuclear power program.

The Japanese government has discussed a variety of administrative reforms which will effectively reorganise the bureaucracy (see Figure 12.1). One reform which has been announced is the merging of STA with the Ministry of Education. It is by understanding the history of nuclear development and recent events that we can comprehend how policy-making is conducted in Japan, and how the future of the STA has become clouded.

CHAPTER 5

Consumerism and Development versus the Environment

Introduction

A feature of the emergence of the consumer society in Japan was the idea that waste, or at least non-utilitarian expenditure, was good, and an indicator of how far Japan had advanced. One cannot but help notice the 'waste' created by excessive packaging and the street pavements piled with no-longer-wanted, unfashionable appliances. While such rejected goods are sometimes sought after by impoverished foreigners, a combination of rubbish and overdevelopment seems to be choking Mt Fuji (Hills: 1995a). Nothing seems to be sacred. A new Recycling Bill for electrical appliances (television sets, refrigerators, washing machines and airconditioners) will come into effect in 2001 (Nagai: 1998). Why has such legislation been so slow to eventuate? The image of Japan as an international economic leader contrasts with that of Japan as an environmental pariah.

This chapter examines this question by first outlining the rise of consumerism in Japan as illustrated by the growing popularity of household electric appliances. The second part of the chapter examines the social costs of the rise in consumerism and economic development, in terms of the impact on the environment. Japan provides a good example of how the environment eventually improves as income increases. Japanese environmental technologies have accelerated that process, but there is still the potential for nuclear power plants and high dioxin contamination from incinerators to cause great harm to the health of the Japanese people. The danger that they represent is but further illustration that the beneficiaries of modern development are often the members of the government, bureaucracy and business, and the losers are the Japanese people. Japanese decision-makers find difficulty in distinguishing between their own interests and that of the nation. It is thus often up to international institutions and non-government organisations to spread new values. While Japan has various environmental laws and regulations in place, it has been slow to establish them. Japan's improving domestic situation and the concern with the global environment disguises the fact that there are still serious pollution problems in Japan, and that pollution in other parts of Asia might well be labelled 'Made in Japan'. Industrial investment in Asia can serve to export pollution.

The Rise of Household Electric Appliances

Household electric appliances grew in popularity from the mid-1950s with increased economic growth. Higher incomes made access to labour-saving devices available to many Japanese. This was especially the case for the so-called 'three sacred treasures' of the television, washing machine, and refrigerator. The Japanese were able to put the unpleasant life of the immediate postwar years behind them and, at the same time, their perception of what constituted 'necessary' household goods changed. The idea of living surrounded by electric appliances became a goal and tangible evidence of having attained a higher standard of living.

The electric fan was the first household electric appliance manufactured in Japan, in 1916, and the first exports, mainly directed to Asia, began in 1922. From about 1930 electric clothes irons entered mass production; by 1935 they could be found in one-quarter of all Japanese homes, and before the Second World War were the most popular electric appliance. Electric refrigerators and vacuum cleaners were also produced but the average wage-earner could not afford them (Morimatsu et al.: 1985). A nationwide survey conducted in 1937 by J. G. Douglas of General Electric predicted that Japan would rapidly become a major market for electric appliances, however this did not eventuate because of the war. The Olympic Games planned for Tokyo in 1940 was seen as a turning point for Japan, and an opportunity to Westernise the Japanese lifestyle. Both the Tokyo Olympics and the boom in consumerism had to wait two decades: with the worsening conflict in Asia, the manufacture, sale, and import of such luxury items into Japan was prohibited in July 1940 (Yamada: 1982, 27–8).

By the Second World War the electronics industry was largely meeting both consumer and industrial demand in Japan, although during the war it generally stagnated. For a short time after the end of the war there was a glut in the supply of electricity, followed by a shortage once industry and transport systems were re-established. By the 1950s a consumer-dominated culture had emerged in Japan. The sudden demand for goods, stimulated by the Korean War in 1950 and 1951, put great strain on electricity supplies, and in January 1952 the Committee on Public Corporations announced a five-year plan for electric power development. The situation was so bad that MITI implemented electricity rationing, with the daytime use of neon lighting and other non-essential uses of electricity effectively banned from January to March 1953 (Tōkyō Shibaura Denki: 1977).

Electric fans and mixers sold well, followed by washing machines. In 1950 Matsushita Electric was able to pay dividends for the first time since the end of the war. Other companies, such as Tōshiba, Hitachi and Mitsubishi, were able to recover financially through increased sales in heavy electric equipment, with household electronics constituting only a minor sideline. The force behind MITI's 'New Trade and Industry Policy Outline' of September 1954, Okuno Kiyomori, perceived that the demand for household electrical goods and automobiles would increase faster than the increase in general incomes, while the demand for foodstuffs and apparel would remain steady. A few months later, the new minister of MITI, Ishibashi Tanzan, expressed the view that it was important to exploit the domestic market as well as maintain exports (Johnson: 1982, 229).

During the *denka būmu* (boom in electric appliances for the home) in 1955, the phrase 'my home' came to be used. It conjured up the image of a home with pristine white washing machines, refrigerators, and electric rice cookers (Tada: 1978, 210). In time, other housekeeping appliances entered the home such as vacuum cleaners and dryers; culture and information goods such as radios, television sets, tape-recorders and stereo sets became commonplace; as did health and beauty items such as hair-dryers and electric shavers; and consumable goods such as light bulbs, batteries and tape (Aoyama: 1991). Many of these items were aimed at saving labour and reflected the increasing liberation of women from the household and the growth in leisure time; they served to redefine gender roles and social hierarchies.

In the first half of the 1950s technological information once again began to enter Japan, and the world's first transistorised portable radio set was produced in Japan in 1955. This enabled considerable reductions in the size of many products and helped improve their quality and reduce prices. The electronics industry underwent rapid growth in the next decade, and by 1965 it had approached the level of industrially advanced nations.

The growth of the consumer electronics industry (for example, hi-fi systems, compact disc players, car audio equipment, television sets, video cassette recorders, video camera recorders) which accompanied rapid economic growth reflected the increasing affluence of the population and the growth of markets for Japanese goods. It also reflected the rationalisation and Westernisation of Japanese life, with the rise of American-led democracy and the nuclear family. The approach to life changed and television sets were an important part of the process. In 1948 the NHK Technical Research Institute resumed work on television experiments in collaboration with Tōshiba. In 1952 it was decided to adopt the NTSC system (the electronic television standard used in the United States) and in 1953 black and white telecasts began. Several educational channels were founded in 1959 although most were forced to change to general channels due to lack of sponsorship. The first domestic television was produced by Hitachi in 1959, helping to introduce American-style family life and the material features of American culture (Aoyama: 1991). Television provided a window to American culture, and promoted middle-class consumerism by transporting viewers to parts of the world they had only dreamt of. In this way, we can see how technology serves to represent and diffuse dominant values, facilitating processes of cultural reproduction and social change (Bray: 1997). In 1960 Sony produced the world's first fully transistorised television set. Colour transmissions began in 1960, with Sony developing an independent system called Trinitron. The wedding of the Crown Prince in 1959 and the Tokyo Olympic Games in 1964 increased the popularity of television (Kōdansha: 1983, 5, 128; Wakamatsu: 1995, 3, 399–400).

The concentration of population in the cities left country farming areas with less than 20 per cent of Japan's total working population by 1967. Television brought images of city life to the country and accelerated the movement of young people to the cities, while many farmers struggled to find the cash to buy agricultural machinery, fertilisers and insecticides. In 1964 Sharp produced the world's first portable computer/calculator (*dentaku*) using transistor diodes, followed by the integrated circuit *dentaku* in 1967 and a model using LSI in 1968. By the mid-1970s Japan produced over half the world's colour televisions and exported three-quarters of them. Since the late 1970s competition has been intense in the electric appliance industry, with major technical advances linked to developments in semiconductor technology. The main consumer electronics manufacturers are Matsushita Electric (which uses the brand names of National and Panasonic), Sanyo Corporation, Sony Corporation and Sharp Corporation. Brother Industries Ltd, established in 1934, was Japan's leading manufacturer of sewing machines, knitting machines and typewriters by the late 1970s (Kōdansha: 1983, 1, 175; Yoshioka: 1995, 2, 416–26; Fransman: 1995, 10–11).

Many of the products were products based on technology introduced from overseas, such as transistors and integrated circuits which were then much improved, and new models of television sets, refrigerators, audio goods and videotape recorders. There has been an emphasis on high quality, low-priced goods. Electronic goods have often been light, thin and small, with miniaturisation often considered a hallmark of Japanese ingenuity and creativity (see Table 7.2). While the Japanese have been accused of a lack of 'originality', there is no disputing the amount of creativity which is required in commercialising ideas borrowed from overseas.

The phrase 'three sacred treasures' (referring to television, washing machine and refrigerator), was first heard in 1954, although its origins are unclear. The three types of goods were not in widespread use at the time, and their high price still placed them in the category of luxury goods for most households, unlike appliances such as electric toasters and mixers. In spite of this, the 'three treasures' gained a rapid hold as the appliances everyone simply must possess. The production of household electric appliances grew rapidly between 1954 and 1958, with televisions occupying 45 per cent of production volume. Sanyo produced a rotary washing machine in 1953 and by 1960 a washing machine was in 40 per cent of households. By 1963, 90 per cent of Japanese households had televisions, a rate of distribution far greater than any other appliance, and which had jumped from 30 per cent to 90 per cent in just four years. The popularity of television is difficult to explain from a pragmatic point of view, other than seeing it as the result of efficient advertising. It may be compared with the United States, where in 1969 refrigerators and washing machines were owned by 90 per cent of households but televisions by 80 per cent.

The so-called 'apartment dwellers' (*danchi zoku*) played a major role in the spread of household electric appliances. The nickname was bestowed on them by the periodical *Shūkan asahi* (*Asahi Weekly*) in 1958. Most residents of Tokyo's big housing complexes had larger incomes, with correspondingly more to spend on such appliances as refrigerators and washing machines. The 1960 *White Paper on National Lifestyle* produced by the Japanese government pointed out an imbalance between the spread of electric appliances and increase in apparel consumption, and other factors such as consumption of animal protein, small size of dwellings, sewerage and paved roads, comparing the living environment factors unfavourably to the United States and European countries, although this made little impact at the time. The rise of consumerism was seen as a milestone in Japan's economic development, an indication that the Japanese people had freed themselves from the struggle against scarcity. The *White Paper on Japan's Economy 1961* bore the subtitle 'Consumption is a virtue: the era of throw-away culture begins', seemingly declaring that waste is a virtue (Yunomae: 1996, 102).

While the Japanese were encouraged to believe that through careful shopping they could acquire good taste, improve themselves, be happier and more attractive, consumer goods did not so much improve the material conditions of families as provide them with symbols of status. Many people bought blenders about 1950 despite the lack of food such as fruit to blend (Tada: 1978, 212). The formation of a mass consumer market and the status associated with goods were part of the social and economic change which Japan underwent in the postwar period (Aoyama: 1991).

Of the 'three treasures', the only one that obviously reduces labour is the washing machine, and advertisements for washing machines in the 1950s emphasised the saving in time for the average housewife with this appliance. However, it is doubtful whether the use of washing machines actually increased the free time available, and a comparison of the time spent on housework in 1951 and 1960 showed that it had increased (Kōdansha: 1962). It is uncertain how the labour and time saved by the introduction of electric appliances was used. Between 1950 and 1960 the number of city dwellers increased dramatically and extended family households declined. The percentage of nuclear families grew to over 60 per cent, thus decreasing the average family size from five to three. Housework would probably therefore have decreased over this period even without the help of household appliances. The use of such appliances meant, also, that a certain standard of housework could be achieved by anyone. Housewives, instead of spending their time in leisure as the early advertisements for appliances suggested, began to use their free time to return to part-time work and gain income to purchase other consumer goods or services, or to pay the educational expenses of the children. In this situation, of course, the true labour-saving aspects of household electric appliances were readily appreciated.

Refrigerators were not considered really necessary until the early 1960s, and both production and consumption showed only slow rates of growth in the 1950s, reaching a distribution rate of 10 per cent in 1960. This grew suddenly to 50 per cent by 1963, when refrigerators with freezers entered the market and consumers began to realise the advantages of long-term food storage. This stimulated the production of good quality frozen foods, which grew by 30 per cent between 1971 and 1972. By 1972, 97 per cent of households had refrigerators, and supermarkets were beginning to stock goods such as 1-litre milk and juice cartons. Even so, there was little consciousness of the refrigerator as a labour-saving device. Refrigerators were not generally used all year until the advent of separate freezer compartments in the 1970s. Microwave ovens were far slower to become popular and reached a distribution rate of 50 per cent in 1987, nineteen years after they appeared on the market.

There are a number of reasons given for the competitiveness of Japanese household electrical goods; these include addressing particular consumer needs and the willingness of Japanese manufacturers to cater for those needs. Success is also attributed to good timing in model changeovers and the exploitation of consumer desire to buy new models. Consumer worries such as safety and low energy consumption, however, became matters of concern in the 1970s; until then, MITI erected buffers against competition from imports and Japanese consumers bought what was available at the price the manufacturers dictated. In 1955 electricity charges were changed and meters were installed in all houses. Electric plugs became a normal part of residential facilities. The Japan Housing Corporation was formed in July of that year. In later years the 'three Cs' (colour television, air-conditioner, and car) joined the 'three treasures' as a representation of the ideal lifestyle. The purchase of items such as household electric appliances served as a way of experiencing economic affluence, despite the fact that improvements in the living environment remained slow, and the increase had a wide influence by stimulating economic growth in the creation of domestic demand, thus increasing employment and also the demand for electricity.

The electric machinery industry developed rapidly, due mainly to the growth of the household appliance and heavy machinery manufacturing industries. In the fields of solid state devices and material science, Japanese research developed unique devices such as the parametron, Esaki (tunnel) diode, and the nickel-cadmium battery. The focus of the electronics industry changed from consumer products to industrial equipment in the mid-1970s, with exceptional achievements in such fields as semiconductor devices. The three main electric manufacturers are Hitachi Ltd, Tōshiba Corporation, and Mitsubishi Electric Corporation. The four major home electric appliance manufacturers are Matsushita Electric Industrial Company, Sanyo Electric Company, Sony Corporation and Sharp Corporation, while the three leading telecommunications equipment makers are Nippon Electric Company, Fujitsu Ltd and Oki Electric Industry Company. Manufacturers such as Casio Computer Company, established in 1957, produce electronic instruments, especially electronic calculators and digital watches (Kōdansha: 1983, 2, 192–5; Itō et al.: 1983, 689).

Home appliances are a part of what has been called 'home automation', the so-called 'intelligent home' and 'intelligent buildings' being an extreme case of how the daily lives of the Japanese can be affected by technology. Since about 1988 the idea of an 'intelligent home' that made use of the latest home electronic goods has been promoted. The home technologies can be broadly divided into: (1) housekeeping systems (home security systems, automated lighting and heating, television camera surveillance); (2) management systems (home shopping, electronic communications, telecommuting); (3) culture systems (distance education, audiovisual systems); and (4) communication systems (upgrading of telephone lines, home fax, computer-based communication) (Aoyama: 1991). They help to provide a total environment, one that distances people from their natural surroundings.

Despite the array of electric appliances available to the Japanese, and the mechanisation of housework that has become possible, it was estimated in 1986 that the 'non-working' Japanese housewife still does nearly eight hours of housework per day (Takahara: 1991). Some Japanese have found their hard-won affluence somewhat empty, and increasingly are concerned with conserving their environment rather than acquiring more material goods.

Consumption versus the Environment

In December 1997 representatives from throughout the world gathered in Kyoto to work towards reducing global greenhouse gas emissions. While the meeting helped put Japan on the map of international environmental diplomacy, it disguises the fact that Japan is still grappling with local pollution problems. Environmentalism is still in the process of formation in Japan. Global environmental problems have become a major international concern in the late twentieth century, often overshadowing serious problems that the Japanese have yet to solve within their own country. The next part of this chapter outlines some of those problems. Unless these problems are dealt with, Japan cannot be considered to be an environmentally-advanced nation capable of showing leadership in the world arena.

Japan's embrace of consumption from the 1960s onwards was accompanied by environmental problems. Such problems remain a potent reminder of the costs of a growth-first strategy which neglects enviromental protection (Kamioka: 1987). Symbolic of the grave pollution problems faced by Japan was the controversy surrounding mass mercury poisoning in the city of Minamata on the coast of Western Kyushu (Popham: 1991; Hills: 1993). Non-material things such as an improved environment came to be more highly valued by the Japanese in the years that followed. The emergence of environmentalism in Japan in the 1970s reflects the correlation between growing incomes and the preference for an improved environment over greater income. Although today's environmentalism has lost much of the radical character of those years, environmental concerns have been taken up by a much greater number of people, and many environmentally friendly practices have entered the domain of being generally accepted, common sense. Whereas previously the private sector was placed in a defensive and adversarial role, its position, too, has changed since the 1970s.

When did the transition occur? In the 1970s the anti-pollution movement tended to be most focused in regional communities directly affected by the source of contamination. It was a grassroots movement with clearly defined victims and aggressors who struggled to protect their interests. In contrast, from the late 1980s until the early 1990s global environmental problems became of more concern. This had been the case in Europe for some time, but in Japan people only became truly conscious of global problems after the end of the Cold War when international meetings of world leaders put environmental problems on the diplomacy agenda. Government research institutes in Japan began to conduct more environmental impact assessments and private companies became more environment-friendly. Citizens, too, became more conscious of the global environment, and in the 1990s there was a marked increase in interest in the environment. Environmentalism emerged from its origins in radical culture to became a mainstream concern.

As mentioned earlier, the anti-pollution movement of the 1970s was most concerned with protecting the immediate surroundings and lifestyle of citizens, and thus differs considerably from the global environmental protection movement which dates from the late 1980s. The former started from the premise of a victim and an aggressor. People living in the vicinity of factory plants where the source of contamination was often traced, can be viewed as the victims. It was these people who organised themselves into a protest movement. The mass media acted as public watchdog and brought such issues to the attention of the wider public. Academics responded to the call for help, and researchers became interested in conducting environmental impact assessments. Bureaucrats, too, showed interest and tried to devise countermeasures. Government bodies such as the Environment Agency were created in response. Pressure was brought to bear on companies so they were forced to implement measures for the prevention of pollution. As a result of this increasing awareness, pollution has mistakenly come to be thought of as being under control. The transfer of the Japanese pattern of development and export of Japan's environment problems to other parts of Asia where much manufacturing occurs deprived the anti-pollution movement of overt targets. The 1980s saw a relative decline in interest in local pollution problems, but growing awareness that Japanese consumption patterns were causing problems for people in other parts of Asia who were helping to meet Japanese demand for resources, such as tropical timber (Dauvergne: 1997).

On the other hand, concerns about global environment problems originated elsewhere. The 1972 report *The Limits to Growth* warned that the earth might not be able to sustain global economic activity beyond 2020. When did most Japanese become aware of such problems? An article on the 'global environment' first appeared in the prestigious newspaper *Asahi Shinbun* in 1985 carrying a report about the ozone hole above Antarctica. Table 5.1 shows how often the words 'global environment' appear in that newspaper's headlines and we can interpret the increase in articles as reflecting a boom in interest in the global environment. There were over a thousand of such articles in 1992 due to the Earth Summit being held in Brazil that year. Since then, the global environment has become a major area of concern, with 400 to 500 articles per year.

The problems discussed in the *Asahi Shinbun* articles can be roughly divided into two types: (1) regional pollution which becomes a global problem, as can be seen in acid rain, land degradation, desertification, and the destruction of rainforests (Aoyagi: 1990; Hadfield: 1990); and (2) destruction of the ozone layer and global warming which are less local in character. The first type has been said to be a 'third world' problem, but it would be more accurate to describe the problems in this category as dilemmas which industrially advanced nations have imposed on developing nations.

How have the groups involved in the conflict changed? In the 1970s, the anti-pollution movement criticised the anti-social behaviour of private enterprise. Since then, companies have gradually taken a position

Table 5.1 Frequency of 'global environment' in *Asahi Shinbun* headlines

Year	Frequency
1985	1
1986	1
1987	10
1988	12
1989	170
1990	356
1991	829
1992	1218
1993	589
1994	429
1995	455
1996	402

Source: Nikkei-Telecom Japan News and Retrieval Database.

more in line with public attitudes to the environment (Yanagawa: 1992). If we compare anti-pollution activists in the period from the early 1970s through to the late 1980s, and those involved in the global environment movement of the 1990s, the people have changed. The former group consisted mainly of local residents who had been adversely affected and were fighting to protect their interests. The profile of the second group is much more elusive. They tend to be well-educated urban dwellers who have an interest in international affairs and are able to use the Internet to obtain information about the rest of the world.

Education about the need to protect our environment has grown since it first emerged in the 1970s, helped by the mass media which reports more frequently about environmental matters. Despite this, there is often a feeling of impotence when articles on the problems of distant places appear in the press. Rather, it has been easier to develop an awareness about disposing of waste thoughtfully, and the need to recycle.

The emphasis on local action is partly the legacy of a 1970s to 1980s ecological movement concerned with reconsidering various aspects of Japanese lifestyle that might have a detrimental effect on human health and the environment. Women were prominent in this movement, despite the growth in the number of women who have jobs outside the home. Women have been particularly concerned with the safety of foodstuffs. Their activities laid the foundation for the wide push in the late 1990s for organic, fertiliser-free vegetables and awareness of the need to recycle waste materials.

While it is possible to identify continuities between the more localised environmental concerns of the 1970s and the awareness of global environmental problems in the 1990s, the latter appears to be more of an externally-driven phenomenon which is concerned less with finding technological solutions and more with international politics. Global environmentalism spread in Japan as a result of government initiatives which, in turn, influenced the attitudes of the private sector, rather than being a grassroots-driven movement. This has moved the spotlight away from pollution problems within Japan and, in so doing, hides the fact that Japan has not overcome them.

In 1989 the Japanese government became aware that the environment was placed high on the agenda of major international problems in the vacuum left by the end of the Cold War. Governments came to see the world and what was ailing it in a different light. Paul James (1993) noted how national laboratories in the United States turned to solving global environmental problems in the search for new research themes in the aftermath of the end of the Cold War. While such a spontaneous response was not evident in Japan, national laboratories tended to take up such research after advice from above, in line with government priorities.

University-based researchers were slower to choose such themes as research topics. It was against this background that the National Pollution Research Institute attached to the Environment Agency was renamed the National Institute for Environmental Studies. Although this move was criticised by anti-pollution groups as an attempt to portray the source of pollution as global rather than local in origin, it spurred the creation of global environment study groups which investigated global warming and other climate change.

As if signalling a transition in concerns, the Japanese government sponsored an international conference on global environmental problems in Tokyo in September 1989. Sixty experts from twenty-three countries gathered there and Japanese government involvement included not only the Environment Agency but also STA, MITI and the Ministry of Construction. While the Meteorological Research Institute and the National Pollution Research Institute had long studied the warming effect of the increase in carbon dioxide, the other ministries also took an interest and successfully argued for their own research funds to study such problems. MITI established a Special Laboratory for the Global Environment in 1989, as well as a research institute for the study of pollution and natural resources. STA hoped to make the study of global environmental problems a national project, and made plans to launch a global observation satellite which would provide information on environmental problems. The Japanese government viewed the problems of a deteriorating global environment as a threat, but there was a strong perception that they presented Japan with an opportunity to leave its mark on the world (Coghlan: 1993).

The Response of Universities

The first manifestations of environmental science in Japan can be traced to the early 1970s, when various fields of S&T for pollution prevention emerged. This was accompanied by the study of ecology, which took on more of an academic flavour and remained separate from the other fields. Rather than concerning itself with human beings, ecology was more focused on animals, plants and the material world. In Japan, instead of adopting an approach of adding humans to the picture as observers, a human ecology approach was taken by some scholars, such as Numata Shin, in which the influence of humans on the environment was studied, and vice versa. Humans appear as actors who can wreak havoc on the environment.

One way of gauging the highs and lows of environmental science in Japan is by looking at categories of grants-in-aid given by the Ministry of Education for research. In the 1960s the serious nature of pollution problems made research aimed at eradicating them a top priority; by the late 1970s such research had largely halted. Although environmental science remained one of a small number of areas of special concern until the late 1980s, it was not treated with the same sense of urgency that it had attracted a decade earlier.

If we examine the establishment of environmental science departments, a similar trend can be observed. The 1960s were the era of expansion of faculties of science and engineering in Japanese national universities. This wave of growth continued as Japan entered the 1970s. Names of faculties and departments changed with the times, and the environment was no exception. In 1968 the first department for environmental protection was created with the establishment of the Department of Environmental Engineering in the Faculty of Engineering at Osaka University. In response to government calls for the establishment of departments and courses to combat pollution there was a veritable rush in 1975 among national universities to set up departments and they came to total over twenty. In 1974, with the promulgation of a law for setting standards for the establishment of graduate schools, universities outside the small circle of former imperial universities began establishing graduate schools. Newly-conceived departments were created in the schools. In the period 1977 to 1978 departments of environmental science were established at Hokkaidō, Tsukuba and Hiroshima Universities. This had a major impact on the establishment of environmental science as a field in Japan, not least through the nurturing of young specialists. The centre of activity was at Tsukuba University, which was geographically close to the National Pollution Research Institute and included many active researchers in environmental science on its staff. Interestingly, during the ten years from 1979, most graduates of the Department of Environmental Science found employment with private companies rather than with organisations expressly devoted to the environment. This was contrary to the hoped-for nurturing of specialists (Uchiyama: in press).

In 1977 the Organisation for Economic Cooperation and Development (OECD) proclaimed that pollution had largely come to an end in Japan. This coincided with a decline in interest in pollution and the environment, and ironically, the establishment of three graduate school departments for environmental science. With their establishment, the boom came to an end. In the 1980s major causes of pollution seemed to have come under control. The focus of environmental activists moved from industrial pollution to lifestyle-related waste and pollution. Given these trends, the budget of the National Pollution Research Institute was cut year after year. In the late 1980s several universities underwent reorganisation. The Department of Environmental Science at Hiroshima

University was abolished in 1988, and there was much discussion about future directions at Tsukuba University. Against this backdrop, in July 1989 the Environment Agency established an Office for Global Environmental Protection. The transition from dealing with pollution to dealing with the environment was further flagged by the renaming, in 1992, of the journal *Kōgai kenkyū* (*Pollution Research*) to *Kankyō to kōgai* (*The Environment and Pollution*). It now not only was concerned with environmental pollution, but also the protection of nature (Uchiyama: in press).

The 1970s anti-pollution movement represented a turning point. It was the first time that an environment protection movement had become a mass movement which mobilised ordinary citizens, helped along by the mass media (McKean: 1981). The number of fully-fledged environmental science programs peaked in the mid-1970s as a result of university expansion, and declined in the 1980s. The words 'environmental science' were used by academics and policy-makers to placate the public. The scientific method and technological solutions were seen as the way to relieve pollution.

From 1991 universities jumped on the bandwagon of the environment boom and departments dealing with the environment suddenly reappeared. While it takes several years for outside trends to affect the makeup of a university department, the majority of the new departments have been given fashionable names in the hope of stimulating interest among students. Such actions might appear superficial, but the current interest in issues relating to the global environment has attracted wider scholarly interest and now includes social scientists. Furthermore, computer simulation and modelling have enabled researchers to deal with problems in a more quantitative manner. Although the discipline of geography has been revitalised as a result of the environment boom, Japanese geographers have not been prominent in debates about the environment.

Response of Citizens

There were mixed responses from citizens' groups to the government-driven concern about the world's environmental problems. For example, according to anti-pollution activist Miyamoto Ken-ichi, if one looks at government policy bodies such as the Environment Agency, it uses problems such as ozone depletion and destruction of tropical rainforests as a scapegoat to divert attention from local pollution problems that could reappear. He advocates a localised approach to environment problems which maintains continuities with the earlier anti-pollution movement. As we shall see later in this chapter, such concerns are not only driven by self-interest but by the continuation of very real pollution problems in Japan (Japan Society for Applied Geology: 1993).

Citizens joined government and industry in their concern about the global environment, but without specific targets it has been difficult for them to act. Not only have the issues changed but the times have also changed. Private enterprise is now not so often the target of government policy. It was difficult for people, including housewife activists (Noguchi: 1992) to decide on whom they should vent their anger. Table 5.2 summarises some of the differences between the concern with local environment (and pollution) and the more recent interest in the global environment.

The Role of NGOs

Ultimately, it is not the public sector, hamstrung by national interest, that can really solve the big problems, but non-government organisations (NGOs). It has been shown elsewhere in this book that the Japanese state has been reluctant to address issues which might clash with the interests of big business. Given the close links between the two sectors, and the absence of a desire to jeopardise such ties, NGOs are an important independent voice, crucial if social change is to truly occur in Japan. Indeed, they provide a moral voice for the Japanese, and are an important part of the expansion of the Japanese environmental infrastructure.

NGOs concerned with global environment problems have been prominent. NGOs became active in Japan in the 1980s and about 90 per cent of Japan's NGOs were established in the 1980s and 1990s. Unlike the anti-pollution movment of the 1960s and 1970s which involved concerned local residents and other citizens, the NGOs dating from the 1980s are more global in outlook, calling themselves global citizens. 'Friends of the Earth, Japan' and 'Greenpeace Japan' were established as branches of international organisations in Japan at this time. Such

Table 5.2 Local versus global environment problems

Pollution/local environment	Global environment
Issues close-at-hand	Seemingly far-off problems
Cause can be clearly pinpointed	Difficult to specify source of problems
Use of technologies to combat problems	Time required to determine ultimate effect
Easy to determine a plan of action	Difficult to know what actions to take
Academics and students versus the government and private sector	Due to competition for international leadership, government takes initiative
Private sector on the defensive	Promotes positive image of private sector

organisations facilitate the spread of new values and are able to address issues which might be politically sensitive. Through the establishment of local branches, they have connected fragmented Japanese environmental groups with other activists overseas.

NGOs came to the attention of most Japanese from late 1991 to 1992, due to media attention at the UN Conference on Environment and Development in Rio de Janeiro, Brazil, in June 1992, the so-called 'Earth Summit'. The perception of a transition from a concern with pollution to the global environment became widespread among the public at this time and the number of newspaper articles dealing with NGOs increased greatly. *Yomiuri Shinbun*, the newspaper with the highest circulation in Japan, carried more than a hundred articles that year on NGOs. The number of such articles in the more liberal *Asahi Shinbun* increased by 300 to total 465 in that year alone. While the Earth Summit was obviously part of the reason for the increased interest, media focus on statements by NGOs reflected their greater credibility when compared with statements by governments which had sometimes been responsible for destruction of the environment (Kawano: in press). Thanks to the processes of globalisation (especially the Internet) in the 1990s and the interest of scholars in the humanities and social sciences, new environmental groups with an international focus have emerged.

Is Japan Advanced Environmentally?

About 1990 Japan was being referred to as an 'eco-outlaw' and environmental 'predator' or 'pariah' (Holliman: 1990, 284; Arafune: 1991), images which stand in stark contrast to those which many Japanese have of themselves. Japanese consumption of endangered whale meat and the killing of whales for 'scientific' research, despite an International Whaling Commission ban on commercial whaling since 1986, have not helped that image. Japan continues to kill approximately 1000 whales annually (Clennell: 1999). Is the negative image fact or fiction? We can determine how far advanced Japan is environmentally by judging it against the following criteria. First, one of the basic conditions for advanced status should be the maintenance of an excellent record in protecting the environment. Secondly, substantial progress in putting into place a regulatory framework for environmental protection would be required. Thirdly, a truly global perspective should be evident. Even if strict standards exist at home, the export of pollution and environmental destruction should not be tolerated. An environmentally advanced nation should show leadership at an international level and actively promote cooperative ventures and treaties. The fourth requirement would be public participation in policy-making. Decision-making needs to be democratic in nature, especially when it comes to the siting of industrial plants that might have an adverse effect on the environment. The more transparent procedures are, the easier it will be to detect any potential problems. Despite the developments outlined in the previous section, Japan fails to meet all the above four requirements.

The Rise and Fall of the Myth

In the 1980s many Japanese came to believe the myth that their country had overcome any pollution problems, and had succeeded in introducing industrial technologies which minimised them. Linked to this was the decline in reporting on pollution and a rise in positive reporting on environment-friendly technologies. In 1978 the Environment Agency put into place what was then the world's strictest regulations on car exhaust emissions. Also, manufacturing companies and electric utilities introduced equipment to purify gas emissions. Against this background the Japanese people came to believe that their country had overcome pollution. Much of what was done was instigated by the private sector and perhaps because of that, there were many areas of neglect which became evident in the 1990s. Even the OECD reported in 1994 that there were severe shortcomings in Japan's environmental performance (Swinbanks: 1994; OECD: 1994). Dioxin contamination is a continuing problem and provides evidence of how systematic rules for environmental protection have not been established. Only in 1997 was a law promulgated that concerned environmental impact assessment. Despite the hype surrounding the 1997 international conference in Kyoto, Japan has adopted a passive and self-interested attitude to global warming. This is perhaps to be expected given that most policy is formulated by bureaucrats who generally take into account the interests of corporate stakeholders, but pay little heed to the voices of regional communities and organisations. The remainder of this chapter discusses these inadequacies in more detail.

Continuing Pollution Problems

It became widely known in the late 1990s that dioxin contamination in Japan was the worst in the world. In the mid-1990s the density of dioxins in the atmosphere averaged one picogram per cubic metre, ten times the level reported in Europe and the United States. As for traces of dioxins in foodstuffs, it is estimated that Japan has the highest levels among industrially advanced nations. The Environment Agency estimates that the Japanese have an average intake of 3.5 picograms per kilogram of body weight. As a result, the level of dioxins in a Japanese mother's milk is among the highest in the world. The toxicity of dioxins (polychlorinated dibenzo-p-dioxins, PCDD) became evident in the large number of children with birth defects born to those who had contact with defoliants used in large quantity by the United States military during the Vietnam War. In 1983 a research team led by Professor Tachikawa Ryō of Ehime University examined ashes from nine city waste incinerators and reported detection of dioxins. There has been grave concern at the lack of policies to combat dioxin contamination.

How do we account for the abnormally high levels of dioxins in Japan? One major characteristic of waste disposal in Japan is the high reliance on the incineration of waste, irrespective of whether its origins are domestic or industrial. This enables authorities to reduce the volume of waste to about 5 per cent of its original volume, and it is considered an effective way to eliminate bacteria and odours. In 1990 about 122 000 tonnes of waste was being discharged every day, 75 per cent of which was being incinerated (Tanaka: 1990). A major problem with this is the high proportion of plastics (such as polyvinyl chloride or PVC), much of which includes chlorides that on being burnt create dioxins. In addition, there are insufficient mechanisms for the public regulation of industrial waste disposal. Much disposal is of an illegal nature, and many regional authorities have been slow to curb it. The shortage of land-fill sites has not helped. At the end of 1998, a national survey of incinerator emissions had yet to be conducted. These structural problems have helped make Japan the world's worst zone for dioxin contamination. In response, the Ministry of Health and Welfare initially decided in May 1984 that dioxin levels beyond 100 picograms per kilogram of body weight were harmful. Twelve years later this was reduced to 10 picograms and, even then, various loopholes made the legislation difficult to enforce. With other major countries creating even more stringent standards, Japan is trailing behind. In the late 1990s many Western countries advocated limits of less than one picogram.

Japan lags behind many other industrialised countries in implementing environmentally-friendly policies. One of the reasons for this has been a desire to allow companies sufficient time to adapt. A notable exception has been the regulation of car exhaust emissions, where Japan has led the world. This owes less to an enlightened bureaucracy and more to Honda beating other automakers in declaring that it was possible. And if it had not been for Toyota and Nissan having sufficient technological expertise to deal with lower gas emission regulations, MITI might well not have supported the Environment Agency in agreeing to them.

Environmental Impact Assessments

Japan is often referred to as the 'construction state' where development takes precedence over public good (McCormack: 1996a). Approximately 10 per cent of Japan's Gross Domestic Product is used in funding 'public' works, comparable to United States and Soviet military expenditure during the Cold War. Japan has enthusiastically promoted many large-scale construction projects, the fervour spilling over into the activities of the Official Development Assistance (ODA) which include dam construction. Other civil engineering projects include roads, estuary and land improvement, and sewerage works. Responsibility for each falls under various ministries and agencies, such as the Ministry of Construction and Ministry of Agriculture and Forestry (see Table 5.3). Once plans are approved it is difficult to have projects reviewed. As a result, the rationality of some projects in terms of public good is often found wanting, and the potential environmental damage can be considerable.

Between 1976 and 1980 the Environment Agency made substantial progress in preparing legislation for environmental impact assessments to which MITI, the business world and the Liberal Democratic Party (LDP) politicians ultimately objected. Finally, in 1981 there was some success, but in 1983 the draft legislation was discarded. There were grave fears entertained by the same groups who had earlier objected to it that the need for such impact statements might put a brake on big, civil engineering projects. The LDP, which had been the political party most closely associated with the construction state, together with big business and MITI, did not want its activities constrained by regulations not of its making. All the organisations strongly opposed the proposed legislation. There were renewed attempts in 1993, with earnest debate really only

Table 5.3 Some environmental responsibilities of ministries

Ministry	Environmental responsibility
Ministry of Health and Welfare	Waste management and treatment
Ministry of Agriculture, Forestry and Fisheries	National forests, fisheries, agricultural chemicals
Ministry of International Trade and Industry	Energy conservation, environmental protection technologies, anti-pollution measures, radioactive contamination from commercial nuclear power plants
Ministry of Transport	Anti-pollution measures for automobiles
Ministry of Construction	Public works and town planning

Source: OECD (1994), 27.

beginning in 1996. Finally, in June 1998 a law was enacted. Japan was the last among the OECD countries to implement this most basic of policies. Prefectural governments have been much faster than the central government to put such policies into place. This has also been the case in the fight for freedom of information, and the expansion of other citizens' rights. The lengthy delay in enacting such legislation illustrates how Japan can be viewed as a developing nation. The legislation described serves as a check on the appropriateness of large civil engineering projects and encourages developers to be more socially accountable. Unfortunately, the range of projects which come under the law is very narrow, with only individual projects being scrutinised and government projects not included. Most nuclear facilities apart from nuclear power plants are also excluded. But for environmental impact assessments to help monitor developments, there must be open access to policy information. Even if residents, local governments, and the Environment Agency do voice their opinions, as is guaranteed by law, the decision to adopt or reject a proposal rests with the relevant agency or ministry. If the company concerned and bureaucrats have shared interests, there is a high possibility that critical views and warnings will not be heeded.

Global Warming

At the Earth Summit in 1992 a document entitled 'Agenda 21' was adopted which argued the need for an international effort. Japan was a signatory to this and other conventions on climate change and bio-diversity, and an agreement to protect forests (Fukukawa: 1992). Since then, various international conferences have been held focusing on individual problems; international agreements have been struck, plans and protocols devised. Of most concern has been the global warming problem. The stance of the Japanese government with respect to the reduction of greenhouse gas emissions has been a passive one. Global warming has been used to justify the expansion of the nuclear power program, but it is possible that such a policy would create more problems than solve them. Even before the Kyoto Conference in December 1997, MITI repeatedly stated that twenty additional nuclear power plants would be needed by 2010 if levels of carbon dioxide were to be stabilised at 1990 levels. As MITI is responsible for the promotion of commercial uses of atomic energy, such declarations involve considerable self-interest.

Public Participation in Decision-making

It is well known that in the bureaucratic state that is Japan, democratic policy-making does not generally occur. Environmental policy is no exception. Before the establishment of the Environment Agency in 1971, MITI and the Ministry of Health and Welfare competed for control (McKean: 1977, 206). Even after its establishment, public participation in decision-making did not improve greatly. Global warming policy was largely decided by MITI and the Environment Agency behind closed doors. Despite the reorganisation of central ministries and agencies that is occurring over the period 1997 to 2001 (see Figure 12.1), the new administrative structure has largely been negotiated by members of the Cabinet, authorised at meetings presided over by the Prime Minister and passed by the Diet. The original Bills submitted by each ministry or agency have been made in secret by bureaucrats. As a result, the Economy and Industry Ministry (which will succeed MITI) will be responsible for policing environment protection regulations pertaining to nuclear power. Despite this being somewhat dubious, there has been little public justification of these decisions.

In the late 1990s Japan is moving towards a more democratic decision-making process. This was the result of public outcry at the role of the Ministry of Health and Welfare in the AIDS controversy discussed in Chapter 11, and the controversy surrounding the 1995 leakage of sodium coolant at the FBR 'Monju', for which the STA was ultimately responsible. A fire at a reactor in Tōkai-mura in 1997 added to the outcry.

For change to occur there must be public access to information. In order to restore public trust in government, public participation in decision-making is essential. The right to know and better accountability are being demanded. In the first half of 1999 a *Freedom of Information Act* was enacted. Greater involvement of intellectuals and experts who are potentially critical of government policy is being encouraged by government councils and deliberative bodies. NGOs have increased in number and are able to provide independent policy advice. Non-profit organisations have also increased, especially in the aftermath of the Hanshin earthquake in February 1995. On 19 March 1998 a *Non-Profit Organisation Law* was promulgated.

There are changes occurring in the relationship between central government and regional authorities. Previously, it was difficult to change national policies once they had been authorised, despite protests at the local level. In August 1996 residents of Maki city in Niigata prefecture opposed the sale of land for the site of a nuclear power plant, which effectively prevented construction.

Conclusion

Since the mid-1970s Japanese manufacturing processes and products have been relatively friendly to the environment. However, much has relied on the superior technology of Japanese manufacturing. The reduction of toxic gas emissions from cars, production of fuel-efficient cars and other environmentally-friendly initiatives have been motivated more by the need to compete in the market rather than any lofty desire to protect the global environment. Furthermore, MITI's administrative guidance has been a powerful influence on manufacturers. All this has contributed to corporate adherence to regulations, but as can be seen in a number of incidents which occurred in the 1980s and 1990s, it has become clear that environmental problems have been dealt with by a bureaucratic state largely oriented towards economic development. Unless the Japanese political-economic system undergoes major reforms that will alter the distribution of power (Maddock: 1998, 245), Japan will find it difficult to become an environmentally advanced nation. But as Gavan McCormack (1996b) suggests, responsibility also rests with the Japanese people, who consume energy and waste-producing non-renewable materials at rates much faster than those of people of most other countries. Real change will only occur if individuals make an effort to consciously change their lifestyles (Barrett & Therivel: 1991).

PART III

The International Dimension

CHAPTER 6

Domestic Development versus Importation of Technology

The Aerospace Industry and the FS-X/F-2
Fighter Plane Controversy

Introduction

The words 'technology transfer' describe the movement of technology from one place to another. While science has often been deemed to be 'universal' and therefore able to be adopted with ease throughout the world, it has not been so for technology. A growing awareness of the problems associated with transferring technology has led to greater use of the words 'technology transfer' since the 1960s. They are still in use today, although applied in two quite different ways. One use refers to the conversion of military technologies for civilian use; the second use relates to the commercialisation of academic research. When the words 'technology transfer' (*gijutsu iten*) are used in Japanese, people generally think of the export of technology from Japan to other parts of Asia. This chapter deals with the joint development of military technology by the United States and Japan which had potential for commercial spin-offs.

The words 'introduction of technology' (*gijutsu dōnyū*) are used to refer to the entry of mainly United States technology into Japan, especially in the decade after the end of the Pacific War, when Japan was intent on catching up and closing the gap in manufacturing technology. Phrasing the process in terms of 'introduction of technology' places the onus on the receiving nation. It describes a one-way traffic in technology from an advanced industrial nation to one which was lagging behind. Now that Japan is a leader in many areas of technology, things have become more complicated.

Has Japan come of age in science and technology? In the field of aerospace technology, Japan is attempting to become less dependent on American technology, but United States firms are suffering withdrawal symptoms and would prefer to sell it technology as before. The 'free ride' alluded to by some commentators actually comes at considerable expense to the Japanese. This became obvious in January 1989, when a small book was published entitled '*No' to ieru Nihon: Shin Nichi-Bei kankei no kaado* (*The Japan That Can Say No: The New Card To Be Played in US–Japan Relations*). The original Japanese version of the book was written by the politician Ishihara Shintarō and the former chairman of Sony Corporation, Morita Akio. An unofficial translation of the book caused such fierce controversy that part of the 'bootleg' English version was read into the minutes of the United States Senate. *The Japan That Can Say No* (Ishihara: 1991) raises issues relating to the need for sometimes costly domestic development over the importation of technology (especially aerospace technology from the United States). These tensions played themselves out in the controversy over the FS-X (or FSX) fighter plane, and a heated debate over the desirability of US–Japan cooperation in its development. It provides a useful case study by which to examine technological transformation in Japan (Low: 1995).

There is a rich literature on the FS-X controversy, but many accounts tend to be journalistic in nature and lack analytical depth. We will first provide brief histories and comments on the aerospace industry in Japan and then discuss the controversy over the FS-X fighter.

Aerospace Industry

While it is possible to point to how Japan is strong in civilian applications of technology (see Table 7.2), Dauvergne (1993) has reminded us that for much of the period since the end of the Second World War Japanese companies assembled and manufactured products, including arms, under United States licence. American technology helped Japan rebuild its military structure and to adapt weapons systems to its own specifications. He points out that between 1950 and 1983 such coproduction agreements provided Japan with about $US10 billion of military technology. In return, United States firms received 30 to 40 per cent of coproduction expenditure in the form of royalties, sales and subcontracting, though the Japanese have not continued to seek greater autonomy in technology.

In the 1960s space exploration overtook atomic energy as the most exciting technological area and Japan did not want to be left behind. But in spite of such ambitious plans and Japan's considerable technological might, the country has yet to build a single wide-bodied, long-range passenger aircraft. As in the case of the nuclear power industry, the aerospace industry was late in developing due to Occupation prohibitions on aviation and military-related R&D.

Even during the Allied Occupation, United States Forces procured aircraft parts from Japanese companies. The repair and overhauling of United States military aircraft created work and contributed to the rebirth of the Japanese aircraft industry, an industry in disarray since Japan's defeat and subsequent demilitarisation. Postwar rocket development began in 1955 soon after the end of the Occupation, when experiments were carried out on a 'Pencil' rocket by Itokawa Hideo at the University of Tokyo's Institute of Industrial Sciences. During the Second World War Itokawa had been an engineer for the Nakajima Aircraft Company. The 'Pencil' was followed by larger rockets such as 'Baby', 'Kappa', 'Lambda' and 'Mu'. For a long period, the Institute and its successor, the Institute of Space and Aeronautical Science (ISAS) conducted the Japanese space program. The Technical Research and Development Institute of the Japan Defence Agency established the Niijima rocket and missile test centre in 1962, but official publications tend not to mention the role of the Defence Agency in the organisation of space research in Japan for fear of criticism over military applications of such technology.

Hall & Johnson (1970) made an important case study of four inter-firm transfers of United States aerospace technology to Japan in the 1950s and 1960s. During this period coproduction of complete aircraft was quite common. In the years 1950 to 1967 more than 10 000 advanced aircraft were produced under licence in various parts of the world. The authors divide the two decades into three periods: 1952–54, repair and overhaul work for the Japanese Air Self-Defence Force and United States Air Force; 1954–64, manufacturing of mainly United States-designed aircraft; and 1965 onwards, commencement of several R&D programs, and production of Japanese-designed commercial aircraft. They see 1957 as marking the beginning of the Japanese aircraft manufacturing effort. Over the next decade, Japan would produce between 100 and 230 aircraft each year.

During the 1960s, MITI launched a project to design, build and export a passenger airplane. The Nihon Airplane Manufacturing Corporation (NAMCO) was created by MITI to develop the plane, the YS-11. It went into full-scale production in 1965, and by 1968 accounted for almost half the aircraft production in Japan that year. The Japanese are divided over whether the YS-11 can be viewed as an historic example of how MITI helped the aerospace industry to recover, or as a tragic failure which lost over four times NAMCO's capital to produce 180 aircraft (Mercado: 1995). Judging the relative success of technological development depends on the criteria by which it is evaluated.

Whatever the pros and cons of having a domestic aerospace industry, the apparent success by Communist China in 1966 in firing a nuclear-capped missile shocked the Japanese into greater activity. The STA proceeded with its own space program, which differed substantially from that of the University of Tokyo. In 1969 it established the National Space Development Agency of Japan (NASDA), with the initial aim of launching a satellite. In contrast to Itokawa's group, which insisted on developing technology domestically, NASDA adopted United States technology for its 'Delta' rocket and built a three-stage rocket capable of launching a 130 kg geostationary satellite. In 1986 NASDA was able to launch a three-stage rocket which could place a 550 kg satellite into orbit.

There are many government agencies, research institutes, industries and committees involved in space research in Japan but the organisation and coordination of research activities has been sadly lacking. The three most important government bodies for space research each have their own facilities and programs: ISAS (now a national research institute) has the Kagoshima Space Centre; the Defence Agency has the Niijima Test Centre; and there is the National Space Development Centre (the centre is linked to NASDA) on Tanegashima. Despite the lack of coordination, it has generally been agreed that ISAS should play the leading role in the development of scientific satellites and that ISAS should not develop launching vehicles beyond a certain size. The National Space Development Centre has taken the responsibility for developing application satellites and for using launching vehicles larger than those of ISAS. In the late 1990s the situation changed somewhat when ISAS engineers were able to persuade politicians that bigger rockets were needed for landing probes on the moon. The result has been that ISAS's M-5 rocket is seen as being commercially viable, more so than NASDA's own rockets (*Economist*: 1998; *Kyodo News*: 1998).

However, until 1968 the situation in the aerospace industry was very different. The United States encouraged aircraft coproduction by providing economic assistance. This can be seen as an example of how military imperatives have taken priority over economic interests. Despite help from the United States and MITI ambitions for an indigenous aerospace industry, Japanese aviation is still in its infancy and is mainly limited to joint ventures. For example, the major fighters (F-15 and F-4) of the Air Self-Defence Force have been produced by Mitsubishi Heavy Industries under licence from the United States firm of McDonnell Douglas. One exception was the independently built F-1 fighter which the controversial FS-X fighter plane was meant to replace (Dauvergne: 1993, 186–8). The next section describes why domestic development of aviation technology is considered important by the Japanese, and why the United States had mixed feelings over the agreement to codevelop it. It is ironical that whereas the United States had previously encouraged the Japanese to exploit American jet aircraft technology, from the mid-

1980s there was a growing belief that the Japanese had become too good at the exploitation and were now adversely affecting the economic competitiveness of the United States in that area.

The FS-X Controversy

The Japanese Viewpoint

The diversity of books on Japanese technology reflects the broad interest in the relationship between science, technology and Japanese economic growth. The literature is of uneven quality, many books falling into the category of what can be described as the 'business school approach'. Accounts such as Ishihara's *The Japan That Can Say No* (1991) strongly reflect national interests and business biases rather than any 'objective' position which an historian might aspire to in their work. However, although Ishihara's work was originally written specifically for a Japanese audience, the book is significant in that it does reflect opinions held by many Japanese on many issues, such as US–Japan relations and American racial attitudes; cultural explanations for Japan's economic success; the trade imbalance and the shortcomings of United States business; the rise of Japanese technology as a strategic bargaining card and Japan's need to say 'no' to the United States when economic and political considerations make this desirable. While this last point comes out strongly in the book, such attitudes and issues have been articulated by Morita, Ishihara and other Japanese writers (Low: 1995).

It was Ishihara's assertions in particular that stirred the controversy. He suggested that American attitudes to the Japanese were racist, and that Japan could sell its technology to the Soviet Union, as it was called at the time he wrote. Technology provides the Japanese with a stick to wave should the United States use bullying tactics. Such a cynical attitude to the US–Japan alliance was not new. Ishihara is a successful novelist who entered politics in 1968. Shortly afterwards, in March 1969, he made known his view that Japan should not rely on the United States for defence and that Japan should arm itself with nuclear weapons (Welfield: 1988, 260–1). Ishihara has subsequently held the position of Minister for Transport, and in April 1999 took up office as governor of Tokyo. His literary aspirations continue and he heads a group which holds a special remembrance every year for Mishima Yukio who committed suicide in November 1970 after a failed attempt at persuading the Self-Defence Force to take up arms in the name of the Emperor (*Business Tokyo*: 1990, 26–9). Given Ishihara's right-wing views, it is not surprising that the development of the next-generation support fighter, code-named FS-X (fighter support experimental) and designed by Mitsubishi Heavy Industries, was so close to his heart. It was seen as representing state-of-the-art Japanese technology. He was alarmed that the then Prime Minister Nakasone Yasuhiro gave in to United States pressure and had agreed to develop and produce the fighter as a joint project. The American company General Dynamics was to provide its F-16 fighter technology, effectively acting as a subcontractor to Mitsubishi Heavy Industries. The fighter's maneuvrability would be increased, and Japanese avionics and weapons systems would be incorporated.

Ishihara's views were revealed in a discussion with the American journalist James Fallows in the January 1990 issue of the general interest, monthly magazine *Bungei Shunju* (circulation in 1990 of 750 000) (*Bungei Shunju*: 1990). Ishihara also voiced his opinion regarding the FS-X project elsewhere. In an article which originally appeared in July 1989 in another prestigious monthly magazine, the conservative *Chūō Kōron*, Ishihara complained that Japan was sold short, claiming that although Japan was able to develop the FS-X on its own, a decision had been made to treat it as a joint development project with the United States. The special characteristic of the fighter was that it would be able to circle quickly with about one-third the turning radius of F-15 and F-16 fighters. According to Ishihara, under the agreement Japan virtually agreed to supply all of its own relevant aviation technology to the United States free of charge, whereas it had to pay for the American technology. The United States would be able to use the Japanese technology without any limitations, whereas the Japanese were unable to use the American technology for purposes outside the FS-X project. Despite this, the Japanese had been accused of trying to steal American technology via the project, in what Ishihara called a display on the part of the United States of 'techno-nationalism' (Ishihara: 1989).

The renegotiated FS-X agreement included the following controversial aspects: American firms would in the future be allocated 40 per cent of the project work; the Japanese would be denied access to United States flight control software yet the United States would have access to technologies, such as carbon-fibre technology, developed in Japan for the project; and United States military patents would be safeguarded by Japan's Defence Agency, not by MITI (Katayama: 1990, 20). It was Ishihara's view that Japan should not necessarily ditch the US–Japan Security Treaty, but observation of the treaty should be secondary to the need for Japan to be responsible for its own defence. Japan, in fact, should use advanced technology as a weapon for nationalistic purposes, to enable Japan's voice to be heard in international politics.

Ishihara was not alone in advancing these arguments. In early May 1989, after the conclusion of the talks over the joint development of the FS-X fighter, editorials of influential newspapers such as the largest business and financial newspaper *Nihon Keizai Shinbun* (circulation in 1991 of 3 million), and two of the three largest national newspapers, the conservative *Mainichi Shinbun* (4.1 million) and more liberal *Asahi Shinbun* (8.3 million), joined Ishihara in expressing concern over the results of negotiations. In the editorials of these papers the agreement was seen as providing little benefit to Japan and causing anti-American sentiment among Japanese (Ōtsuki: 1990, 81–2).

The strong feelings aroused by the FS-X agreement and *The Japan That Can Say No* created enough interest to warrant publication of an official translation of the book by the New York publishing house Simon & Schuster, without the chapters by Morita (Ishihara: 1991). As a result of the public response to the original publication, Ishihara teamed up with Watanabe Shōichi and Ogawa Kazuhisa to produce a sequel (Ishihara et al.: 1990).

Ishihara is proud of the Japanese defence industry and his books reflect this pride. This attitude can also be seen in government policy. The Defence Agency, for example, is keen to buy Japanese products and as a result, all major manufacturing companies in Japan have become involved in supplying military products. The Defence Agency has been responsible for 70 to 80 per cent of Japanese aircraft production for many decades (Davis: 1992, 11; Samuels: 1994, 261). Even if the initial knowledge is from overseas, ships and aircraft have been made in Japan under licence by companies such as Mitsubishi Heavy Industries and Kawasaki Heavy Industries. Weapons systems, on the other hand, have been purchased mainly from the United States, but in the future Japanese advances in semiconductor technology and other high-tech areas will mean that in the fields of targeting, guidance, communications and manufacturing techniques, Japan will be taking the lead (McIntosh: 1986, 52–3).

The American Viewpoint

Noble (1992) spells out the underlying reason for United States' concern over the development of an indigenous Japanese aerospace industry. Fear of a decline in economic competitiveness in the United States has prompted moves to encourage allies to contribute money and tech-nology to various large-scale projects such as the human genome project, the (now defunct) superconducting supercollider, and a space station. Japan has also been asked to bear more of the financial burden of keeping United States troops in Japan.

Formal agreements have also served to provide frameworks for co-operation in strategic areas. In 1983 a military technology transfer agreement was made between the United States and Japan; this related

especially to the exchange of electronics technology with military applications from Japan to the United States (McIntosh: 1986, 51). In April
1988 a US–Japan agreement was reached which would allow the transfer
of information on classified United States military technology to Japan
(Swinbanks: 1988). Later in 1988, a new science agreement was signed
which included provisions to safeguard military research and prevent its
transfer to other countries (Anderson: 1988). The concern on the part
of the United States to maintain access to sensitive technologies with
military applications was confirmed by an NHK (Japan Broadcasting
Corporation) survey which showed that one in three electronic companies in the United States, which it surveyed from a total of thirty, use
Japanese electronics in military products (Hartcher: 1988).

Given these attempts by the United States to secure strategic Japanese
technology (Drifte 1990, 41–3), it is understandable that the United
States would pressure Japan not to develop its new fighter independently.
It is ironical that when an agreement to codevelop it was reached, there
was American indignation that it would allow the Japanese to gain
unfair technological advantages. What added further fuel to the fire was
Ishihara's threat that the Japanese would consider diverting defence
technology to the Soviet Union during the Cold War.

The November 1988 Memorandum of Understanding to codevelop
the FS-X fighter provided a further framework for US–Japan technology
transfer. Under the agreement, five Japanese companies would receive
60 per cent of development funds, and a United States subcontractor,
General Dynamics, would receive the remainder in return for providing
F-16 fighter plane technology and other equipment. When the FS-X
codevelopment agreement was submitted to the United States Congress in May 1989, a heated debate erupted over whether it was in the
national interest to participate. This illustrates how difficult it was for
Americans to negotiate the best possible outcome without antagonising
the Japanese and undermining cooperation on the FS-X and future projects. Commentators such as Dauvergne (1993) suggest that irreparable
damage has been done as a result of the controversy.

As in many popular American accounts, Shear (1994) has depicted the
FS-X story as a case of the United States handing the keys to the aviation
kingdom to Japan – a case of giving away strategic technology to the
Japanese. Many Americans preferred to see Japan buy United States
aircraft or to develop the fighter on their own. Shear provided a dramatic
account of the key events and players, and wrote unabashedly for
an American audience. The FS-X codevelopment scheme, he argued,
provided the Japanese with the foundation for a commercial aviation
industry. The Japanese argued that they had learnt little which was new
but Shear was not convinced. He viewed the Japanese manufacturing of

components, subsystems, electronics and instrumentation as eventually leading to a more fully-fledged aviation industry, and a growing threat to United States component makers.

Walsh (1993) provided a more carefully considered study of the controversy. He portrayed the United States as rather paranoid given that the United States government had licensed the F-16 technology to ten other countries. Also, since the United States dominated the aerospace industry globally, there was not a great deal to fear from the fledgling Japanese aviation industry. Some American industrial groups recognised the benefits of codeveloping the FS-X. The Aerospace Industries Association of America drew attention to how dated the F-16 technology was, compared to the more complex F-15. By the time that the FS-X was actually produced, the United States would be well ahead developing the next generation of fighters. Furthermore, it was argued that commercial spin-offs from codevelopment of fighter planes would be less important than benefits accruing from Japan's coproduction of civilian aircraft with the United States and European firms. The American Electronics Association opposed codevelopment as it provided no tangible benefits to the electronics industry (Walsh: 1993, 385). Why the difference? Noble (1992, 53) states that there are huge barriers (arising from the non-cartelistic structure of the United States aeronautical industry in Western countries in which contractors compete with each other) compared with other industries which protect United States aerospace firms, whereas the electronics industry is much more vulnerable.

Despite such differences of opinion, the agreement was passed by Congress in June 1989, with an amendment that forbade the transfer of certain jet-engine technologies, and prohibited the Japanese transfer of FS-X technology to a third country. The agreement to codevelop the fighter plane showed the effectiveness of *gaiatsu* (foreign pressure) in shaping Japanese policy. The United States has been careful to withhold sensitive software and design data, and there has been little in the way of transfers of Japanese military technology to the United States (Shear: 1994, 280–1). The United States policy think-tank RAND (a contraction of the term 'research and development') has explored some of the issues surrounding the FS-X project. A RAND technical report on technology transfer from the FS-X project to the United States (Chang: 1994) cites several obstacles, such as a lack of knowledge and access of Japanese FS-X technology by United States firms, complex transfer procedures, conflicts over proprietary interests, differing program needs, and overall difficulties associated with transferring industrial property. Chang soberly suggests that rather than expecting gains in actual technology, it might be more realistic to expect to learn from Japanese practices in industrial R&D and defence acquisition.

Another RAND report published the following year, written by Mark Lorell (1995), attempted to look at the history of US–Japan collaboration on the FS-X fighter. One of the aims of the report was to assist United States government officials to formulate better policies and strategies for military technology collaboration with allies. As Lorell (1995, 357) pointed out, the question of which side would benefit most was at the heart of the controversy. His opinion was that neither side would gain dramatically from the direct technology transfer through the program. However, he believed that the Japanese military aerospace industry would benefit greatly due to their success in pursuing many of the initial objectives of domestic development, albeit within a collaborative framework. Lorell argued that it was necessary for full production of the aircraft to occur in order to promote United States security and economic interests, and he was right.

The first of four FS-X flight-test aircraft was completed on 12 January 1995, and the first flight occurred on 7 October 1995. The Japanese Diet (national parliament) approved production in mid-1996, and it is envisaged that the Japanese government will procure 130 of what the production phase agreements renamed 'the F-2 aircraft', with delivery commencing in 1999 and stretching into the first decade of the twenty-first century. Lockheed Martin was awarded a $US75 million contract by the prime contractor Mitsubishi Heavy Industries in October 1996. Lockheed Martin, the principal United States subcontractor during the development phase, will continue to have a major involvement in production, one which is estimated to be worth over $US2.5 billion in contracts (US Government: 1997; Dewitte & Vanhastel: 1997).

Theorising the Debate

Itō (1992, 365–6) portrays the 'traditional' pattern of US–Japan economic conflict as involving an increase in a particular type of export to the United States, the Japanese then being accused of dumping by American manufacturers, subsequent US–Japan government negotiations followed by price controls and export restraints. This pattern changed, however, in the mid-1980s to include 'structural' problems in Japan which acted as barriers to foreign products. Also, the Americans adopted a 'result-oriented' policy with respect to access to the Japanese market. High technology, in particular, became the focus of bilateral trade conflicts.

The rich literature on the FS-X controversy provides a number of perspectives on the role of technology in the US–Japan relationship. Spar (1992) sees the act of 'framing' an issue as an important variable that intervenes between political structures and the decision-making process, and suggests that the domestic groups framed the problem of the FS-X project differently from the central decision-makers. Benefits accruing from any potential cooperation were consequently viewed differently. Ultimately, the actors who were able to frame the problem most compellingly were the winners.

No matter what the viewpoint of the individual actors or groups, dramatic events in 1989 which effectively saw the ending of the Cold War placed the United States in a changing world order. Tuathail (1992) saw the questions posed by the FS-X as symbolic of a series of larger issues which the United States had to confront. These revolved around whether it could continue to define national security in military and geopolitical terms, or whether it was better viewed in terms of economics and technology. The United States was in the difficult position of seeing Japan as both its leading strategic ally and its greatest economic threat. Tuathail described the debate in terms of 'discourses' which these contending perspectives generated. The geo-economic discourse tends to adopt a revisionist view of Japan, its key advocates being Clyde Prestowitz, James Fallows, Karel van Wolferen and Chalmers Johnson.

If we look at the details of the story, what lessons do these discourses teach us about US–Japan technological cooperation in the future? Dauvergne (1993) drew the conclusion that codevelopment was not such a plausible model for future US–Japan high-tech military cooperation. It has contributed to the emergence of barriers to future cooperation: caused Japanese wariness of cooperative ventures; revealed strong American opposition to such cooperation; blurred the boundaries between military and trade issues and negotiations; and encouraged the Japanese to pursue greater technological self-reliance. Japan may well look more to Europe for codevelopment opportunities in future as a result (Davis: 1992, 15). But wherever Japan turns, what will be necessary will be a 'strong confluence of perceived interests' among the major players (Lorell: 1995, 403).

Noble (1992, 4–6) examined the controversy as a case study in bilateral negotiations, and found that certain dynamics came into play. First, national priorities can determine bargaining advantage. The United States, for example, has emphasised military and diplomatic goals over economic and technological gains, and this can effectively place the United States in a weaker position in negotiations. But Noble found that in the case of the FS-X, Americans were keen to protect their economic interests. Secondly, he observed that national power was a major factor in bargaining advantage. A stronger country can bully a weaker country into submission. We have seen that the United States was able to persuade Japan to allow American participation. And thirdly, Noble found domestic and economic structures (and the conflict they can create) can improve bargaining terms by providing a pretext for demanding certain concessions. Both Japan and the United States have attempted to gain leverage using the domestic political situation as reasons for demanding certain outcomes.

Conclusion

This chapter has shown that Japan had long viewed national security in terms of economic, political and military considerations. Japanese support for a domestic defence industry reflects the belief in the deterrent potential that such an indigenous capability would have, part of a quest for self-reliance which dates back to early in the twentieth century. The FS-X controversy was significant for the United States in that it linked economic and defence issues, and showed how important trade considerations would be for the US–Japan relationship in the 1990s and beyond. In June 1997 the United States Defense Intelligence Agency expressed concern to the Senate Select Committee on Intelligence that American S&T corporations were threatened by foreign governments, and that the flow of high-tech data overseas might have implications for United States national security (*Japan Washington Watch*: 1997a). Such fears will not go away.

In today's global economy, the dichotomy of 'domestic development' versus 'importation of technology' discussed in this chapter is becoming less valid. The development of Japanese technology will increasingly occur overseas, where much manufacturing already takes place. The internationalisation of Japan's R&D effort has seen the establishment of major R&D centres in Western countries: for example, Canon in France, Hitachi in California, Kobe Steel in Surrey, Kyōcera in Washington, Matsushita Electric in Frankfurt and San Jose, Mitsubishi Electric in Boston, NEC in Princeton, Nissan in Detroit and Bedford, and Sharp in Oxford (Kahaner: 1993). Is this domestic development or imported knowledge?

The establishment of such 'think-tanks' has been prompted by a realisation that while 'shopping' for technology has been a successful characteristic of postwar Japanese economic growth, the Japanese may not be able to continue to buy all the technology they require in a ready-made form. Although Americans would prefer the Japanese to simply continue to buy United States aircraft, the Japanese are keen to develop their own indigenous capabilities. The United States tends to place restrictions on technology transfers which makes outright purchase of technology or coproduction unattractive.

An understanding of the actions of policy-makers, personnel and organisations helps provide a better insight into Japan's economic growth than do stereotypical views of Japanese culture and so-called special characteristics of Japanese society. In studying Japanese technology today, we need to reconsider the extent to which geographical boundaries determine the dynamics of the spread of Western technology, whether the idea of a region is sometimes more useful, and how far a nation's borders define a national technological system. Perhaps the way many historians, and certainly many businesspeople, have mapped the development of technology in terms of nation-states needs to be reexamined.

Looking at technology as an artefact, the labels 'made in Japan' or 'born in the USA' hide their significance as forms of knowledge which sometimes owe less to national characteristics than to negotiation, bartering and flows of information. Japan and the United States can attempt to say 'no', but there are strategies and complexities in place which make the flow of knowledge and expertise difficult to police. The history of technology and technology transfer can become richer by being aware of the multiple factors affecting the technology that makes the border crossings. We also need to be aware that there are varying levels of technology, such as the mature dot-matrix printer versus the leading-edge laser printer, which can be transferred. Second-hand technologies and technological waste can be transferred to nations just as easily, or more easily, than that which is at the cutting edge. The division between military and civilian technology is also unclear. Six Japanese companies are among the top 100 arms manufacturers in the world, a seemingly small number but large when one considers that theoretically Japan bans the export of military technology. The next chapter continues this look at the international dimension of Japanese technology by focusing on its outward transfer.

CHAPTER 7

Domestic Technology versus the Export of Technology

Introduction

This chapter further examines the question of what Japanese technology is. We then look at its outward transfer in the form of consumer electronics products which have been increasingly made overseas in order to minimise costs and improve profitability. Such products are highly suited for global markets as they are mass-consumption items which require little customisation (Zampetti: 1996). The export of consumption patterns and the outward transfer of technology can also be accompanied by environmental problems.

Japanese Technology: What is It?

Does Japanese technology or, put in a different way, the Japanese development of technology, have any special characteristics? We saw in the first part of this book certain features of the Japanese model of R&D. But if we compare the types of technology developed with those of the United States some broad generalisations can be made.

Shimura's tendency to attribute features of a nation's S&T to 'traditional' culture is not entirely convincing, but there is an element of truth in the features listed in Table 7.1. Customs and habits may owe more to a region rather than to the space confined within national borders. Even when trends can be identified, the speed of technological change often renders them short-lived. It could be argued that Japan's strength in technology (especially consumer electronics) can be traced to factors such as the applied nature of its R&D, incremental improvements, emphasis on commercial applications, quality control, and miniaturisation. These characteristics may not be so much national attributes as current features of its technology, which may

Table 7.1   Features of technology development in Japan and the United States

Japan	United States
Applied research, product development	Basic research
Incremental improvements, technology fusion	Major innovations
Civilian applications	Military applications
Process and manufacturing technology	Product technology
Parts technology	Systems technology
Hardware	Software
Predictable technologies	Unpredictable technologies
Quality control	Creation of new product features
Miniaturisation	New design concepts
Standardisation, mass production	Customised goods

Source: Shimura, 1993, 17.

be transitory and not so prominent in the future. As Okimoto suggests, Japan's distinctiveness may lie in the mix of organisational, social, and cultural characteristics (Okimoto: 1989, 175). A study of the growth of consumer electronics in Japan enables an exploration of these questions.

Manufacturing Moves Overseas

In the 1960s the first major postwar wave of foreign direct investment by the Japanese was directed towards Asia, and to a lesser extent the United States. In order to overcome impediments to exports in the early 1970s, Japanese firms established manufacturing facilities in developed countries. Sony was the first to do so with its colour television assembly plant in the United States in 1972. A couple of years later a United Kingdom plant followed. Matsushita and other companies who were keen to avoid protectionist measures did so as well, in an attempt to defend their market share (Belderbos: 1995, 107).

In the 1980s a feature of the 'internationalisation' of the Japanese economy was a dramatic increase in direct investment abroad, especially in industrialised countries and less so in Asia and Latin America. The 1990s, however, saw the reverse occurring (Sachwald: 1995, 1), with the Japanese again turning towards Asia and establishing new offshore manufacturing facilities. This industrial restructuring was accompanied by increased shipments of finished goods back to Japan.

With the shift of high-tech manufacturing offshore, the transfer of actual knowledge about the production of computer parts, telecommunications equipment and video cassette recorders may become a reality. Electronic parts are no longer sourced just from Japan but come from throughout the world. Sony, Matsushita and Toshiba procure parts from Southeast Asia. Firms such as Sharp produce 85 per cent of their overall production overseas (*Tokyo Business Today*: 1993). Hitachi, JVC and other firms now re-import 'Japanese' video cassette recorders that have been made abroad. Japan became a net importer of colour television sets in 1993, the overseas-assembled sets coming mainly from Malaysia, South Korea and China, in descending order (*Japan Times*: 1993). Table 7.2 lists the proportion of Japanese manufacturing of electrical appliances which are now produced overseas and the figures suggest that national borders are becoming less relevant and that techno-nationalism will be more difficult to enforce. Nevertheless, the Japanese are still reluctant to part with their knowledge and expertise.

If we look at the activities of multinational firms in Asia, American and European firms appear to be more willing than those from Japan to give local people strategic positions within their operations. The 'Japanese-type' of technology transfer apparently places a great deal of emphasis on training local engineers and operators, thus requiring a large number of Japanese technical experts. It is claimed that the continuing presence of these experts is to provide on-the-job training and ensure that local employees have an understanding of the processes beyond basic operations, especially important in the event of sudden changes to model design and production methods (Thee: 1992). Globalisation here means the transfer of knowledge with control still held firmly in the hands of the Japanese.

In today's global economy, technology transfer no longer follows a simple linear model. This is particularly so in the case of Japan. Japan has

Table 7.2 Proportion of Japanese products manufactured overseas

	1985 (%)	1990 (%)	1993 (%)
Colour televisions	38.8	60.1	71.9
Videotape recorders	6.3	18.7	41.6
Tape-recorders	26.1	55.0	58.8
Radios	55.2	56.9	63.4
Refrigerators	18.6	30.9	40.6
Washing machines	5.9	12.8	20.9
Microwave ovens	22.7	45.3	63.3
Electric fans	32.9	48.7	67.8

Source: MITI: 1996, 138.

previously been accused by politicians and industrialists of avoiding meaningful technology transfers, particularly to the newly industrialised economies of Asia. It has been argued that Japanese firms tend to rely on Japanese technical experts for a longer period than do American or European companies which operate offshore production facilities. Consequently, the Japanese have been accused of being unwilling to transfer technology and skills. Japanese companies, it is claimed, only license the technology of older products and processes, such as that of the dot-matrix printer, whereas that of laser printers is not made available. Even with joint ventures, there is often insufficient information disclosed to the other partner to make any meaningful transfer of technology. In the case of the offshore manufacture of televisions and cameras, technology transfer is avoided by procuring parts from local subsidiaries of Japanese firms (Normile: 1993). These networks ensure that the competitive edge of Japanese products, based on the advantages of new technologies which accrue to the owner of the knowledge, is maintained. Wide access to these technologies greatly diminishes potential profits, whereas 'mature' technologies can be more readily transferred.

More than 10 per cent of United States private company research is conducted overseas whereas the figure for Japan is about 2 per cent. Japanese R&D personnel in Japan and employed by United States firms amount to approximately 1 per cent of total United States private sector spending on R&D (Sigurdson: 1992). These percentages do not, however, necessarily reflect the proportion of information flow between countries. Japanese R&D facilities in the United States engage in joint arrangements with American research organisations, whereas Japan-based R&D facilities of American companies tend to confine their relationships to universities and university professors, in order to recruit the best graduates (Serapio: 1994). But it would be simplistic to portray such operations as being biased. Due to the recession and lack of capital in Japan, joint ventures between Japanese and European firms, for example, have seen a flow of marketing, design and production expertise from Japan, rather than cash (Rappaport: 1993). Furthermore, American access to Japanese R&D and vice versa is only one small part of the story. About 80 per cent of the Japanese researchers and engineers who have gone abroad have gone to developed countries, especially the United States. On the other hand, 90 per cent of foreign researchers and engineers in Japan come from developing countries (NISTEP: 1991). This globalisation of company research confounds simplistic attempts to restrict information flows but we do need to see it in perspective. Less than 20 per cent of total technological activities of most highly industrialised nations occur outside the home country, suggesting that most national technological systems are still relatively confined to their own borders (Foray & Freeman: 1993).

Diana Hicks and her colleagues have attempted to measure the extent of international exchange in Japan's R&D (Hicks et al.: 1994). Japanese companies publish scientific papers in international journals but these are often produced by laboratories in their home country which are staffed by Japanese, rather than by foreign affiliates where some non-Japanese might be employed. Collaborations tend to occur with Japan-based institutions, and citations reflect this emphasis. The conclusion is that the Japanese remain dependent on the national science system, despite contributing to the international literature. And the internationalisation of Japanese corporate scientific research is still very small. The results are not surprising. Japanese scientists and engineers are socialised to a high degree within national boundaries, and are unlikely to leave their company let alone their country. Overseas think-tanks have been established, but international contacts are still slow to occur though the Japanese certainly do not ignore overseas literature.

Despite the increasing internationalisation and globalisation of Japanese firms, almost 80 per cent of corporate laboratories can be found in the Greater Tokyo and Osaka areas. We must be beware of labelling technology as an artefact 'made in Japan' or 'born in the USA' (brand loyalty and country loyalty can be misguided), since it sometimes might be more accurate to describe the technology as 'designed in Tokyo'! The region around the capital is one of the most high-tech industrial areas in the world (Castells & Hall: 1994). Japan's so-called 'internationalisation' has occurred around the same time as opposing currents have been set into place. MITI's technopolis program was partly born out of the desire to develop regional areas of Japan. It may be more appropriate to describe the current technological paradigm shift as 'glocalisation' rather than 'globalisation' (Courchene: 1995). 'Glocalisation' here refers to the manner in which, at the same time as R&D becomes more international, there are localising tendencies at work which seek to emphasise place-specific knowledge, processes and resources.

The recent nature of the multinationalisation of Japanese firms and the way it has been achieved over a short period, especially when compared with European and American firms who have a long history of investment abroad, has drawn adverse attention, despite the scale of investment sometimes being much smaller. One early type of Japanese investment took the form of reverse vertical integration which saw firms become involved in mineral extraction and processing in countries such as Australia and some Latin American countries. Another form was horizontal investment in manufacturing in neighbouring Asian countries. After the oil shock of the early 1970s Japan took care to diversify its sources of energy and raw materials. It began to globalise its production too, investing in the United States, Europe and elsewhere.

Japanese investment in Europe, Australia and no doubt elsewhere is heavily skewed towards non-manufacturing activities. In the case of Europe, this represents 78 per cent of total investment, and is concentrated in banking, finance, insurance and real estate (Nicolas: 1995, 31). Of the direct investment in manufacturing, about half is in electronics and transport machinery. One source of complaint is that the majority of Japanese subsidiaries operating in the European Community are wholly owned subsidiaries (Nicolas: 1995, 39).

Japanese manufacturing in less developed Asian countries seems to consist mainly of relocation of mature industries in order to exploit some competitive advantage such as lower labour costs, cheaper land and raw materials. In the process, the transfer of technology occurs. Manufacturing often involves assembly of parts and components, with relatively little value being added. In the case of the Association of South-East Asian Nations (ASEAN) countries of Indonesia, Malaysia, Philippines and Thailand, relatively low-tech technologies found in radios and standard television sets have been common, whereas in the newly industrialised economies (NIEs) of Singapore, Hong Kong, South Korea and Taiwan, where a more highly skilled workforce is available, intermediate technology occurs, such as that in simple videotape recorders. High-tech products tend to be manufactured in Japan, where automation can help to lower some of the costs of production.

In the case of Europe and North America, a major reason for Japanese investment appears to be access to markets. Local production enables firms to tailor their products to the needs of European consumers (Sachwald: 1995a, 61). The decision to establish a manufacturing subsidiary can depend on trade policy and whether there are anti-dumping measures which need to be overcome by local production.

Technology Flows

Since the 1960s Korea and Taiwan have both sought to introduce technology in the same way that Japan did after the Pacific War. The problems of technology transfer were raised at the United Nations General Assembly in 1961, especially the relationship between technology providers and the receiving nation. Developing nations were keen to remove barriers to the flow of technology from the more industrially advanced nations and place more responsibility for the promotion of technology transfer on the nations where much of the technology originated (UNCTAD: 1974). It was in such a context that technocrats in developing nations began to use the words 'technology transfer'.

Three Elements of Technology Transfer

Technology transfer is often thought of in terms of three key categories: technical information which has become (1) documents (patents, blueprints, technical diagrams and manuals); (2) equipment (machines, manufacturing plants); and (3) personnel and institutions (technical education and traineeships) (Chin & Hayashi: 1995, 51). In the case of categories (1) and (2), when they are acquired by the receiving nation, that completes the transaction, at least from the viewpoint of the country of origin. However, whether it be information or equipment which is purchased, that attitude to technology transfer leaves the receiving country with problems. To really complete the transfer, appropriate training from technical experts dispatched to the receiving nation as well as technical traineeships in the sending country are necessary. In 1994 about 10 000 Japanese technical experts were sent to other parts of Asia, and 30 000 to 40 000 technical trainees received instruction.

Transfer is possible at every stage of the life of the product, from R&D design until the time the product hits the market, depending on the technological sophistication of the receiving nation. Immediately after the end of the Pacific War, in many fields Japan's technological gap with the United States was not wide, and technology transfer at the earlier stages was possible. However, in the case of other parts of Asia, even when information and machinery have been acquired, the requisite technical understanding to see the process through to production has often been missing. What is missing is the embodiment of the know-how in the local people, through training. The responsibility to address this situation lies with Japan and the United States, who together constitute 80 per cent of the trade in technology with East Asia.

In the United States many patents are quite elementary. A feature of Japanese technology transfer is the importance of people as facilitators. Many Japanese companies prefer to train local personnel in Japan rather than in their home countries. There is considerable potential for Japanese manufacturing plants to become important professional training sites for the rest of Asia (Chin & Hayashi: 1995, 59–67).

The NIEs and ASEAN nations are obviously at different stages of assimilating foreign technological knowledge. The sending of technical experts to and the receiving of trainees from NIEs peaked in 1990, after which numbers have declined. In contrast, the exchange of personnel between Japan and ASEAN countries has grown. Furthermore, it can be seen that Japan is performing a role for ASEAN countries which it had earlier served for NIEs. While Japan still transfers sophisticated technologies to NIEs, the transfer of manufacturing technology is now occurring between NIEs and ASEAN countries. One can describe this technology transfer in terms of a cascade model from Japan to NIEs to ASEAN countries. Furthermore, one could also depict Japan as a node in a NIEs–ASEAN network (Chin & Hayashi: 1995, 67–71).

We can say that there are three types of international technology transfer (Chin & Hayashi, 1995):

1 *Intra-firm Technology Transfer*. As this occurs in a local branch of the parent company, the sending of personnel and technical training is part of the transfer process.

2 *Inter-firm Technology Transfer*. When technology is transferred to a potential competitor (for example, the United States to Japan, Japan to NIEs), agreements are entered into and technology transfer occurs within the confines of a specific licensing arrangement. Often, the technology provider is not anxious to transfer the knowledge, giving rise to international trade friction. The receiving country is often keen to acquire more knowledge than has been agreed to, giving rise to criticism of countries such as Japan, which is then viewed as wanting to keep its knowledge and skills to itself. However, when the techno-logical standards of both are close, there is a period after transfer when the receiving nation becomes a threat to the provider-nation's markets. Examples of this have been the transfer of textile technologies from the United States to Japan, and Japan to Asia. Recently, this has been the case in the trade in personal computers.

3 *Network Model Technology Transfer*. This type of transfer falls between types 1 and 2. The technological level of the receiving nation is increasing and there is a pool of capable, local technicians to draw on. The relationship between provider and receiver is not so hierarchical, nor is it one of foe against foe. The relationship between companies is one of cooperation, such as with Original Equipment Manufacturing where Japanese brand names are used in various parts of Asia. With the rise of the Japanese yen in the second half of the 1980s, this became more prevalent.

A feature of Japanese technology transfer has been the selling of small-scale, simplified technologies which are useful for immediate, short-term, manufacturing purposes. This scientific and technical knowledge has not been of a particularly original or high level, requiring only an incremental increase in technological understanding. It is unsuited for the training of S&T personnel to doctorate level, for this takes time, and diverges somewhat from the immediate needs of firms from advanced nations. Training at doctoral level cannot be achieved within the frame-work of technology transfer which occurs within firms and between firms.

The growth of manufacturing in other parts of Asia has resulted in a huge excess capacity in manufacturing. Asian nations have been so zealous in investment in manufacturing that sufficient buyers for the increasing number of products may be difficult to find. This has already resulted in a widespread fall in prices, and shows how investments in manufacturing capacity can exceed demand for products; the cost of machinery cannot be recouped through the sale of goods (Garran: 1997b). The Asian economic crisis of 1998 exacerbated the situation.

Conclusion

For a while, Japan's economic miracle appeared to have been exported to other parts of Asia, along with Japanese capital, but the breaking-down of national barriers has also enabled the transfer of reject technology and nuclear waste. This is useful for industrially advanced nations such as Japan where, as a result of strong public opposition, it has become increasingly difficult to begin the construction of new nuclear power plants within the country (see Chapters 4 and 5). Mitsubishi Heavy Industries, one of the leaders in the atomic energy industry, has therefore chosen to expand business overseas, especially in the developing countries of Asia (Sato: 1990). While environmental groups have successfully opposed further development of atomic energy in 'industrialised' countries, nuclear plants are perceived or presented in Asia as the 'wave of the future'. China, Indonesia, South Korea, Taiwan, Malaysia, and Thailand are just some of the Asian countries that have expressed interest in establishing nuclear power plants within their borders (Oishi: 1990).

Perhaps people of other Asian nations have become 'fashion victims' of a sort, following the path of development created by Japan. Gavan McCormack has highlighted the environmental problems created by the pursuit of leisure in Japan, whether it be on golf courses, at theme parks or tourist resorts (McCormack: 1996a, 78–112). People in Southeast Asia are dying from illnesses caused by record-high levels of smog. There is an increasing feeling that people should aim for socially responsible levels and types of consumption which do not impact negatively on the lives of others.

Recent years have seen the emergence of a substantial middle class in Asia which constitutes new markets for Western-style products. In the NIEs of South Korea, Taiwan, Singapore and Hong Kong, it is Western culture mediated by the Japanese that seems especially prominent. For example, whether in Hong Kong, Tokyo or Hanoi, karaoke machines have been reshaping how people socialise, using technologies that are sometimes Asian in origin. In 1992 the karaoke trade alone was estimated to be at least $7 billion.

The globalisation of culture is an exciting one and offers the chance of bonding with the rest of the world. But the establishment of manufacturing plants offshore to satisfy Japanese consumption needs and export strategies has served to export environmental problems (Holliman: 1990). McCormack argues that 'In per capita terms in the early 1990s, Japan was consuming energy and non-renewable materials, while producing carbon dioxide and other wastes, at rates around 10 times greater than would be its entitlement under any equitable global "ration"' (McCormack: 1996b).

Household electric appliances have grown in popularity in Japan and other parts of Asia. Increasingly, these goods have been made outside Japan, but R&D continues to be centralised in the Greater Tokyo and Osaka areas. Some of the problems associated with the rise in consumerism have been exported, while the technical knowledge has been retained. The next part of the book looks more closely at the social dimension of Japanese S&T.

PART IV

Science and Technology for the People?

CHAPTER 8

Information Society versus Controlled Society

Introduction

In mid-August 1998, as the world was approaching a new millennium, Japanese Prime Minister Obuchi Keizō was blissfully unaware of what the Y2K (Year 2000) problem was (Boyd: 1998). Although he was the leader of one of the most technologically advanced nations, Obuchi was ignorant of the consequences that recording the date of the year in only two digits might have for software in 2000. This reflects how many Japanese lack a knowledge of information technology and the way it can create economic growth (Boyd: 1998), a puzzling situation given that the Japanese were the first to coin the term 'information society' in the 1970s (Morris-Suzuki: 1988, 7–8). It was some two decades later, in the 1990s, that the Internet began to be widely used and personal computers became commonplace. While there is the potential for an 'information society' to be an information-rich society, we have seen in Chapter 5 that this is not the case, especially when it comes to the environment policy-making process. Japan is not an information utopia. Public access to information is severely constrained. Japan appears to be more of a controlled society, constrained by a preference for visually based technologies, and by companies who manipulate technological choice. Japan is a nation known for the production of computer hardware and video games, but it is generally considered to lag behind the United States in information technology (see Table 7.1). Indeed, Japan's use of computers is behind that of many other countries. Given the convergence of computers and telecommunications, this is likely to restrain Japan's economic advance. Despite being a country known for embracing technology for economic growth, why have the Japanese been so slow to make it part of their lives? This chapter examines some of the reasons.

The Information Society

Tessa Morris-Suzuki pointed out in her book *Beyond Computopia* (1988, 8–9) how the term 'information society' was used in Japanese publications in 1969 in three distinct ways: (1) the Industrial Structure Council saw it as a society in which computerisation would provide access to information, free people from clerical work, and encourage creativity; (2) Hayashi Yūjirō saw the information society as being characterised by how the price of goods tends increasingly to be a result of 'information costs' associated with the requirements of fashion, style and quality. The importance of labour and material costs declines; (3) the third approach combines part of the previous two and predicts that the rise of the information society will be characterised by computerisation of commerce, finance and manufacturing and the growth of information industries such as software production. Thus, in the information society both the method and content of production will be changed. While Morris-Suzuki (1988, 154) was particularly concerned with the potential for information technologies to provide political, bureaucratic and managerial élites with the means by which to accumulate information, and thereby have power over individuals, this chapter is more concerned with how technological choice is shaped by both cultural and economic factors.

Since the world oil shortages and price rises of the 1970s there has been a trend away from the manufacturing of products which are heavy, thick, long and big, to those which can be described as light, thin, short and small. In contrast to the late 1970s when the new technologies associated with computer numerical-controlled machinery and robot micro-electronics influenced manufacturing systems, the 1980s were a period of the 'new media' when the communicative capabilities of micro-electronics became the centre of attention. Since the 1980s the development of personal computers has become less of a MITI concern and has entered the domain of the private sector. Other ministries and agencies took an interest in information technology, competing with each other for any potential spoils. In 1983, the Ministry of Posts and Telecommunications proposed a 'teletopia' scheme which involved choosing twenty model regions in which to introduce new communications infrastructure. MITI devised the rival concept of 'new media communities'. A few years later, in 1986, the Ministry of Construction proposed the 'Intelligent City' plan. Again, in 1984, Nippon Telephone and Telegraph (NTT) proposed the establishment of an optic fibre information network system which involved the Ministry of Post and Telecommunications. The commercial network INS Net 64 commenced a few years later in 1988. As can be seen in the first phase of Japan's telecommunications deregulation in 1985 with privatisation of NTT, there was a marked shift in leadership from the public to the private sector, something that can be said to be a feature of this period.

In 1984 the Murai Jun research group at Tokyo Institute of Technology worked with groups from the University of Tokyo and Keiō University to establish the Japan University Network (JUNET) by connecting phone lines with university mainframe computers using a UNIX operating system. UNIX, a brandname, was originally developed by Bell Laboratories in the United States. In 1986 JUNET obtained connectivity with the rest of the world. The Japanese scientific community was quick to take advantage of the network.

Commercial, online services to libraries began in the late 1970s. The use of CD-ROMs and online databases for patent information, literature searches and scientific data has increased since that time. Greater usage has been accompanied by a lowering of costs. From 1990 electronic journals covering a wide range of fields emerged and, at the same time, university library budgets declined. To some extent digital media information has replaced printed matter, causing an adverse effect on academic publishing and book distribution. The trend is not unique to Japan. With the circulation of preprints of scientific research, the significance of publishing in academic journals has less to do with speed and more to do with academic prestige. The advent of the Internet has meant that the importance of journals has declined even more in terms of conveying timely knowledge. The circulation of scientific preprints relied on the availability of airmail and photocopying, they were not refereed and only reached a limited audience. In contrast, the Internet has overcome both of these problems: anyone can submit material and everyone can evaluate what is distributed.

In the early 1990s it was unclear what NTT's future would be and the anticipated competition in telecommunications was slow to occur. Although Japan was the first country with a cellular telephone service, subscriber numbers were relatively low until 1994, partly because Japan was using its own cellular standard, thereby limiting the use of the cellular phones to Japan (Puffert: 1997, 91). The entry of three personal handyphone system providers in 1995 changed the position, as did the decision in December 1996 to reorganise NTT and restructure it as NTT Corporation, NTT East, NTT West and NTT Long Distance. In addition, NTT would be allowed to enter the international telecommunications market and Kokusai Denshin Denwa (KDD), which had previously enjoyed a monopoly over that market, would gain access to the domestic market. In May 1998 further deregulation occurred with carriers being allowed more autonomy to change telephone charges (Nishimura: 1998, 2).

Despite the hopes of many Japanese for the emergence of an information society, Japan's communications network still mainly relies on the telephone. In the 1992–93 financial year, 79.4 billion phone calls were made in Japan. This grew to 109.2 billion in 1996–97 (Nishimura: 1998, 9). The Internet has been slow to become established, but by July 1997 there were a million Internet hosts in Japan.

White-collar workers have been slow to familiarise themselves with the potential of new information and communication technologies (Murakami: 1998), and the growth in the use of computers which has occurred has not generated the benefits which were hoped for. For instance, the emphasis on information processing was seen as allowing women to compete equally with men for jobs (Ekusa: 1992). Morris-Suzuki (1988) pointed out how information technology was not, in fact, enabling the majority of Japanese to pursue more creative work or to have greater leisure time. It meant a shift from routine manual work to routine 'information transfer' work, service work in the household to paid service work. The number of insecure and transient jobs has increased and by 1999 Japan experienced a postwar record level of unemployment of more than 3.39 million people (Stokes: 1999). Morris-Suzuki accused knowledge-intensive industry of being more concerned with producing sophisticated, 'value-added' products for the rich than with trying to upgrade the quality of life of most Japanese.

How do we account for all this? What has gone wrong? The private sector has long been aware that the use of computers requires workers with the appropriate skills. The nurturing of younger personnel with such skills has been considered important, but the government has been slow to act on it. Even with the microelectronics revolution of the late 1970s, there was a feeling that the effects of the technological change on work practices would be delayed. At the time, cumbersome, Japanese-style typewriters were still used in offices in Japan, and wordprocessors were seldom used. In the 1980s the use of Japanese language word-processors became much more common (Gottlieb: 1993, 1995). During that decade in the West, computers were introduced into schools but in Japan they have been slow to be introduced. Part of the blame can be traced to government and industry's focus on the production of hardware and the neglect of software. With the spread of computers this emerged as a serious problem. Japanese computer education in primary schools and junior high schools has been weak, largely due to the lack of ability of young people to romanise Japanese in order to use the keyboard. Furthermore, the Ministry of Education has been reluctant to recommend specific hardware and software lest it be viewed as favouring one company over another. As a result, much computer training occurs in privately-run computer schools. Since 1988 more than half of those who were trained in the information sciences at high school level were trained at such schools. In 1987, 80.6 per cent of companies sent staff to these schools for extra training, contributing to a veritable boom in the establishment of information science departments in many private universities in the late 1980s.

Why has the public education system been slow to introduce computer education? Not only has the required infrastructure been lacking, but students have often been quicker than their teachers to embrace new technologies. Until the 1970s most Japanese would not have dreamt of using a wordprocessor to type Japanese, let alone a fully-fledged computer. The subsequent popularity of wordprocessors may well have discouraged the use of computers even if they had been equipped with Japanese wordprocessing software.

Japanese manufacturers were buoyed by the success of wordprocessors in the late 1980s, and employed Chinese workers to create Chinese versions of the products in the hope of establishing a network of user countries which would include the People's Republic of China and Taiwan. Unfortunately for Japan, people in these countries preferred to develop their own software which would be compatible with American technology. As a result, Japan was left behind in the introduction of personal computers.

In the 1980s Japanese hardware and software differed depending on the maker. Sakamura Ken at the University of Tokyo decided to create Japan's own computer architecture (including operating system) with his The Real-time Operating-system Nucleus (TRON) project which commenced in 1984. At the time, Nippon Electric Company (NEC) acounted for 70 per cent of Japan's personal computer market. In order to challenge this domination of the market, other makers united to support the TRON project and build an original Japanese computer. In contrast, NEC continued to promote the MS-DOS system which its computers used. In late 1998, declining equipment investment by Japanese corporations in computers contributed to an overall slump in sales of personal computers and a sharp decline in profit for Japan's major electronic firms.

Due to the wide penetration of the education sector and business world by Japanese wordprocessors, the Japanese were slow to take to the conventional alphabet-based keyboards which are an essential part in operating a computer. Rather than adopting an electronic culture that relied on a keyboard, many Japanese preferred a more visually-oriented culture as can be seen in the popular use of facsimile (fax) machines, reading of 'manga' comic books, popularity of video games and karaoke.

Why have the Japanese lacked originality in developing uses for computers? The absence of computers has already been referred to yet Japan is the leading producer of video games with companies such as Nintendō enjoying large market share. Whereas children in the United

States and Europe often play games on a computer using a keyboard, the Japanese have tended to design game products which can be used more on their own, rather than rely on other technology. These games often depend on the speed of reflexes, whereas computer games arguably permit greater contemplation and use of intellect. In terms of developing computer literacy, cognitive powers and imagination, the computer games are better than the video games made in Japan.

Many people envisaged that the Japanese would be quick to adopt fax technology. In contrast, the Japanese have never really taken to using telexes. The popularity of visual-based communication which allows handwritten messages and pictures was to be expected in Japan. Cultural factors have clearly influenced the speed of adoption of technology. Japanese manufacturers are also at fault. Sony has been very slow to show interest in wordprocessors and computers. Only in the 1990s, when computers became such an important part of communications, did Sony produce its own.

Another example of slow social acceptance of new technology is the case of mobile phones. Mobile telephone services started in Japan in 1979; in the late 1980s they became popular in Europe. But in Japan, due to the monopolistic role of NTT in telecommunications, the spread of mobile phones lagged behind that of Hong Kong and Taiwan. At last, in 1994 the phones had gained a degree of popularity among young Japanese, reaching a level of ownership of 4 million people. A system of having three or four carriers in each area was introduced and subscribers were able to actually purchase the mobile phones (Nishimura: 1998, 8). The number of subscribers doubled the following year and reached 40 million in 1999. As this suggests, choice in technology can often be limited by the private sector.

There are limits to the growth of such non-keyboard based culture, at least until the day when information can be largely conveyed by sound rather than text. Unfortunately for the Japanese, multimedia culture is centred around the alphabet-based keyboard, and this is perhaps central to understanding why Japan has a handicap in upgrading computer literacy.

The Internet, which initially was limited to use by university academics in the late 1980s, should (in theory) easily spill over into use by everybody. Much has been written of how information has become such an integral part of the social system in the age of the Internet and Japan is similarly experiencing this. But the high-tech technology that Japan excels in is centred on hardware since language poses a problem for software. It is not clear how this can be remedied.

Internet use has grown rapidly in recent years. In 1993 the first commercial Internet provider started business. By July 1994 the number of hosts connected to the Internet throughout the world totalled approximately 3.2 million and users numbered more than 30 million. Japan ranked number six, with 72 409 hosts. 1995 is considered the first year in which the Internet really took off in Japan, helped along by the development of the World Wide Web. In 1997 the number of Internet users in Japan were estimated at over 5 million (Jiji Press: 1997). A survey of these users (March 1997) found that most (94.2 per cent) were male; 51.9 per cent were engineers; and that most people (74.6 per cent) used it for both work and pleasure. Almost half (46.4 per cent) used it at work or at an educational institution, and about a third (34.3 per cent) used it mainly at home (Takagi: 1997, 4). By October 1997, Internet users were estimated to have reached 10 million (Nishimura: 1998, 9). While it is difficult to obtain exact figures, these numbers reflect an explosion of growth. As might be expected, among those who use the Internet in Japan, around half of high-tech researchers use e-mail, with the highest percentage of such users being located in universities and colleges. Those aged up to thirty-nine years most often used e-mail, with usage declining with age.

Japan became the second-largest Internet market in the world by the end of 1998. In the six months to January 1997 the number of Japanese host computers connected to the Internet increased by 48 per cent to 700 000 (Holley: 1997). The high cost of being connected to the Internet works against its popularity. It is also not helped by NTT's unwillingness to embrace new information technologies. A monopolistic environment discourages risk-taking (Boyd: 1998). NTT is still effectively the sole provider of ordinary local telephone services to approximately 60 million subscribers. Ando (1998, 14) also suggests that consumers have been slow to shift to new service providers, preferring to continue paying NTT's higher prices, which in turn encourage consumers to keep telephone calls to as short a time as possible. In an attempt to remedy this, NTT is being reorganised into Nippon Telegraph and Telephone Corporation (Holding Company), NTT East, NTT West, and NTT Long-Distance. NTT East and West will both offer a service covering the whole of Japan. If this reorganisation leads to lower service costs and lower access charges, the Internet boom may well lead to greater growth in the development of multimedia.

The Japanese were slow to become aware that the Internet would become one of the most basic parts of social infrastructure. As we have seen in this chapter, one of the major reasons for this is the Japanese reliance on Chinese characters, but also because the use of keyboards in Japan was not widespread. With the advent of the Internet, mastery of the keyboard became necessary, and it has been said that those over the age of thirty-five years have found it difficult to keep up with the new multimedia culture as a result. It has also been suggested that Internet networks do not suit Japanese corporate culture since the Internet does not lend itself to strict rules, regulation and management. It is a type of medium with a loose structure that is cheap and liberating. For security-conscious companies, in-house intranets are a better option. There is considerable scepticism that the rush to install computer networks is nothing more than an attempt to keep up with one's neighbours. Ironically, the information age may not guarantee greater freedoms. Technology can lend itself equally to liberating computer users as well as monitoring them.

Japanese Software

Japan's software technology is not noted for its originality, and it often modifies or extends ideas from overseas, as evidenced by the software factories of computer manufacturers (Cusumano: 1991; Takeshita: 1996). Video game software and Sakamura's TRON project are two notable exceptions. Part of the reason for this lies with the state of computer science and software engineering. Aoyama (1996, 134) identifies the following special characteristics of the industry: (1) domination of custom-made software; (2) hierarchical structure of the industry in which large computer companies outsource work to subsidiary software houses who in turn outsource their work; (3) a people-centred approach influenced by the Toyota production system.

The TRON project is divided into two broad sub-projects. One is devoted to applications, especially the concept of incorporating intelligence in ordinary objects, as seen in an intelligent house where doors might be linked to a security system, windows linked to the air-conditioning system, and lighting is activated by sensors. The other sub-project is the development of a computer architecture which would provide the infrastructure for computerised environments (Sakamura: 1996).

As part of the push to commercialise TRON, a new company with the name 'Senetto' was established and started business on 1 February 1999. Emboldened by the court cases involving Microsoft in the United States and the spread of Linux (a UNIX-type open architecture operating system) in Europe, Sakamura and his supporters have decided to attempt to use TRON as an alternative operating system to Microsoft Windows. Efforts will focus on commercialising the personal computer operating system B-TRON. A personal computer using B-TRON has already gone on sale in Tokyo. Part of the plans includes the establishment of a company 'Global OS' in Silicon Valley, and the development of English and Chinese language software (Nikkei Telecom: 1999).

Another research program of interest is the Real World Computing Program launched in 1992 to succeed the Fifth Generation Computer Project discussed in Chapter 2. MITI encouraged foreign companies and organisations to participate, but as might be expected from the FS-X fighter plane experience, the United States was cautious. Americans ultimately became involved with people from other countries in the Joint Optoelectronic Program (Mikami: 1998, 5). While such cooperation is mutually beneficial, it is also motivated by a broader political agenda of nurturing relations with economically powerful groups.

Seven-Eleven Japan, a chain of 7300 convenience stores, has completed its Fifth Integrated Information System. In contrast to the Fifth Generation Computer Project, its aims are more modest, namely, to install a computer system which will link all the company's stores by satellite and Integrated Services Digital Network (ISDN) line. The system features a large 3-terabyte database which enables the collection of point-of-sale data (Mitsugi et al.: 1998). The network is but one example of how retail network systems are being transformed by communications technology.

The Rise of the Video Game Industry

The most obvious manifestation of the information society has been the Japanese video game, a complex mix of computer graphics, communication technologies and software. Recent products are more sophisticated than ever before, with features that are realistic and interactive. Japanese video games lead the world. Nintendō, Sega and Namco pioneered the new industry in the mid-1970s (Sunagawa: in press). Domestic sales and exports are estimated to have topped 1 trillion yen in the 1997 financial year (Arai: 1998, 24). In 1992 Nintendō Company ranked third in Japan, after NTT and Toyota, in terms of operating profits. Sega Enterprises came thirty-ninth.

Nintendō was orginally a Kyōto-based manufacturer of playing cards and games. In 1975 the company worked with Mitsubishi Electric to develop a video game system which made use of an electronic video recorder. The following year microprocessors were incorporated into the system, and in 1977 video games for home use were developed by the two companies. By 1978 Nintendō had begun selling coin-operated video games (Nintendō: 1998). Sega is less of a 'Japanese' company, having been established in 1954 as the Service Games Company. An American, David Rosen, founded the company in the aftermath of the Allied Occupation of Japan, with the aim of developing amusement machines. In 1956 he imported coin-operated equipment, buoyed by the demand for them from American military bases in Japan. Rosen turned to making his own machines in 1965. In 1966 he sold Sega to Gulf and Western Industries, but bought the Japanese assets of Sega with Nakayama Hayao and other Japanese investors in 1979. In 1984 the company was bought by Japanese, and the Japan-based company Sega Enterprise Ltd was born (Sega: 1998).

Both Sega and Namco introduced microelectronic technology about the same time as Nintendō. All three pioneered the new industry in the mid-1970s, and increasingly moved in the direction of computer games. Computer technology had been introduced into coin-operated game machines in amusement centres in the 1970s, but thanks to advances in semiconductor technology, home-use video games became possible in the 1980s. In the early 1980s Nintendō dominated the market for 8-bit and 16-bit generation game products. Sega, Casio, Bandai and other companies competed with Nintendō to produce cartridge-style home entertainment games (Sunagawa: in press).

The video game industry became truly established in 1983 when Nintendō started selling the home video game console 'Family Computer' with a television-like monitor and controller in place of a keyboard. As a result, computer games went beyond amusement centres and firmly entered the domain of the home. Early software included the popular 'Mario Brothers'. Nintendō increasingly focused on the home-use market and by 1984 accounted for 90 per cent of the home game market. In 1985 the 'Family Computer' went on sale in the United States. With the expansion of home computer games in 1987 the NEC Home Electronics' 'PC Engine' caused a move away from 16-bit home video game systems. There was a slump in demand in the early 1990s due to the lack of original software and declining overseas markets. With the transition to the 32-bit and 64-bit game consoles, the industry entered a new phase of growth. In 1994 leading electronics companies Matsushita and Sanyō introduced the '3DO Real', and Sony entered the market the following year with its 'Playstation' (Nintendō: 1998; Sunagawa: in press). These units can now be found in 15 per cent of Australian homes, along with Nintendō game player consoles which are found in 600 000 Australian homes (Chester: 1999).

As with comic books, video game consumers are not limited to high school students. Companies such as Kōei have specifically developed the computer game market for adults, with games simulating historical events (Iwasaki: 1991). Sony has sought to attract female users with games such as 'PaRappa the Rapper', and Nintendō is targeting primary school children with the popular 'Pokemon' ('Pocket Monsters'). Both groups constitute new markets for the video game industry (Arai: 1998, 2).

Does playing video games promote computer literacy? At the moment, games on personal computers are quite distinct from games with their own dedicated consoles. The dedicated consoles are much cheaper than personal computers, as is the software. The personal computer video game market is still relatively small. Furthermore, the development of software using open platforms is less attractive to hardware manufacturers as they lose control over the content of games. Parents and retailers sometimes have an aversion to the violence and sex which is often part of games software for personal computers (Arai: 1998, 26). Greater availability of games on the Internet may encourage more users to switch to personal computers. At the moment, though, Japanese video games, like Japanese wordprocessors, appear to be an intermediate technology which, due to their popularity, have slowed the transition to personal computers and the more widespread use of keyboards. It is thus a combination of cultural, political and economic factors which has hampered computer literacy. An understanding of them helps us to better understand Japanese society.

The success of the Japanese video game industry is testimony to the visual nature of Japanese culture, and provides convincing evidence of Japan's software potential. One of the most popular new coin-operated video games in amusement centres is called 'Dance Dance Revolution' manufactured by the Konam Company. Users step on a small raised platform and dance with a virtual partner on a video screen (Sullivan & Jordan: 1999). To what extent 'information' consumers who purchase the products have control over what is created is difficult to measure. In the case of video games such as 'Dance Dance Revolution', it can be argued that the software largely determines how the games are used, and they are a poor substitute for real human relations. Because of this, the industry has sometimes been viewed negatively in terms of its social impact. Eugene Provenzo Jr (1992, 1997) has found wide evidence of sex bias and gender stereotyping in Nintendō games. Violence and aggression are also common aspects of the games. Most of the video games examined by Provenzo had violence as their major theme.

Such features can be found in other forms of Japanese popular culture, especially comic books, and are not unique to Japan. What is most worrying is the fact that how the game is played is determined by the computer and how it has been programmed rather than by the free-ranging imagination of the player. The information society may result in pre-programmed players rather than the creative, innovative individuals that many had hoped for.

Conclusion

Computer and video games, along with wordprocessors, are aspects of Japan's information society. Whether this technology leaves the Japanese more resistant to the use of computers in the workplace has been the subject of concern. The popularity of the Internet encouraged many Japanese to use computers, but the decline in profits of major electronic firms such as NEC in the late 1990s suggested that the market for personal computers was nearing saturation. Perhaps there will be new innovations, new products, which will capture the interest of the market in the twenty-first century. There is the potential for mastery of computers to nurture creativity and problem-solving abilities. We should remember, however, that technology is a two-sided coin. Just as information technology can liberate the Japanese people by providing access to an information-rich world via the Internet, it can also serve to control them by enabling easy surveillance by the state, and encouraging consumption over education.

CHAPTER 9

Science, Technology and Gender

Introduction

We have found that the sources of 'Japanese' S&T are home-grown or derivative of imported innovations. The sites of domestic R&D are diverse, located in both the public and private sectors, and there is considerable variation according to corporation and institution size, prestige, region, funding body and industrial sector. A major factor which has yet to be considered, though, is the role of gender. This chapter focuses on gender inequalities in the S&T workforce. As gender cannot be discussed without also referring to questions of race, class and ethnicity, these factors are also briefly touched upon towards the end of the chapter.

In order for Japan to create new S&T, an educated workforce is vital. Koizumi (1995), like Morris-Suzuki (1994), has focused on the social networks and the people power necessary to develop such a capability. Koizumi emphasises the role of engineers in accumulating the technical knowledge, rather than the machinations and policy decisions of businessmen and bureaucrats. Engineers, he argues, are like black boxes. Although it is possible to measure outcomes, it is difficult to gauge what is inside. But are these 'black boxes' gendered? To what extent is there gender inequality in S&T-related careers and is the ratio changing? To what extent do women represent an under-used or exploited workforce and how does class and ethnicity serve to stratify the workforce? This chapter raises such questions by suggesting that representations of S&T are gendered, and explaining that this affects career perceptions. Women have been spoken of as an untapped S&T workforce, but the reality is that they tend to be exploited as part-time and casual labour. During the 1990s recession, more than ever before young men were encouraged to pursue careers as scientists, engineers and technicians, but they were opting for more lucrative careers in the service industries. Who will create Japanese S&T in the future? This chapter suggests that a non-Japanese, Asian workforce may partly fill the gap (Low: 1992).

Is Japanese S&T Gendered?

The form and content of S&T is, as we have seen, governed by power hierarchies in Japanese society, whether it be within the confines of a university department or a laboratory, within the bureaucracy, or among firms competing in the marketplace. What is often forgotten is how gender affects who controls S&T, how it serves to control people, and how gender issues affect the way policy is formed and implemented. Individuals make choices and gender bias can affect what is decided.

'Gender' is a term that refers primarily to sexual identity but also embraces other associated characteristics. Hence, while nature or biological makeup determines a person's sexual identity, gender also reflects the culture, society and history in which a person is immersed. It can be argued that it is not nature which determines the profile of Japan's S&T workforce, but Japan's history and culture (Jehlen: 1995).

Many accounts of Japanese S&T are concerned with showing how Japan has advanced, taking on a Western veneer of rationality to succeed in the Western world. Cultural historians tend to argue that under this veneer of 'modernisation' lies the traditional Japanese who is more emotional, irrational and at one with nature (Watanabe: 1990). This dichotomy resembles attempts to use female metaphors for nature and natural metaphors for women in the Western world, such as 'women as part of "the natural order"', 'women at one with nature'. Reason and objectivity have been portrayed as being largely masculine traits which have shaped the present Western vision of science. But interestingly, the conceptual dichotomies which have been used to divide the masculine from the feminine (culture versus nature, mind versus body, reason versus emotion, objectivity versus subjectivity, public versus private) (Wajcman: 1991, 5) in Western scientific thought, have also been used to separate Western thought from Eastern. It is Asians who are then dominated in place of women, it is the East which is portrayed as the Other (Minear: 1980; Said: 1978, 1985; Wilkinson: 1983).

Historians of S&T have often unwittingly presented an image of S&T as having been monopolised by men, through the pronounced absence of women from their accounts of the development of the 'scientific method' and its application. Even when inventions are not attributed to males, there somehow seems to be an assumption that they can be given credit for all technologies since early times. It is easy to point out the selective nature of history writing and the weighted absence of mention of workers or women, and the preoccupation with wars and 'major' political events in official histories.

We need to question basic assumptions regarding Japanese history and the roles and images of men and women. The lack of women figuring in stories of S&T tends to be explained as due to their lack of education or technological skills. Although it remains a major task for historians of Japan to document the gendered division of labour, it can be pointed out that women have traditionally been involved in agriculture in roles such as gathering of crops, threshing grain and processing of food. Little has been written of their possible role in the spread of pottery and cooking utensils during the Neolithic period and important innovations during the Tokugawa period such as irrigation and the 'senba koki' (a wooden frame equipped with a row of long teeth to strip grain) (Smith: 1959, 102). One easy way of putting women and gender relations back into accounts of history is by looking at traditional Japanese S&T, especially in the private domain. During the Tokugawa period, cotton cloth was popular among the people and women spun cotton manually; the thread was then made into cloth by using hand looms. The rural production of silk was also the province of women, who reeled and wove silk for their own use at home, as part of the domain tribute, and also for sale. One can therefore argue that women provided a skilled, technical workforce. They had acquired reeling techniques as part of their home or farm responsibilities, and they were also used to teaching these skills to others (Bernstein: 1988, 59).

Major studies of Japanese women scientists can still only be found in the Japanese language, reflecting their rather peripheral place in English language accounts of the history of Japanese science. The most important publication in Japanese in this area has been the book by Yamashita (1983). Yamashita outlines the background for the careers of the women scientists she discusses, and then tackles each discipline: biology, chemistry, pharmacy, medicine, mathematics and physics. Another important book was written by the historian of science, Miyata (1985). Unfortunately, the only Japanese woman scientist Miyata feels worthy of including alongside the likes of Marie Curie and Lise Meitner is the nuclear physicist Yuasa Toshiko. Yuasa (1909–80) is considered to be Japan's first professional physicist; she graduated from Tokyo Bunrika University (now known as Tsukuba University), was later awarded a French doctorate in science for research in nuclear physics and spent much of her life in Paris (Tsugawa & Kanomi: 1996, 117–38; Yagi et al.: 1997). This approach to correcting histories of science is limited to finding exceptions rather than in eliciting any general pattern of women's involvement.

Textile industries have been important to Japan's modernisation and the part played by entrepreneurs and female textile workers has been considerable. The latter tend to be neglected or omitted from many histories as the modern Japanese vision of S&T (which has long been promoted) appears not to include women, partly due to a preoccupation with paid production and its inputs. But a close examination of Japan's industrialisation from the 1870s to the First World War shows that there were probably more women in Japan in the industrial labour force than in any other country during this time. Over 80 per cent of workers in the textile industry were female (Bernstein: 1988, 54; Saxonhouse: 1976, 100). Furthermore, we need to understand that the introduction of Western S&T in Japan affected both public and private aspects of the lives of Japanese. Women have tended to be viewed as being confined within the private sphere which has been associated with emotion and subjectivity. The Western scientific skills of reasoning and objectivity were employed in the public sphere in Japan for often military-related purposes. Despite some interpretations of women as being highly skilled in domestic textile production, they were nevertheless considered by their employers to be unskilled labour worthy of only low pay. The role of women in spreading new silk technology is often forgotten. One well-known example is that of Yokota Ei, the author of *Tomioka Nikki* (*Tomioka Diary*). Yokota's father was a former samurai and council elder who was involved in the silk business. She went to work at the Tomioka Silk Reeling Mill in Gunma prefecture when she was fifteen years old as one of its first workers. A year later she returned to her home town to become a 'technical leader' at the new silk mill there (Bernstein: 1988, 58–9). Yokota kept a diary of her time at Tomioka and of her initial months at a mill in Rokku in Nagano prefecture. This diary was later published under the name Wada Ei (Hunter: 1984, 20–5; Wada: 1931).

One can highlight the effects of scientific and technical change on women and men during the Meiji period, and how these differed. This can be shown by the history of women textile workers. Matsuda Michio pointed out: 'The brunt of industrialisation as practised by the Meiji government was borne by the peasant girls. Hundreds and thousands of young girls became workers in textile mills and died of tuberculosis. Guns and battleships were paid with the profits made from their silk and cotton fabrics' (Matsuda: 1966, cited in Watanabe: 1990, 126).

An increasing number of English language books have focused on the plight of the factory girls. Textile exports enabled Japan to build up heavy industry and military strength without extensive borrowing, courtesy of Japan's women workers (Saxonhouse: 1976; Sievers: 1983; Tsurumi: 1990). But how do we go beyond this limited approach of depicting women as victims of male domination?

An examination of the history of the education of girls and their options at tertiary level in Japan provides evidence that S&T have successfully been portrayed as masculine culture (Collins: 1989). By looking at how separate streams have served to channel girls away from mathematics and science, we can arrive at structural reasons as to why women are under-represented in areas of S&T (Levine & Kawada: 1980). This is not to say that there have been no female scientists and engineers. Ben-Ami Shillony has written that, largely as a result of the Second World War, by 1945 the number of women in higher education had almost quadrupled compared with the number in 1935. The national total of forty-four women studying science at tertiary level in 1935 had increased to 1470 in 1945, the number of women studying engineering had increased from zero to sixty-two in the same period (Shillony: 1986, 775–6). Despite such increases, the nature of teaching programs at women's tertiary institutions certainly served to constrain them. Ronald Dore has shown that schools generate their own values and motivations, irrespective of their instrumental links with the outside world (Dore: 1986, 349–50) and this has caused Japan's two-year women's courses to maintain a gender-biased attitude towards S&T which discourages women from pursuing careers in S&T. However, most national universities are coeducational.

A closer examination of women's wartime activities shows how their role in the S&T sphere was constructed according to the social requirements at the time. During the Second World War it was socially appropriate for women to assist in the war effort. One example is the manufacture of balloon bombs by women. In November 1944, 9000 balloons (made of paper or rubberised silk) were released from Japan bearing bombs. Thousands of Japanese, especially high school girls, were mobilised to paste and stitch the balloons. While the role of Japanese women in the design of such weapons is unclear, throughout the world women munitions workers often have had input into what they produced. The potential for Japanese women to invent and innovate is likely to have been considerable (Mikesh: 1973; Hayashi: 1985).

Shioda (1994) emphasises how technological advances have created new work opportunities for women. During the postwar period of rapid economic growth from 1955 to 1973, factory automation in the production of electrical appliances and precision instruments created job opportunities for women workers beyond the textile industry. The spread of domestic, labour-saving technologies such as washing machines, refrigerators and vacuum cleaners enabled women to pursue paid work outside the home. Labour shortages encouraged women to shift from primary to secondary industries. Whereas in 1954 women constituted only 14 per cent of workers in the metal and machinery industries, by

1970 this figure was 42 per cent. Technological advances enabled experienced male workers to be replaced by unskilled female labour, though not without problems. Shioda (1994) explains that while the larger, prestigious corporations that manufactured electrical appliances, metal products and chemicals aggressively hired women in the late 1960s, the work was semi-skilled, women filled only subsidiary positions, and it was young, single women leaving junior high school who were employed, and at low wages. The repetitive, monotonous work of assembling products resulted in a high turnover of workers.

Gender and the S&T Workforce Today

Women account for nearly half of Japan's workforce, but most have part-time jobs with little security or chance of advancement (*Australian*: 1999b). Is Japan now any different from elsewhere in terms of gender inequalities in the workforce? Shirahase & Ishida (1994) provided some empirical evidence and argued that the degree of gender segregation in Japan is smaller than that in the United Kingdom and the United States. They accounted for this by pointing out the smaller proportion of managerial and service occupations in which men or women were over-represented, and explained that there was a more equal gender composition in clerical jobs, blue-collar production work and the agricultural workforce. The authors concluded that Japan's lower degree of gender segregation was the result of a smaller proportion of male or female-dominated occupations. The picture, however, is not rosy. They pointed out the likelihood of gender inequality in career prospects, access to authority, employment status and full-time/part-time distinctions within occupations. To this list of inequalities, Aiba (1995) added size of firm. Women change their type of workplace as they grow older. They go from working in larger firms as full-time workers to part-time jobs in smaller firms. The same, vaguely defined, occupational title disguises differences in work tasks. Likewise, similar pay for men and women may not mean similar job content. The predominance of part-time, female workers means there is a large difference in average wages earned by men and women.

Indeed, women's participation in the S&T workforce has tended to be in casual, part-time positions requiring little in the way of skills. Before the skills of this hidden workforce can be mobilised, S&T may have to be reshaped to accommodate them and a good start would be in schools and universities. Women need to be shown that they are as capable of success in S&T as men, and that it is socially appropriate for them to be so. Despite many barriers, women high achievers and schools which have encouraged their academic success have been able to overcome problems of access to education. While engineering may have been the largest area of tertiary enrolments in Japan in 1986 with 19.2 per cent, as opposed to 7.4 per cent in Australia, only 2.3 per cent of Japanese students were enrolled in science courses whereas the figure for Australia was 14.3 per cent. Engineering is a male-dominated area in Japan. In 1984, for example, 25.1 per cent of male university students chose engineering whereas only 2.2 per cent of female students opted for that choice. The situation in science, however, was more equal, with 3.6 per cent of males and 2.6 per cent of females pursuing such study (Collins: 1989).

Once women graduate and find research positions in the public and private sectors, do they experience much gender bias at the workplace? The problems experienced by women in the general workforce are also apparent in a study (Endo et al.: 1993) of sixteen female researchers employed at national research institutes, universities and private laboratories. In national laboratories, the women interviewed suggested that there were no perceptible gender differences in work and educational opportunities. Research showed both men and women often working overtime during the week, and on Saturdays and Sundays. At one laboratory, there appeared to be a gender bias in favour of men when it came to overseas trips. At universities, women experienced difficulty in being considered for new positions. Family and home duties cut into their research productivity, and even if their academic standing was equal to that of male candidates, it was thought that the male would probably be chosen. At private laboratories, there was a perception that women tended to be assigned work which was less urgent and less crucial to the company.

When pondering the question of how S&T has affected the lives of women, it is important to not only consider the situation in Japan, but also the way in which Japanese management and Japanese technology has affected the lives of women workers in Asia. There is a growing literature describing the transfer of technology from Japan and industrialised nations and the way this tends to reinforce their domination over developing countries, reproducing the male dominance which somehow seems to be encoded in the machines themselves. Examples can be found in Matsui (1987), such as the case of Malay women in Japanese factories suffering from mass hysteria, unused to working on assembly lines and in a new environment of concrete buildings and complicated machinery. The 'boss' is likely to have been male. Not only is the impact of technological change different for men and women, but gender relations in the workplace can also determine the direction and pace of that change. Tessa Morris-Suzuki has written of a dicing section in a microchip factory. The work, cutting microchip wafers, involved a great deal of concentration and manual skill. All the workers in the section were women, whereas the machinery repair workers were men. Female workers were not given advanced technical training because of the perception of them as a short-term workforce (Morris-Suzuki: 1988, 111–12).

The sexual division of labour is one barrier, but technology itself can be regarded as being gendered. The assembly-line system which transformed the Malay women into 'robots' was designed for repetitious work, allowing the exploitation of 'unskilled' women workers for long hours at low wages, and placing men (who could 'understand' the system) in supervisory roles with higher remuneration. The relationship between science and patriarchy only became clear in the 1980s. Easlea (1983) has shown how the arms race was the inevitable outcome of a science in which 'feminine' values, women and 'female' nature were resisted.

Beyond the Workforce

Another way in which we can consider the gendered nature of S&T is by asking how S&T has affected the lives of women. A distinctive feature of Japanese technological development has been the social costs of Japan's high economic growth. The characteristics of policy-making in S&T in Japan include the activities of small lobby groups in which women are active. Women have certainly been active in anti-pollution campaigns and peace movements. In 1954, the anti-nuclear movement in Japan was initiated by a women's group in Suginami, Tokyo, outraged at the 'Lucky Dragon' incident in which Japanese tuna-fishermen suffered from radiation during a United States nuclear test at Bikini Atoll (Toyoda: 1984).

Watanabe (1990, 112) writes of the common practice of conceptualising nature as a mother. Unfortunately, 'mother' nature was overloaded with industrial waste during Japan's period of rapid economic growth. From the late 1960s much anti-science literature focused on the social costs of industrial development, emphasising that pollution and war were evidence of how science had been abused. Science has been shown as being tied to the capitalist system of production. When capital was exported, so were the techniques of oppression.

Japanese women, often out of concern for their children, have been a major force in grass-roots opposition to Japan's rearmament and the development of atomic energy. While lacking in political power, women have indicated their displeasure at the local level (Ishizuka: 1985, 6). Such protests by women are considered politically 'respectable' by the Japanese population as they reinforce the image of women as concerned mothers (Buruma: 1985). Although their individual voices may have lacked impact, the cumulative effect of their protests cannot be negated. Protests by women may not be the most effective way of changing things but they do have an effect in shaping a political consciousness which has tended to take an adversarial approach to S&T.

The push for ecologically sustainable development and interest in environmental issues can be interpreted as a celebration of a less patriarchal science where humans work with nature. Rather than championing a science in which one must detach oneself objectively from natural phenomena and then attempt to dominate or master them, we are seeing an increasing tendency for scientists to immerse themselves in nature in order to obtain a more holistic understanding of it.

The position in which women find themselves, and the damage done to the environment in the name of economic growth, can both be partly attributed to the links between science, technology and the ideology of masculinity which have served to limit women's input into science, the production of technology and even its use. Nowhere is it more strongly reflected than in medical science in Japan, a stronghold of patriarchal values that have served to divest women of control over their own bodies. Margaret Lock has written of this and examined how the rise of the nuclear family and the social role assigned to middle-class housewives has supposedly given rise to various syndromes and neuroses. She suggested that attempts by gynaecologists to medicalise menopause were not unconnected with the desire by the medical profession to receive government reimbursement for women undergoing treatment (Lock: 1988). Oral contraceptives are difficult to obtain in Japan, serving to enhance the interests of the part of the medical profession that is responsible for abortions (Coleman: 1983; Djerassi: 1987, 157–61; *New York Times*: 1992; Shibuya: 1997).

While the role of women as consumers of goods is an important area of research, their choice of appliance has often already been limited by political factors impacting on the design and technology. Although market research in Japan does place importance on the response of housewives to products, the relative absence of women at the design and technical level reflects the power distribution within Japanese society. Not all household goods are considered the domain of women. Video cassette recorders, for example, tend to be associated with fathers and sons in Western countries (Wajcman: 1991, 90; Keen: 1987). The gendered use of technology in the Japanese home poses further questions worthy of exploring.

Even the home can be considered a technological construct designed to isolate women from men, to domesticate them, and to separate the public domain from the private. Despite international interest in Japanese architecture few publications seek to address such issues, preferring to focus on architecture as works of art and public monuments. In an appropriately titled book *The Hidden Order: Tokyo Through the*

Twentieth Century, Ashihara Yoshinobu writes of Japanese houses which have been vulnerable to fires and burglaries. Housewives consequently have felt obliged not to leave their home for more than two or three hours lest they tempt fate. As Ashihara pointed out, equal rights for men and women and the problems of urban development and housing are very closely related (1989, 48–9). Large-scale 'danchi' housing blocks may have partly solved this situation, but may have served to further isolate the housewife from the local community by interring her within a concrete box.

S&T, Race and Ethnicity

Scientists have rejected the notion that 'race' can explain a person's morals or intellect, but racial classifications continue to be used to differentiate people and account for perceived differences (Appiah: 1995). Ethnicity, like racial or national identities, is arbitrary in that it is often defined by stating what it is not, rather than by any pre-determined, biological makeup. The American reports referred to below tend, however, to use the word 'race', perhaps due to the perception that the term represents a more objective form of classification than ethnicity (Sollors: 1995). Despite the problems with the term, the American authors are motivated by a desire to be inclusive rather than exclusive, driven by the hope of describing a 'multiracial' S&T workforce.

The Japanese tend to portray their population as homogeneous and middle-class, thereby ignoring inequalites related to race, class and ethnicity. They do, however, recognise gender differences and the effect these might have on the labour force. For example, the Research Institute for Future Engineering has recommended the increased use of female researchers in its survey report for the STA of Japan. By the year 2005 it is estimated there will be a shortfall of 480 000 researchers, with 300 000 persons required in engineering and about 130 000 more researchers needed in the sciences. It is hoped that by retaining older researchers, encouraging women to pursue research careers and encouraging foreigners to work in Japan, this shortfall may be met. In contemplating Japan's future, the impact of such gender changes on the profile of S&T workers may be considerable (*STA Today*: 1991, 8).

One concern is the trend over the past few years for science and engineering graduates to opt for careers in the tertiary sector rather than in manufacturing. Most science, engineering and technical personnel employed in manufacturing now work in just six high-technology industries: instruments, chemicals, transportation equipment, electrical and non-electrical machinery, and refined petroleum products. Of the 192 400 'scientists' working in manufacturing in 1989, more than half were computer analysts (US Government: 1991). But if Japanese men are avoiding careers in these industries, and women are discouraged from taking their place, who will? Japanese firms hope that Asian personnel offshore and resident in Japan will fill the gap.

Americans have come to realise that they need to make the most of their multiracial workforce if they are to maintain the lead in S&T. Recently, they have addressed the underrepresentation of minority groups (African-Americans, Hispanics, native Americans, native Alaskans and native Pacific Islanders) in the S&T workforce. Some Americans are concerned that if action is not taken educational and economic apartheid could eventually occur. This has resulted in almost a 100 per cent increase over the period 1977 to 1989 in people belonging to United States ethnic minorities who obtain a bachelor of engineering degree, a growth in numbers from 2654 to 5239. Despite this, minorities who obtained doctorates increased from only twenty-seven in 1975 to seventy-one in 1990. Those receiving doctorates in the physical sciences saw a growth from seventy-one to 111 over the same period (US Government: 1992a; US Government: 1993a). Growth in the award of doctorates to women and minorities has hidden the decline in white male recipients. The overall number of science and engineering doctorates awarded to United States citizens differed little in the years 1990 and 1991, despite a 5 per cent increase in total doctorates awarded (US Government: 1992b). In 1990, 14 per cent (3200) of total doctorates in science and engineering were awarded to students from China, India, Japan, Singapore, South Korea and Taiwan. These countries effectively rely on the United States to educate over a quarter of their doctoral students, however, there is great variation if we look at each individual country and field. In engineering, about three-quarters of Taiwanese doctorates were awarded in the United States, whereas less than 1.8 per cent of Japanese doctorates were obtained there. The figures for South Korea and China are 44.4 per cent and 21 per cent respectively (US Government: 1993b).

In 1991 foreign citizens gained 38 per cent of science and engineering doctorates conferred by United States universities. During the previous ten years the proportion of foreign recipients increased most markedly in computer science, rising from 26 per cent to 51 per cent. Increases in mathematics and physics were similar, 32 per cent to 55 per cent and 26 per cent to 46 per cent respectively. Large increases occurred in doctorate recipients from Asian countries, especially Korea and the People's Republic of China (US Government: 1992b).

The centre of manufacturing has shifted from the United States to Japan, and then on to Asia. Technological innovation is leading to a revision of the political and economic map. The direction of this shift is unmistakable and the process has been accelerated by the phenomenon of 'brain reverse' whereby scientists and engineers from developing nations elect to leave the United States and return to their home countries. The 'brain drain' becomes the 'brain reverse'. Sometimes they are attracted by job opportunities at newly established high-tech facilities in their own countries. But more often, there is a heightened sense of contributing to the economic well-being of their own people.

The 'brain reverse' will undoubtedly contribute to further industrial growth in Asia, but to what extent it is extremely difficult to forecast, given the nature of the technology behind its rise to power. Previously, each time the centre has shifted the technology has differed too, but the shift to Asia is complicated by the accompanying transition from secondary industries to the tertiary sector. This process is not merely one of production, capital accumulation and living in comfort. The economics of the computer age defies such simple characterisations. The language used to describe it requires re-examination.

S&T and Class

Grouping all S&T workers together may be impractical because it does not recognise class differences between scientists and technologists, but there is nothing to prevent further fine-tuning by incorporating class into any analysis. To what extent are the differences inherent to S&T and what is in place through force of habit? We need to consider the nature of the divisions between soldier and officer, doctor and paramedicals, company clerk and factory worker.

We can attempt to draw fuzzy lines between S&T according to content, but if we look at Western history we see clearer differences relating to class. An intellectual class in Europe shaped scientific discourse whereas an artisan class was largely responsible for what we call technology. Such class differences have been perpetuated and are especially apparent in England and Germany; they are also common in Asia. In Japan, as in China, craftsmen were often illiterate and deemed to belong to a low social class. But with Japan's industrialisation in the Meiji period of the late nineteenth century, such class connotations were often forgotten. The offspring of the impoverished samurai class who had lost their stipends sought new sources of income and were drawn to the fields of science and engineering. They did not care to distinguish between the two fields. To these budding technocrats, they were merely new forms of knowledge written in foreign languages; it was Japan's 'modernisation' which mattered.

This is not to say that there were no class distinctions made in Meiji Japan – we can talk of a pluralistic structure of private and public

S&T. The establishment of pilot factories and telegraph services can be linked to the samurai-technocrats who oversaw the state-run projects, whereas the development of technology for private profit can be traced to industrial entrepreneurs such as Toyoda Sakichi, founder of the Toyota company.

These two traditions have intersected and fused into what is called modern-day S&T, taking some hundred years to do so. During the early Meiji period, graduate engineers showed contempt for amateur inventors and craftsmen and were reluctant to join private enterprise. The class consciousness can also be seen in the long-established field of public works, where class distinctions between the engineer and local foreman meant travel in different train carriages and the use of different toilets. In contrast, in the relatively new field of electrical engineering, graduates were eager to join the private sector. In the early days before university programs in electrical engineering had been established, budding students went abroad to study in the United States, not at universities but at factories where they worked and learnt from the technology and those around them. In this way, private Japanese technology has been able to reach levels of excellence.

It has been observed that Japanese engineers are 'socially and economically closer to production workers', and often work in close proximity to them (Kinmonth: 1991, 345). The lack of divisions between scientists, engineers and technicians in Japan, and growing computer literacy may require the development of new occupational categories, such as 'scientific worker', which conflates them. Perhaps even management executives may fall into this category. A British publication *Engineering Our Future* (1980), also known as 'The Finniston Report' (cited in Kinmonth: 1991, 338), has suggested that another factor in Japan's technological development has been the unusually high status which engineers enjoy in the private sector, where many engineers occupy seats on company boards. If true, this is perhaps a legacy of the late Meiji period when government enterprises were being closed and graduate engineers of samurai background were forced to seek positions in private enterprise. The historian, Earl Kinmonth, disputed this and suggested that it had been the United States corporate élite and not Japan's which had a disproportionately high number of executives with a science or engineering background. He argued that, compared with other Western nations, Japan had the lowest proportion of such people and that a careful empirical study was needed (Kinmonth: 1991).

Many books describe how university graduates joined technical school graduates to form effective corporate R&D teams. Technological innovation had no time for class distinctions based on education. But the notion of an equal society can be deceiving. At the macro-level, there is evidence of differences in remuneration if we compare secondary industry to tertiary. There appears to be a widening gap between salaries in banking and finance and those in manufacturing which, if extended to the global level, means a widening gap in wealth levels between Asian countries which rely on manufacturing and other creditor nations such as Japan and some Western countries. It is no coincidence that New York has lost its garment industry and replaced it with one devoted to the production of debt and capital (Harvey: 1989, 331).

Conclusion

Gender issues come to the fore in studies of Japanese S&T if we realise the contingent nature of traditional portrayals of Japanese history, widening the concept of S&T to include public and private spheres of production, providing details of gender differences in participation in areas such as education, and emphasising the social aspects of Japan's industrialisation. A wide interpretation of the role of women in Japanese society is necessary. In addition to gender, issues of class, race and ethnicity also come into play.

This is not surprising as the culture of S&T is not very different to that of society. Norms in scientific practice can also be found in other forms of social practice, and technology can be likened to a social system which organises space and human actions, creating relationships which maximise profits or achieve managerial goals.

How will the gender balance change as a result of the Asian economic crisis of the late 1990s? The so-called 'hollowing out' of manufacturing (Takayoshi: 1995) may well have exported gender inequalities overseas along with the factory plants, but the difficulties associated with the decline of Asian currencies created large-scale unemployment in Japan and many other Asian countries. Although Japan was experiencing postwar record-high levels of unemployment in the last year of the twentieth century, the figures appeared relatively low when compared with those of other Western nations. The low unemployment figures reported in Japan often disguise the extent of hidden unemployment, especially among women who opt for part-time work due to the unavailability of full-time work. While it can be argued that increased opportunities have been created for women in the workforce, it has become apparent that during the recession in Japan in the late 1990s, male graduates have often been favoured over women in company recruitment.

CHAPTER 10

National Interest versus Local Interests

Civil Aviation and the Construction of Narita Airport

Introduction

Early in the morning on Monday, 15 December 1997, members of a radical, leftist group visited the home of Sawada Jun in Tama ward, Kawasaki city, in the south-west of Tokyo, and set fire to his car and garage. The incident appears to have been carefully planned; batteries and a timing device were used. Sawada is a 55-year-old public servant who works in the Minister of Transport's secretariat, where he is a technical councillor. He is in charge of a project to extend the Shibayama railway which serves the Narita airport. The arson was not an isolated occurrence. Radicals are also suspected of setting fire to two cars parked outside the home of an airport official in September 1997. There has been a long history of such incidents, which have pitted 'national' interest against local interests. The incident at Sawada's home shows the controversy surrounding the construction of Narita airport (formally known as 'New Tokyo International Airport') has not abated. Travellers departing from Narita airport have their travel documents checked on their way there; many are surprised that there has been a history of conflict which has made such checks necessary. This chapter outlines the history to illustrate that not all Japanese agree with the national agenda of development, and that public policy has at times been flawed. The continuing opposition to Narita airport is testimony to that (*Japan Times*: 1997b).

As one of the largest government projects in Japan's postwar history, the problems surrounding the building of the airport near Sanrizuka deserves attention. Narita airport has been the focus of great conflict, often arising from the attempt by local farmers to protect their land. They were joined by sympathetic, left-wing groups. The protests attracted the support of anti-war, anti-nuclear and anti-pollution activists. The construction of the airport has galvanised citizen protest in a way which other issues have not. It throws light on some of the inadequacies of policy-making in Japan, especially the lack of consultation and the ineffectiveness of local government to pursue the concerns of local inhabitants. The book *Against the State* (Apter & Sawa: 1984) shows the political issues involved and the lack of effective community consultation and transparency in policy-making in Japan. This chapter attempts to analyse the conflict, and to show the problems with how 'national' interest (as opposed to public interest) has been pursued. Such problems are not isolated to Narita airport but also apply to Japan's other big projects, projects which involve large-scale facilities that are troublesome to local inhabitants.

In order to understand the Sanrizuka dispute more fully, this chapter first outlines the rapid development of civil aviation in Japan in the 1960s and early 1970s, and gives an historical overview of the problems associated with rapid growth in this sector, focusing especially on the dispute surrounding Narita airport.

The Growing Popularity of Air Travel

Japan saw rapid growth in civil air transport in the 1960s and it grew in popularity among the Japanese people from the early 1970s. The number of passengers using domestic air routes with the three main airline companies increased 12.5 times in the decade between 1960 and 1970, an annual increase of 28.7 per cent. International passengers also increased during that period by 9.5 times, or an annual increase of 25.2 per cent. One of the reasons for the steady growth in international travel was the relaxation of restrictions on leaving Japan. From April 1964, the year of the Tokyo Olympics, it became possible to make one visit overseas per person per year without special government approval, and to leave the country with a maximum of US$500 in foreign currency. In 1966 the 'one person – one trip a year' rule was abolished, and in 1969 the currency limit was raised to US$700. Group discounts were also introduced in 1969, and in 1970 changes in the passport system allowed permission for multiple journeys for the purpose of tourism as well as for business, with passport validity lengthened from two to five years. The above conditions contributed to the extraordinary growth in international travel by Japanese in the 1970s (Yoshioka: 1995).

The growing popularity of civil air transport was made possible by the large-scale introduction of jet aircraft. On international routes, the use of Boeing 707 and Douglas DC-8 aircraft by Pan-American Airlines from 1955 prepared the way for a world-wide boom in jet travel, and in 1958 new jets were introduced on a large number of routes, such as BOAC's Comet IV and Pan-American's Boeing 707 on the trans-Atlantic flight. In April 1959 BOAC began regular flights between London and Tokyo, and in September of the same year Pan-American started a service between San Francisco, Honolulu, and Tokyo. The large jets could carry twice the number of passengers in half the time of propeller-driven planes, thus further reducing the cost of a seat.

Japan Airlines was slow to take advantage of the new aircraft, finally introducing the Douglas DC-8 on the Pacific route in August 1960, a year later than Pan-Am. The DC-8 was the backbone of Japan Airlines' international fleet until the Boeing 747 arrived in 1970, servicing not only the Pacific route but also the northern European route. The next aircraft used by Japan Airlines was the wide-bodied Boeing 747, originally designed to be used as a cargo transport once the next generation of Boeing jets were introduced. This plan failed, however, and the Boeing 747 has been the mainstay of international air travel for nearly a quarter of a century. Japan Airlines bought its first 747s in June 1966, stimulated by Pan-Am's purchases in April of the same year. As in the case of the DC-8 a decade before, Japan Airlines was motivated by the need to compete with Pan-Am. The first Japan Airlines 747s flew in July 1970.

On the domestic front, the introduction of jet aircraft began in earnest with the simultaneous use of Boeing 727s by Japan Airlines and All-Nippon Airlines in 1965. This aircraft dominated the main domestic routes in the latter half of the 1960s. Rapid growth in the domestic market, however, forced both companies to consider using larger jets. Japan Airlines used Douglas DC-8-61s (234 seats) as a stopgap measure, then in 1972 used 747s from the international routes and planned the introduction of more in 1973. All-Nippon Airlines, on the other hand, planned the introduction of wide-bodied aircraft in 1972 to replace their Boeing 727-200 (178 seats). There were problems with the choice of plane, however, as in 1970 the new president cancelled a previous order for Douglas DC-10s and decided on the Lockheed L-1011 (Tristar). This culminated in the 'Lockheed Incident' involving former Prime Minister Tanaka Kakuei, who was arrested and accused of accepting bribes from the Lockheed Corporation to influence the granting of aircraft contracts.

The confusion arising from the All-Nippon choice of a wide-bodied plane resulted in a delay in the introduction of this type of aircraft on domestic routes. In 1971 All-Nippon petitioned the Ministry of Transport to delay introduction of wide-bodied aircraft until 1974, and the ministry complied, instructing both companies to begin use of the new planes at the same time. Japan Airlines employed Boeing 747s on its Tokyo to Okinawa run from August 1972, but their introduction on other routes was delayed until April 1974. On the same date in 1974 All-Nippon began using Tristars on the same routes.

Towards the Establishment of a Three-Company System

About 1960 civil air transport in Japan followed a two-company system, by which Japan Airlines serviced all international routes and the main domestic ones, while All-Nippon Airlines served some main domestic routes and all local ones. Both companies were strictly controlled by the Ministry of Transport and built up close managerial ties. The main shift in this relationship in the 1960s and early 1970s was from a two-company to a three-company system. During this period the Ministry of Transport maintained complete control over the civil aviation industry. First, it conducted aggressive administrative guidance, and secondly, it adjusted each company's share of the profits by strategic allocation of the right to use transport routes. The ministry also placed strict limits on competition, applying complete control over the framework of the entire supply system of civil air transport, a control which showed no signs of wavering throughout the 1960s and in the first half of the 1970s. The ministry aimed at strengthening the ties between Japan Airlines and All-Nippon, and the organisation and amalgamation of small local airlines, in an attempt to centralise the civil air industry.

At first, the activities of Japan Airlines and All-Nippon Airlines were clearly defined and separated, leaving no room for competition. From 1959, however, All-Nippon was permitted to service the main domestic routes of Tokyo to Osaka and Tokyo to Sapporo only, which was the start of intense competition. In 1962 Japan Airlines initiated talks aimed at amalgamating the two companies. The Ministry of Transport responded with policies to limit competition, such as equalising the number of flights from each company on major domestic routes, and suggesting the use of identical aircraft. It continued to offer administrative guidance to keep both airlines on an equal level. Talk of amalgamation arose again in 1966, following several accidents by All-Nippon aircraft, and the Ministry of Transport seized the opportunity to centralise air transport by proposing the assimilation of All-Nippon by Japan Airlines. Finally, however, it had to be content with conducting a special investigation into All-Nippon and appointing a Japan Airlines executive as vice-president (later to become president).

In this period, the Ministry of Transport was also faced with the problem of seven local airlines that were running regular local flights, although not licensed to do so. The ministry decided to offer each airline a regular licence, and proposed they merge to offset their deficits, and so All-Nippon formed an administrative partnership with four of these companies (Tō-a Kōkū, Fujita Kōkū, Chū-Nippon Kōkū and Nagasaki Kōkū). Later, these companies, except for Tō-a Kōkū, were either assimilated by All-Nippon or passed their regular licences to that company. The remaining three local companies (Kita-Nihon Kōkū, Nittō Kōkū and Fuji Kōkū) formed Japan Domestic Airlines (Nihon Kokunai Kōkū), and the Ministry of Transport recognised its right to run flights on certain main domestic routes as well as regular local flights. All-Nippon and Japan Domestic Airlines each serviced separate local routes. Japan Domestic Airlines was soon in financial trouble and in 1966 the ministry proposed that it merge with Japan Airlines within a period of five years, and set up plans for personnel changes. The rise in demand for domestic air transport in the latter half of the 1960s saved Japan Domestic Airlines from this action, and in 1971 it merged with Tō-a Kōkū to form Far East (Tō-a) Domestic Airlines. The structure of civil air transport then remained unchanged until the mid-1980s, with Japan Airlines monopolising regular international flights, all three companies servicing major domestic routes, and All-Nippon and Far East Domestic servicing local routes.

The legal basis for this system may be found in the Cabinet Agreement of November 1970, 'Regarding the form of the air transport industry', and instructions from the Minister of Transport on 1 July 1972, 'On the system of air transport'. The system was abolished by Cabinet decision in December 1985, when Japan Airlines was privatised and All-Nippon and Far East Domestic (in April 1988 it changed its name to Japan Air System) commenced flights on regular international routes.

Air Accidents and Their Significance

There were three main problems associated with the increasing popularity of air transport. The first was a series of air accidents involving large numbers of fatalities. The second was the increased social interest in the problem of noise pollution from aircraft. The third was the worsening of problems encountered in the construction of New Tokyo International Airport at Narita, namely the protest movement by local residents.

From 1958 to 1971 thirteen fatal air accidents occurred in Japan, eleven of them involving Japanese airlines. Accidents in 1966 (an All-Nippon 727 over the coast near Haneda; a Canadian-Pacific DC-8 at Haneda airport; a British Airways 707 on Mt Fuji; an All-Nippon YS-11 in the sea off Matsuyama Airport) and 1971 (a Far East Domestic Airlines YS-11A on a mountain in Hokkaido; an All-Nippon 727-200 collision with a Self-Defence Force training jet) resulted in considerable fatalities. There were a number of elements contributing to these accidents: bad

weather conditions, structural weakness, pilot error, and mid-air collision. It is certain, though, that the use of large and wide-bodied jets
increased the scale of such accidents. Government response was to
strengthen safety protocols by establishing a permanent investigative
body for aviation accidents, including a team of experts; making flight
recorders and voice recorders standard equipment; and completely
separating civil airspace from that used by Self-Defence Force (SDF)
aircraft: all SDF flight training was located over the sea.

Noise pollution became a major social problem from 1959, when Pan-
Am Boeing 707s began flying to and from Haneda airport. In December
1960 a council of concerned residents from areas near the airport was
formed, and negotiations with the Ministry of Transport began, with the
result that in April 1963 a curfew from 11 pm to 6 am was placed on the
airport. The next large-scale protest came from Osaka, where jets first
flew into Itami airport in June 1964. In October of the same year, citizens
from the eight cities adjacent to the airport formed a council to protest
against the noise pollution and demanded an airport curfew and the
legislation of compensation rights. The Ministry of Transport applied the
same curfew as that of Haneda airport to Itami, and introduced the *Act
Concerning the Prevention of Pollution* (officially issued in October 1967),
which made provision for government responsibility for anti-pollution
constructions and moving costs. Not satisfied with these measures, thirty-
one citizens of Kawanishi sued the country for past and future damages
and demanded a curfew of 9 pm to 7 am, and the case was tried at Osaka
District Court. This was the first litigation concerning airport noise
pollution in Japan. The case, and other similar ones, was won by the
complainants at Osaka District Court (1974) and later at the Osaka High
Court (1975), but the Supreme Court in 1981 rejected all claims except
that of compensation for past damages. Since then, other claims have
been similarly rejected.

The citizens' lawsuits had the effect of placing pressure on the Ministry
of Transport and airlines to improve anti-pollution measures, such as
increasing airport environment budgets, reducing the number of jets
flown each day, and self-imposed curfew restrictions. In spite of these and
other technological measures, the basic problem remained: a lack of
space to build airports on a scale large enough to keep noise pollution at
an acceptable level.

The Continuing Dispute over New Tokyo International Airport

In order to overcome some of these problems, it was proposed to construct a New Tokyo International Airport. The result, often referred to
as Narita airport, boasts a great number of flights per day and large

numbers of both passengers and freight, but it also suffers from poor weather conditions, insufficient runway, terminal, and facility space, and bad access from the centre of Tokyo. The level of noise pollution is high, and because of this there is a curfew from 11 pm to 6 am, and it is surrounded by wire fences and armed guards, creating tension in users and surrounding residents.

The faults of the airport can be traced to a bad choice of site and the fact that the construction of the airport was forced to proceed without the complete consent of the local residents. The poor choice of site may be traced to a desire to avoid SDF and United States Air Force training areas, and to a disregard for the many demerits of an inland airport. Almost no efforts were made to gain the consent of local residents in the planning process, and this has caused their protests to continue.

In 1965 the Japanese Cabinet decided to construct an airport at Tomisato, near Narita city, in Chiba prefecture. Local farmers protested violently, so much so that a decision was made to move the site to near-by Sanrizuka, a less-populated area, much of which was owned by the Imperial Household. The ensuing dispute between the government and local inhabitants, which is referred to as the 'Sanrizuka dispute', has continued for over three decades.

Postwar development in Japan has forced people to leave their homes to make way for construction, and those who remain on the fringes of such development have often been adversely affected. Disputes have often arisen as a result. In most cases involving the construction of large-scale facilities, the cooperation of three parties is necessary: central government, the government authority or private company directly responsible for the facility, and local authorities. Responsibility for construction approval generally lies with central government agencies rather than local authorities. And in most cases, local authorities make little effort to seek the views of local inhabitants. Instead, they focus their energies on eliciting the support of the local assembly and powerful figures in business groups. More often than not, they take the side of the central government and those seeking to establish the facilities in the first place. Local authorities have long attempted to attract government-funded projects to their region, with the benefits tending to flow to local construction companies and powerful business concerns. More bluntly, Japanese local authorities are a vehicle for the flow of government funds to local companies. They generally encourage government-funded construction projects, and tend not to be overly concerned with the interests of the local people, apart from business interests.

Given this situation, local inhabitants who object to such construction projects have few avenues available to register their protest. One common way people seek to prevent the establishment of such projects is by refusing to relinquish their land ownership and fishing rights. Most of Japan's coastal waters are subject to fishing rights. In order for a facility such as a nuclear generation plant to be established on the coast, it is necessary to appropriate land and local fishermen are required to relinquish fishing rights. Apart from residents who are directly affected, there are others who object to decisions made by central government. Due to the lack of other means by which to express their protests, such people have often joined forces with the local opposition movement.

In order to overcome this opposition, those promoting construction projects frequently resort to one of three methods. The first method is to buy up land under various pretexts prior to the announcement of construction. If the site selection is kept secret, it is usually not difficult to acquire the land. The second method is to encourage cooperation by providing facilitation fees, subsidies and bribes. Those not able to be bribed can be singled out for discriminatory treatment. One often-observed strategy is for local authorities, when ordering goods, to favour only those companies who support its projects. Furthermore, the families and relatives of those who support the project receive preferential treatment when it comes to employment in local government and local companies. The door to employment closes for those opposing projects. The third method is to acquire the land of those who oppose the project by force, using appropriate legislation. Such laws have, since the 1970s, been severely criticised as being a misuse of state power. Unless the situation is an extreme one, the exercise of this forced acquisition power has become rather difficult.

Due to this polarisation of attitudes and behaviour, it is relatively easy to characterise disputes centring around the construction of large-scale, problem-fraught facilities as a conflict between those promoting construction projects and those opposed to them. The Sanrizuka dispute was no exception.

The decision to construct the New Tokyo International Airport at Sanrizuka, Narita city, Chiba prefecture, was announced in June 1966. The basic plans for construction of the airport announced by the Transport Minister that December called for a 1060 ha site consisting of three runways (4 km, 3.2 km, and 2.5 km). By the end of the 1990s the airport was still not complete. Narita airport was opened on 20 May 1978, but only the 4 km runway was complete. The acquisition of land for the other two had yet to be finalised and the situation remains unaltered (New Tokyo International Airport Authority 20-Year History Compilation Committee: 1987). The vicissitudes of the plans for the construction of Narita airport has been the result of a strong and tenacious opposition movement based around the Hantai Dōmei ('Opposition Alliance') which has enlisted the support of New Left political groups and other volunteer supporters to resist the moves to acquire the land selected for the runways.

An Outline History of Construction of the Airport

The history of the airport project and the dispute surrounding it can be understood in terms of three stages. During the first period (1961 to 1966), the concept of a new airport emerged. After some powerplay among politicians with vested interests, it was decided that Sanrizuka in Chiba prefecture would be the location. The dozen tumultuous years after (1966 to 1978) was a period of armed battle from the time of the announcement of the construction plans to the partial opening of the airport. A violent conflict occurred between the promoters of the airport and the opposition movement and its supporters. Though there has been no end to the dispute, there has been an uneasy stalemate and thawing of hostilities in the following years (1978 to the present day). In the 1990s some dialogue occurred between promoters and one part of the opposition movement. This contributed to a thawing in the relations among the major players.

The concept of building the New Tokyo International Airport can be traced to Marui Kanichi, head of the section for airport management in the Administration Department of the Transport Ministry's Civil Aviation Bureau (Japanese Government, Ministry of Transport: 1987). The need to extend Haneda airport offshore had already been discussed by his colleagues in the ministry, but Marui persisted with the idea of having a second airport which could take over from Haneda. The grounds for his argument were that extending Haneda airport offshore would be difficult given the severe constraints arising from plans for the harbour and bay, shipping and navigation needs, and the limits of land reclamation technology. It would not be able to cope with the large increase in departures and arrivals likely to accompany high economic growth. (There were, however, moves later to explore the possibility of an offshore extension to Haneda airport. Also, Marui's estimates of the likely increase in arrivals and departures were excessive, as they did not take into account the advent of large passenger planes, such as airbuses.) Marui's second argument in support of a second airport related to having an airport which could cope with supersonic passenger planes. Such planes, he argued, required an airport with a 4 km runway. Without such an airport, Japan would be left behind by other countries, and Tokyo would be rendered a mere local air terminal rather than a world-class airport. (As supersonic travel has not become commonplace, this argument tends to be conveniently forgotten.)

In response to these two arguments, which now appear rather weak, the Ministry of Transport began a process of negotiations behind the scenes. Following these talks Cabinet decided on the construction of a second international airport (the New Tokyo International Airport) on 16 November 1962. In response to this, moves to select a site began at the beginning of 1963. On 20 August the Transport Minister Ayabe Kentarō requested the Council for Aviation to provide advice on and investigate the appropriate scale and location of the airport. A report was submitted three months later, on 11 December, which recommended Tomisato-mura in Chiba prefecture. This site would provide access to the eastern zone of the upper air space of the capital region. (The western zone was ruled out of contention due to the presence of a group of American air bases at Irumagawa, Yokoda, Tachikawa and Atsugi.) As for the scale of the proposed airport, it was recommended that there be two 4 km runways, two secondary runways, and one cross-wind runway. It was envisaged that the airport would be 2300 ha in area. However, during the ensuing two years there was a major dispute among the politicians with vested interests. Kawano Ichirō, who had consistently argued for a location in Tokyo Bay, remained intransigent, supported by a group of like-minded bureaucrats in the Ministry of Transport. With the death of Kawano on 8 July 1965, this group lost their leader, and Tomisato-mura became the favoured location. It was against this background that it was recommended as the site on 18 November 1965. Meanwhile in Tomisato-mura itself, a strong opposition movement had emerged since late 1963 which resisted moves to designate their village as the site.

After further deliberations by the governing LDP, the vice-president of the LDP, Kawashima Seijirō, proposed to Tomonō Takendo, governor of Chiba prefecture, on 17 June 1966, that the nearby Sanrizuka replace Tomisato-mura as the airport site. Governor Tomonō approved this two weeks later on 2 July. Cabinet approved the change on 4 July, and on 12 December that same year the Basic Plan for Airport Construction was presented by the Transport Minister to the New Tokyo International Airport Authority, which had only been set up several months earlier on 30 July. This plan recommended a site of 1060 ha, half the size of that recommended for Tomisato, one runway of 4 km, a second runway of 3.2 km, and a third of 2.5 km. The plan called for an airport which was open 24 hours a day. It was envisaged that the major runway would be completed at the end of the 1970 FY, and that total construction would be completed by the end of the 1974 FY (Japanese Government, Ministry of Transport: 1970).

The reason why Sanrizuka suddenly became the airport site can largely be attributed to two things: land acquisition would be relatively easy as one-third of the site consisted of imperial estate land and prefectural forestland; secondly, the bulk of the land that was in private hands was owned by people who had settled there after the war and the group's cohesion was relatively weak. Many of the farmers were only part-time farmers and had second jobs. In short, the choice of Sanrizuka was a political one based on the perceived ease of acquiring land. The decision was made suddenly by Cabinet without consultation with the local inhabitants.

Negotiations for land acquisition by Chiba prefecture and the Airport Authority went on steadily, amid attempts by residents to resist the plans. Their protest efforts were frustrated by a decision by the prefectural assembly to support plans for the airport. Those residents who opposed the airport formed the group Sanrizuka Shibayama Rengō Kūkō Hantai Dōmei (hereafter referred to as Hantai Dōmei), with Tomura Issaku as president. The opposition movement thereby became more organised. At first it was comprised solely of local people, members of the Socialist Party and Communist Party, but the usual demonstrations, meetings and petitions did not halt the construction plans. In the summer of 1967 Chiba prefecture and the Airport Authority moved in the direction of land acquisition by force using legislation. As a result the resolve of the opposition movement strengthened, and they turned to using force in order to resist. New Left political groups offered the Hantai Dōmei their assistance, and an escalation in the hostilities followed.

Armed conflict commenced in 1968, with four clashes occurring between 26 February and the end of March. Many people were wounded. This became known as the 'first Narita incident'. Weapons used in opposition tended to be things like stones, metal pipes and bamboo poles rather than firearms, knives and explosives. The opponents did not resort to what could be termed terrorist activities, but as violence became an everyday occurrence supporters from the Socialist Party and Communist Party distanced themselves from the Hantai Dōmei, and the organisation was largely left to New Left political group members. Apart from the Red Army and a small number of exceptions, Japan's New Left groups tended to be fairly moderate when it came to disputes which involved force.

During these clashes, the Airport Authority went ahead with construction plans. Building was divided into two parts: the first centred around the main runway and passenger and freight terminals; the second had the other two runways and a second passenger terminal at its core. On 13 September the president of the Airport Authority (and former head of the Civil Aviation Bureau of the Ministry of Transport), Imai Eisaku, requested approval for airport construction which necessitated land acquisition legislation. He received the approval from the Minister of Construction three months later. The Airport Authority next requested a judgement on the proposed site of part one of construction, from the prefectural expropriation committee; by the end of the year the prefecture handed down a favourable decision. On 1 February 1971 the Airport Authority then requested that the prefecture forcibly expropriate the land which fell within the designated area, a request carried out from 22 February until 6 March. A second round of land consolidation occurred during the period 16 to 20 September when public-held land was targeted for acquisition. The Sanrizuka dispute escalated as a result.

At the 'Tōhō Crossroads incident' of 16 September, the first day of the second round of land acquisition, three police officers were killed. Amid a retaliatory offensive on the part of the police, one member of the Hantai Dōmei committed suicide. By Spring of 1973 the opening of the airport was in sight. There were other problems which the Airport Authority encountered, such as difficulty in obtaining approval for construction of a pipeline for carrying jet fuel, but despite these small hitches the airport opened on 20 May 1978. It had been planned to open the airport within the 1977 FY, but due to an incident involving fourteen activists who occupied a control tower on 26 March 1978 (just before the end of the FY), the opening was delayed two months (Tōkyō Shinbun & Otsubo: 1978).

From Stalemate Towards Dialogue (from 1978)

With the opening of part of Narita airport the era of large-scale violent conflict came to an end. The Airport Authority began construction of the remainder of the airport fairly early after the initial opening, but buildings and land owned by many members of the Hantai Dōmei happened to fall within the site that had been selected. While there were those who argued that the land should be acquired by force, as in 1971, many people were reluctant to become the target of the harsh public criticism and were not keen to raise the prospect of more violent battles (Gijutsu to Ningen: 1979; Matsuoka: 1981). There was a possibility that such action might paralyse Narita airport and expose the arrival and departure of planes to danger. There was also a risk that as Narita airport was now an international facility, a replay of the earlier violent clashes would see a loss of credibility in the eyes of other countries by the Japanese government. The government's own public opinion polls found that people did not support compulsory acquisition of land.

The Airport Authority decided not to proceed with forced acquisition and instead strongly promoted a strategy of attempting to convince landowners to part with their property. There were attempts behind the scenes to open up dialogue with members of the Hantai Dōmei, but these did not meet with much success and a stalemate ensued for most of the 1980s. Stage two of construction began in October 1986, but as land for the second and third runways had not been finalised it was more or less limited to the building of the second passenger terminal. In September 1989 the chairman of the Chiba prefectural committee for expropriations was physically attacked, and all members of the committee resigned as a result. The committee remained indefinitely dissolved so, in effect, the forced acquisition of land was no longer a real option (Uzawa: 1992a).

The Hantai Dōmei fragmented into three factions. The charismatic leader Tomura Issaku, who had been president, died in November 1979 and with him went the binding force of the organisation. Despite this, the members continued to protect their land. In 1990 moves were made to break the stalemate (Furihata & Ichinose: 1991). On 1 November a liaison committee for regional development was established. Members of one of the Hantai Dōmei factions participated, along with those involved in local policy-making. As a result of discussions, fifteen symposia were held to discuss problems relating to Narita airport over the period November 1991 to July 1993 (Narita Airport Problem Symposia Record Compilation Committee: 1995). The organisers of the symposia were a group of five academics led by Sumiya Mikio (Sumiya: 1996). From September 1993 to December 1994 discussions continued in the form of roundtable conferences (Narita Airport Problem Roundtable Conference Record Compilation Committee: 1996). At the roundtable conferences, government representatives and Hantai Dōmei members exchanged their views. The government apologised to the local people for the violent oppression which had occurred, and it was generally agreed that plans for the airport should proceed on the basis of democratic discussion and a perspective centred on the coexistence of the airport with the local community. A consensus was reached about the second (3.2 km) runway, and it was decided that construction of the third (2.5 km) runway should be re-examined on completion of the second runway. Only one of the three faction groups participated in these meetings, so the agreements reached did not extinguish the stalemate which existed with other members of the Hantai Dōmei. However, even some of the members of the non-participatory groups responded positively to attempts to purchase land for the airport, so undeniably there was some thawing of the icy relationship which had existed (Kitahara: 1996).

The Pursuit of the National Interest

If we view the construction plan for the New Tokyo International Airport in terms of national interest, the project was questionable, not only in terms of the outcome but also in the process of construction. If the 'national interest' had truly been given priority, a rationally conceived project would have been the best outcome for the Japanese people. A democratic method of consultation would have been the best way of ensuring that the interests of the people were met. The New Tokyo International Airport construction project was a 'national project' which the central government took upon itself to promote. The construction program should have been required to satisfy 'national interest' even more than the usual large-scale project, but as we have seen, this was not the case.

Most people would agree there was a need for a large-scale international airport close to the capital. However, in terms of policy choices which optimised public benefit, site selection should have been made after a comprehensive assessment of the most appropriate type of airport. Narita airport was a total failure on this count. As the airport is 70 km from the centre of Tokyo, access is difficult. Furthermore, since the airport is located inland and is rather narrow, aircraft noise is a grave problem and in order to contain it, there is a curfew: planes are only able to arrive and depart between 6 am and 11 pm. New Tokyo International Airport would have been better built out into the sea, in Tokyo Bay as was proposed in the first half of the 1960s.

Due to the machinations of politicians bent on looking after their interests, the best choice in terms of national interest was not made, and Tomisato-mura was first chosen. Once it was found that it was impossible to construct the airport there, it would have been responsible policy-making to abandon the plan and seek alternatives, but this did not occur and a decision was made to opt for the narrower Sanrizuka site, without the benefit of expert assessment. Sanrizuka was far from being the most appropriate site and was, in fact, among the worst possible sites. Given this, the construction of the airport there can scarcely be considered a policy in the national interest, and it might be more appropriate to consider the airport as a project which was not based on rational policy-making. Furthermore, the project went ahead without following democratic procedures. There was no effort to achieve the agreement of local inhabitants. Only Chiba's governor Tomonō and his colleagues were consulted by politicians and the Ministry of Transport. But even for Tomonō, the decision to choose Tomisato-mura in November 1965 came as a surprise, as was the decision to then opt for Sanrizuka. Such decision-making was highly secretive, and it is not clear who really took the initiative. It may have been the LDP, the Ministry of Transport or perhaps Chiba prefecture. In addition, only two weeks after being announced, the construction plan for Narita airport was authorised by Cabinet, and became a 'national project'.

Conclusion

For large-scale national projects like the airport, decision-making processes should be impartial, objective and transparent, and open to public scrutiny. Project sites should be decided after the agreement of local residents has been obtained. The construction plan of Narita airport failed on these counts alone. However, it would be fair to say, and at the risk of defending the actions of the Transport Ministry, that in the mid-1960s, community consultation and objective decision-making were not necessarily common practice. Until the 1950s, for 'national' public projects the following was common: first, it was generally thought that land development involving large-scale construction projects was desirable, and that achieving such development was a great achievement for the bureaucrats who promoted the projects. Secondly, as there were great economic benefits for the region selected for the large-scale construction projects, they became the object of much political action. This was the case until the early 1960s for nuclear power plants. Thirdly, local inhabitants and the living conditions they had to endure were not a major consideration. The idea of building an around-the-clock airport for supersonic aircraft on a very narrow strip of land in an inland, densely populated location does not seem logical, but thirty years ago this was not considered. Fourthly, the secretive decision-making which occurred among the bureaucrats, politicians and businessmen was regarded as a normal procedure. The concept of democratic procedures was viewed as permitting the unreasonable interference of outsiders. These generally accepted ideas about 'national' public projects have increasingly become a thing of the past, and it would be fair to say that the Sanrizuka dispute made a considerable contribution to the changes in thinking which occurred (Uzawa: 1992b).

CHAPTER 11

The Patient versus the Doctor

Changes in Medical Care and Attitudes to the Body

Introduction

This chapter deals with the doctor–patient relationship in Japan and how advances in medical care achieved in developed nations from the 1960s through to the 1980s were received there. An argument has been made in Japan that due to unique cultural characteristics and attitudes to the body, concepts such as informed consent are inappropriate, as are oral contraceptives. This chapter suggests that ideas about the body, and even resistance to organ transplants from brain-dead donors, have much to do with the prevalence of long-standing power relationships where doctors have the upperhand, rather than because of any innate need to respect cultural traditions. While religious beliefs play a part (Ōmine: 1991; Aono: 1995), the doctor–patient relationship is a major contributing factor.

Medical Care in Japan

Advanced medical care is readily available in Japan, and the national health insurance scheme ensures that the cost of medical care is afford-able for most Japanese (Gyoten: 1992). The Japanese medical system is a predominately private system with the bulk of medical care provided by the private sector (Watanabe: 1998). The system is centred on physicians who provide a service for a fee to patients who belong to a compulsory health insurance scheme. Patients who work for large companies enjoy private policies with better coverage than the government scheme, leading to a two-tiered system of medical care. Health insurance coverage encourages longer hospital stays in Japan. The average length of stay in hospitals is a relatively long 38.3 days, in contrast to eight days in the United States (Lock: 1987, 5).

174

Many Japanese doctors have small private practices staffed by one doctor and a nurse. In contrast to many Western countries where prescriptions are filled at pharmacies, doctors not only prescribe drugs but also dispense them. This situation lends itself to excessive use of medication in Japan. As health-care consumers, the Japanese shop for Western-style medicine and also for Asian medical techniques, such as *shiatsu* and acupuncture, as well as herbal medicines. Japanese patients are becoming more demanding of medical care. They expect high-technology medical services and are calling for a more equal relationship with their doctors, one that is less paternalistic and more of a partnership. Patients are increasingly seeking more information about their illnesses and the options for treatment.

The Doctor–Patient Relationship

In his classic study of the history of tuberculosis in Japan, William Johnston (1995, 126–30) relates the story of a doctor–patient encounter during the late nineteenth century, and how the patient suffering from tuberculosis, her mother-in-law, and the physician (who had studied overseas) all engaged in a game which eliminated the need to know the identity of her disease. Such games are still being played in Japan today, especially when a patient suffers from cancer or AIDS. Physicians and families are faced with the moral dilemma of whether or not to tell patients the truth about their illness. If they do, they risk possible accelerated deterioration in the patient's condition and, if word spreads, the patient might be ostracised by society. Most of the 200 000 cancer sufferers who died in Japan in 1990 had not been told before their death of the diagnosis by their physicians or families. Even Emperor Hirohito who died of cancer in January 1989 was not told (Ormonde: 1990). While ostensibly the interests of the patient are all-important, such dilemmas tend to place final authority in the hands of physicians. A survey conducted by the Ministry of Health and Welfare in 1994 found that only one in five cancer patients are told that they have cancer, and the Supreme Court made a ruling the following year that doctors were not obliged to do so (White: 1997, 38).

There has long been a stigma attached to leprosy, tuberculosis, psychiatric illnesses and now AIDS. Japan's some 6500 lepers have been isolated in special colonies, and hospitals are reluctant to publicise that they treat AIDS patients for fear of being shunned by people seeking other medical treatment (Hills: 1995b). The social stigma, combined with long-standing tendencies for physicians not to be forthcoming in diagnosis, has contributed to a situation where it is unclear how many people actually live with HIV/AIDS. This has hampered AIDS education (Hills: 1994a; Saphir: 1994).

Late in the nineteenth century, cuts in government funding of public hospitals saw a subsequent rise in private hospitals, often attached to the offices of individual physicians. The quality of care at small private hospitals has been varied (Johnston: 1995, 172–3). As we have seen in earlier chapters on R&D, the bulk of medical care is provided by the private sector. All this has resulted in a largely private, fee-for-service medical care system centred on physicians, which is highly competitive and variable in the quality of care on offer (Lock: 1987, 5–6). The authority of physicians is further reinforced by their ability to both prescribe and dispense drugs, leading to a tendency for over-medication and an overly close relationship between doctors and pharmaceutical companies (Sugaya: 1981, 185). Under the national health scheme introduced in 1962, the government pays a set price to doctors, clinics and hospitals for the drugs which have been dispensed, irrespective of whether they have been bought at a discount (often about 20 to 30 per cent). The more drugs prescribed and the closer the links with the drug companies, the higher the earnings. Doctors augment their income significantly by freely prescribing drugs and taking advantage of the disparity in prices (Okimoto & Yoshikawa: 1993, 257; Hadfield: 1996). As a result, Japan has the heaviest use of prescription drugs in the world. A third of the health budget is spent on drugs. This exceeds defence spending and is more than double the amount spent on rice. It constitutes about twice the amount per capita spent on pharmaceutical products in the United States, and triple that spent in Britain (Hills: 1994b, 5; Garran: 1997a).

The medical profession consists of various interest groups which make it difficult to achieve consensus on issues relating to health care policy. As Lock (1987, 7) pointed out, tensions exist almost at every level, between national and regional medical organisations, between doctors based in hospitals and in private practice, specialists and general practitioners, and practitioners of traditional medicine and those who practise Western biomedicine.

Concern about these issues was heightened when a scandal occurred with the import of tainted blood products into Japan. A former director-general of the Bureau of Pharmaceutical Affairs of the Ministry of Health and Welfare was made president of Japan's largest pharmaceutical company, Green Cross. Many other senior bureaucrats have joined the same company (Miyamoto, M.: 1996). This is an example of *amakudari* (literally 'descent from heaven'), used to describe a common practice whereby retired bureaucrats take up highly paid positions in companies which they dealt with formerly. This company and four others sold HIV-infected blood products until at least 1988, despite knowing since 1986 that such products would lead to AIDS. In the 1980s, Japan imported one-third of the world's blood products, mainly from the United States

(White: 1997, 43). The Ministry of Health and Welfare was culpable too, as it knew as early as 1983 that unheated blood products were dangerous. Although a decision was made in 1985 to treat these products, earlier blood products were not recalled in Japan. This disregard for patient welfare resulted in approximately half of Japan's haemophiliacs being infected with HIV, and a further third contracting AIDS (White: 1997, 44). As Feldman (1997) points out, Japan was not alone in its late approval of heated blood products. Britain was slow to approve as well, with the result that there, too, about half of the haemophiliacs are infected with HIV.

In Japan, the public outrage drew attention to the collusion of pharmaceutical companies, bureaucrats and doctors, and especially to the inadequacies of the Ministry of Health and Welfare (Talcott: 1996). HIV-positive haemophiliacs are suing the government for infecting them with the tainted blood products (Komatsu: 1997; Skelton: 1996; *Weekend Australian*: 1996). Miyamoto Masao (1996), a former employee of the ministry, suggests that the following characteristics of the ministry may have contributed to the scandal: the importance of harmony in the ministry over reality; emphasis on the protection of industry over the welfare of the public; the dogma of continuity clashing with the need for crisis-management; the seniority system which makes criticism of superiors difficult; lack of leadership in decision-making; system of *amakudari*; lack of a Freedom of Information Act; lack of respect for individual rights; use of clinical trials for new drugs as a non-tariff barrier; tendency for Japanese to consider themselves unique.

The slow Japanese response to the possibility of HIV infection from blood transfusions and tainted blood products can be seen as symptomatic of a medical system (bureaucracy, health industry and practitioners) out of touch with the needs of the Japanese public and more motivated by a desire for greater profits. The erosion of trust in the system has led to calls for greater autonomy on the part of patients and more consumer choice.

Death by Overwork

There have also been concerns that Japanese companies have been neglecting the health and welfare of workers in the pursuit of profit. One manifestation of Japanese-style management has been the phenomena of *karō shi* (death by overwork). Despite record increases in unemployment in Japan in the late 1990s, the reality is that some Japanese are working longer hours than ever before. There is concern that individual rights are being ignored, and that harmful work practices and conditions are being tolerated for the greater corporate good.

The National Defense Counsel for Victims of *Karō shi* (1990) has documented many cases of workers dying from overwork. It cites the case of Yasuda Shinji (name changed) who was an automobile engine designer. He died at work from a stroke at the age of thirty-seven after working from 8 am to well after midnight every day for three years. Any spare time was devoted to the study of English in case he was required to travel overseas for work purposes. When he died from overwork, his wife and three young children received no workers' compensation from the company as such funds were only made available to those who had lost a limb while working with machines. Thousands of people in their forties and fifties, but some in their thirties as well, have died from strokes or heart disease arising from overwork. The National Defense Counsel for Victims of *Karō shi* estimated in 1998 that 10 000 people die from overwork in Japan per annum (*Asia Inc. Online*: 1998). Whereas it was previously thought that this was most common among shiftworkers and drivers, it seems to afflict all kinds of professions, including white-collar workers in general office and management jobs. The long work hours, heavy work schedules, job-related stress, extensive travel, job transfers, long commuting time, and the need to often live away from one's family have taken their toll on the Japanese worker.

Japanese companies are trying to reduce their reliance on lifetime employment and the previously rigid, seniority-based salary system. In the late 1990s major manufacturing and construction companies slashed staff in unprecedented numbers in order to survive Japan's worst postwar economic recession. The economist Jesper Koll summed up the situation as follows: 'Mrs Watanabe is saving her money because her husband is bringing home less pay, his job security is gone and her daughter just got fired' (cited in Skelton: 1998). Despite the changed conditions, Mr Watanabe may be working harder than ever. At the same time, however, there is a growing perception that Japanese workers must look after their own health and welfare.

Towards a New Doctor–Patient Relationship

In recent years, medical care has come to be thought of as a service provided to patients, and there is a growing recognition that patients have the right to choose and make decisions. The Japanese have become health care consumers and they expect and demand medical services which make use of advanced technology (Lock: 1987, 5). The problem is that such services can vary greatly, as can the technology used, and it is often difficult to ascertain who are the best service providers. There seems to be a lack of health care accountability. White (1997, 42) points out that there are only around 400 medical malpractice suits filed in Japan each year, with only about one in five ending in a decision which favours the patient. Appeals result in a final decision often occurring long after the death of the patient. The concept of informed consent provides medical care users with a way of changing the power relationships in the health industry.

One way of overcoming some of these problems, and the basis of the hope for greater freedom in medical care and a new doctor–patient relationship, is the concept of informed consent. By looking at its reception in Japan and the controversy surrounding it, we can come to understand how Western ideas are being adopted. The idea of informed consent dates back to 1957 when it was first used to refer to the need for patients to be informed of risks associated with medical care, but it has been used in industrially advanced nations since the 1970s. Miyamoto Shōhei (1988) views this as a revolutionary change in thinking about medical care, a change that has been imported into Japan but has still not adequately taken root. The idea of informed consent is by itself not necessarily a positive thing from the viewpoint of patients, rather, it can be seen as a quality assurance mechanism for medical technology. One major fault of the Japanese medical system is the difference in the quality of medical technology between various institutions. The fate of the patient can depend on the institution and on the doctor providing appropriate medical care. The spread of informed consent can provide a useful role in eliminating the disparities in the quality of both medical care and the technology used to provide it.

The idea of informed consent started to spread in Japan from the 1980s, as a result of a study by a group of lawyers and medical professionals who produced a draft report, 'Declaration of the Rights of Patients' (1984). This proposed: that the rights of individuals be respected; the recognition of the right to receive equal medical treatment; the right to receive the best possible treatment; the right to know; the right to decide for oneself; the right to privacy (Ikenaga: 1994); the last two matters are directly related to informed consent. This group became active in propagating the idea of informed consent.

By the late 1980s the idea of informed consent had begun to take root against the background of its establishment as an international rule or standard. It was impossible for the medical community in Japan to resist it. First, the systemisation of informed consent was viewed as the 'internationalisation' of the medical system, and as partly the result of Japanese doctors working abroad, the increase in Japanese patients going overseas for treatment and the increase in non-Japanese patients in Japan. If the Japanese had resisted such ideas it would have meant relegation to underdeveloped-nation status.

Secondly, advances in medical technology make it increasingly possible to control life or death by machines, and give rise to the possibility of organ removal from brain-dead patients. Thirdly, there was a need to protect the profits of pharmaceutical companies. Japanese companies had to comply with rules for registering pharmaceuticals by testing, based on the idea of informed consent, lest they risk being marginalised in international markets. But it is said that compliance is still insufficient, and Japan is still far behind the United States in evaluating and monitoring drugs.

In the 1990s various government committees, medical associations and law societies produced reports and statements which incorporated the idea of informed consent. It became more socially accepted. There has been growing agreement that the doctor–patient relationship needs to be changed. Some medical professionals argued that the Western idea of informed consent needed to be propagated in a form that took into consideration the cultural characteristics of the Japanese, one which placed more emphasis on the authority of the doctor. Two reasons are given to justify this: the first that informing patients of the truth is not necessarily always in the interests of the patient. In the case of illnesses such as cancer there is the danger of patients losing the will to live. Those who support this view consider it appropriate for doctors to consult with the patient's family when deciding whether or not to inform the patient; a viewpoint which maintains that doctors should retain authority. If one acknowledges the right of patients to informed consent, doctors are unable to deal with such situations on a case-by-case basis. The second reason is that the Japanese are family and group-oriented and, because of this, Western rules such as informed consent which are based on the concepts of the primacy of the individual are not appropriate for Japan. This view tends to deny that patients have the knowledge to make decisions and treats them as people who are controlled by their feelings.

The weakness of such views is the lack of proof and objectivity. Doctors may not necessarily be the best judges of whether or not to inform patients of their illnesses. There have been attempts to fashion a Japanese style of informed consent which considers accepted Japanese cultural characteristics, but there is no consensus among sociologists of the veracity of such claims to uniqueness.

As previously mentioned, a major flaw of the Japanese medical system is the variation in medical technology used by doctors and found in institutions. Standardisation and quality control is inadequate compared with that in Europe and the United States. As a result, advised medical treatment can differ and there are differences in testing and ability to diagnose illness depending on the doctor and the institution. At times, many doctors are lax in staying up-to-date with new developments in medical science and fall behind in keeping up with international standards. This is in contrast to the United States, where checks are in place to ensure that the level of medical care is relatively standard throughout the country.

Given all of the above, patients are faced with the major dilemma of deciding which medical institution to choose. This is exacerbated by the lack of information which might assist in making such decisions. If there are problems after the choice is made, it is then difficult to change. Furthermore, the choice available in the selection of doctors and hospitals can depend on personal connections and gratuities. There are numerous factors which contribute to this situation. One of these is the inability of the factionalised medical community to regulate itself and to offer a united front to tackle major issues on a national basis, despite the existence of the Japan Medical Association. Because of this leadership vacuum, it is difficult to implement quality assurance measures aimed at improving the delivery of medical care.

The Medical Manipulation of Life and Death

The advances in modern medicine have led to remarkable developments in life-prolonging technology. For people who have lost some of their normal bodily functions, medical technologies have come to the rescue. The ability to provide nutrition to people through tubes has made it possible to prolong the lives of people for several years beyond what would otherwise be possible. Furthermore, the use of respirators enables people who have lost the ability to breathe in the normal manner to survive for many years. Kidney dialysis can enable people to enjoy life for up to twenty years or more. Those with faulty hearts, livers and lungs can live for several years through receiving a transplant of healthy organs. Those who receive heart or liver transplants can have an average life-expectancy of seven to eight years, two-thirds of successful transplant patients can thus live for five years or more.

The development of such life-prolonging technologies should not be welcomed without reservation. First, the prolonging of life may not be in the patient's interests. Secondly, the prolonging of the patient's life may endanger the lives of other people in the process. Thirdly, it promotes a culture which approves of the medical manipulation of human life and death. Despite acceptance of this in many Western countries, not everyone may see this as a positive thing.

The development of medical technologies has many merits for those who are ill, but positive benefits are not guaranteed. For example, for those declared brain-dead the use of respirators is nearly meaning-less. Similarly, there is almost no hope of reviving people who are in a vegetative state. Life-prolonging technologies can exacerbate the physi-cal and mental pain of those who are sick. For those who are close to death, it can be distressing to have multiple tubes connected to one's body in order to prolong life just a little longer. And when organs are transplanted, there are certain trade-offs involved. The interests of potential donors are not always central in the minds of the doctors.

Medical technological advance has enabled people with certain conditions to largely control when death will occur. The hospital environment has become a technological one and the right of patients to decide for themselves has become increasingly enshrined legally and more accepted socially. The concept of 'death with dignity' has attracted the support of many people. The change in attitude has been the result of a strengthening body of opinion which believes in euthanasia, that is, that people in certain circumstances have the right to choose when to die. However, strict conditions must be imposed.

While medical technologies have, on the one hand, brought life to patients, they can also have a negative side. For those in a vegetative state with no hope of regaining consciousness, the use of an intensive-care unit for an indefinite period at great cost is a drain on medical resources. It is difficult for physicians to declare that all hope of life is lost, but it is debatable whether life should be prolonged in such a state. In the case of those receiving heart and liver transplants, it is basically a case of 'killing' the donor and enabling the recipient to live. Donors might not only be brain-dead patients or those in a vegetative state and there is a danger that those whose lives are deemed dispensable will become donors in the future.

For a country like Japan where the social welfare system is inadequate, a system where dying with dignity and euthanasia is possible would relieve families of the crippling cost of medical care. If patients were given a choice, it may be that some might prefer to relieve their families of this burden. We need to be mindful that the attitude of prolonging life at all costs takes away the right of people to decide their fate themselves.

Let us next examine the impact on Japanese society of the development of life-prolonging technologies, especially the transplant of organs from brain-dead patients and the concept of death with dignity. For many Westerners, these topics are not as controversial as they are in Japan, for it is often thought that one must respect the wishes of the patient. In Japan, the authority of medical practitioners is extremely strong. There are many cases where it is the physician who controls the life and death of patients. There is little in the way of protection of patients' rights, and death-hastening technologies have started to become available. Given this situation, the debate regarding organ transplants and death with dignity occur within a cultural context different from that of Europe and the United States. This does not mean, however, that the introduction to Japan of Western cultural attitudes to the body might not be a positive thing but it does mean that the reception of technologies needs to be examined within a cultural context. Changing that context involves introducing a value system that sees brain death as an adequate definition of death (Lock & Honde: 1990).

Organ Transplants

On 17 June 1997 the *Organ Transplant Act* was passed by the national parliament, the Diet, and it became effective as of 16 October that year. This Act formally allowed the removal or organs from brain-dead patients for transplant purposes. The legislation meant that an estimated 8000 people in Japan at that time could be taken off artificial life support as the law recognised the concept of brain death (Wise: 1997). Japan's first heart transplant, however, had occurred on 8 August 1968. It was carried out by Professor Wada Jurō of Sapporo Medical University. Since that time, not one heart transplant had been conducted, not one case of a liver transplant from a brain-dead person occurred. Since Wada's operation, organ transplants had come close to being taboo. As a result of the desire by many people to change this situation, the law came into being but in the year following the passage of the legislation, not one case of an organ transplant from a brain-dead person occurred. In contrast, each year several severely ill Japanese patients venture overseas for costly heart and liver transplants. For people living in Europe and the United States this is an extremely odd state of affairs, since thousands of heart and liver transplants are performed there each year. Many Westerners wonder why organ transplants are not carried out in technologically advanced Japan.

There is a historical reason for this taboo. Wada's heart transplant (the thirtieth to occur in the world) was accompanied by so many doubts that it created a very negative attitude to transplants among the Japanese people. The 18-year-old recipient of the heart transplant was Miyazaki Nobuo. His health deteriorated after surgery and on 29 October, eighty-three days after the operation, he passed away. Japan's first heart transplant was celebrated with much fanfare by the mass media at the time, but doubts arose with the death of the recipient. Professor Wada's behaviour was viewed as possibly constituting murder and the Sapporo Regional Prosecutor's Office carried out an investigation. Another doubt concerned whether the medical care of the donor, Yamaguchi Yoshimasa, and diagnosis of his brain death were appropriate. And there were doubts about the medical procedures involved in the heart transplant.

The 22-year-old student, Yamaguchi, drowned while swimming at a beach (Gotō: 1992). He stopped breathing and his heart arrested but he was revived in the ambulance. While receiving medical care at a hospital, he was moved to Sapporo Medical University where despite still being conscious and able to breathe for himself, he was not given the appropriate life-saving assistance. Rather, he was targeted to be a donor and Wada persuaded Yamaguchi's family to agree to this. The patient was not declared brain dead, and various pieces of evidence suggest he had not yet reached that point. The recipient, Miyazaki, was deemed by another physician as being able to live several years more without a transplant. Wada was considered to have carried out 'unnatural' procedures though it was not proven that his medical treatment was inappropriate. The medical profession carried out its own investigation without releasing the results. Three leading physicians who were asked by the Prosecutor's Office to provide expert reports gave ambiguous findings. In the wake of the Wada transplant incident, both the medical profession and citizens came to regard heart transplants from brain-dead donors as taboo.

In Europe and the United States, organ transplants came to a temporary halt due to the absence of an immunosuppressant drug which would inhibit rejection of organs. In 1978, a new drug, Cyclosporin, proved to be remarkably effective. Organ transplants entered their second phase. As Japan entered the 1980s preparations were made by the medical world to again consider organ transplants from brain-dead victims. In Japan, under the *Organ Transplant Act*, the removal of organs can now only occur with the written consent of the donor and his or her family. However, because of the poor distribution of donor cards, lack of approved hospitals, and cases where families do not agree, the first organ transplant did not occur until early 1999. The distrust of doctors prevalent among the Japanese people since the Wada incident is deep-rooted, and there has been resistance to donor cards and a reluctance to donate organs (Aono: 1995). This distrust is not just an emotional feeling, but a response to the overwhelming authority exerted by physicians, the lack of effective checks on the activities of the medical world and the lack of respect of the wishes of patients. The legacy of the Wada incident is a serious one, but the reasons for the situation lie not only with what occurred then. Features of Japanese culture have also worked against the spread of organ transplants from brain-dead donors. In Japan, harming one's body is viewed negatively: one's body is not only one's own. As Nudeshima (1991) suggested, many Japanese view personhood as a collective reality. He argued, however, that it was not cultural barriers which had been the main obstacle to organ transplants, but the medical community. The medical profession is so factionalised that it is difficult for peer review and assessment to occur. He called for a quality control system for medical procedures. In contrast, Namihira (1991) explained that the remains of deceased people have an important role in the mourning rites and cutting open a body for organ parts interferes in this process. Despite this, Nudeshima (1991) pointed to a 1990 survey in which 40 per cent of respondents agreed with the donation of organs from brain-dead relatives, whereas 16 per cent would refuse; 11 per cent of respondents would only donate to recipients they knew.

Euthanasia and Death with Dignity

Since 1993 there has been a widening acceptance in the West to euthanasia and the right to death with dignity. Many Japanese thought that such changes in attitude to death might also eventually reach their own country. The less powerful members of society, such as elderly people and accident victims, have considered euthanasia and there have been cases where patients and their families have agreed to euthanasia after having been convinced by physicians.

Euthanasia is a medical procedure which a physician allows in accordance with the wishes of patients who desire to be released from harsh physical pain which they experience when dying. A drug is administered that hastens their death. In contrast, death with dignity is when a physician stops life-prolonging treatment in accordance with the wishes of the patient. The patient may not necessarily be near death and may not actually be conscious of pain. It is possible for patients in a vegetative state to continue living for several years with the help of medical technologies: they may be diagnosed as not being conscious of pain but such cases also can be considered for death with dignity.

In Japan, the first court case in which close family members were accused of killing occurred in 1949 when a Korean woman resident in Japan became bedridden and half-paralysed due to a cerebral haemorrhage. She asked her son to end her life and he responded by giving her potassium cyanide which she drank; she subsequently died. He was sentenced to one year of imprisonment, suspended for two years. Similar incidents occurred throughout the years, and the criminal case was considered as having set a precedent. Lawyers gradually came to a common understanding of when a mercy killing could be deemed appropriate. Japan's legal and justice system effectively took the position of controlling euthanasia. One person, Ōta Tenrei (1900–85) took exception to this. Ōta was a physician based at the Kyūshū Imperial University who felt that all citizens should enjoy access to essential medical care. He had been a socialist member of parliament and began to speak out on the subject of euthanasia from 1963. He also started moves to legalise euthanasia. In 1976 Ōta established the Japan Euthanasia Society, but due to a strong public outcry attempts to legalise euthanasia collapsed. The society decided on a new strategy which involved a 'living will' in which one writes a statement requesting death with dignity. In 1983 the organisation changed its name to the Japan Society for Death with Dignity.

The contents of the 'living will' was similar to that in the United States and Europe, but there appear to be some areas of variation. First, in the West, patients have the right of informed consent and the concept of death with dignity has been widely debated. In the case of Japan's 'living will', if the doctor diagnoses that the patient is beyond medical help and already dying, the doctor can carry out death with dignity without the agreement of the patient. Secondly, in some Western countries, when the patient has lost the ability to express his or her own free will the 'living will' can come into effect at any time. In Japan, even if the patient still shows signs of being able to express their own will, doctors can carry out death with dignity without the informed consent of the patient. Thirdly, in the case of the West, the physician is not exempt from responsibility whereas in Japan's version of the 'living will', promoted by the society, this is emphasised. In the Japanese 'living will', informed consent and the right of patients to decide for themselves is ignored, with patients giving doctors an unconditional right of approval to carry out death with dignity. Furthermore, it involves exemption of doctors from responsibility. This is an extremely paternalistic approach which reflects characteristics of Japanese medical care (Nudeshima: 1991).

In the 1990s two cases of mercy killings by doctors (described by the mass media as euthanasia) have occurred in Japan. The first case occurred in April 1991 at the Tōkai University Hospital. The research associate, Tokunaga Masayoshi, acting on the fervent wishes of the patient's family, killed a 38-year-old unconscious male patient by an injection of potassium chloride, despite the protests of the nurse. The Yokohama District Court found the doctor guilty of murder and sentenced him to two years of imprisonment, suspended for two years. The second case involved a death in April 1996 at the Keihoku Municipal Hospital in Kyoto. Without ascertaining the wishes of a 48-year-old male patient suffering from terminal cancer, the hospital injected a muscle relaxant to ease his pain and thereby hastened death. The physician did not inform the family and did not obtain the family's agreement. There is debate about whether the physician could have employed other more established forms of pain control, rather than one which resulted in the death of the patient. This case illustrated the paternalistic nature of the Japanese medical world: the danger of euthanasia without the involvement of the patient. Many Japanese commentators approve of euthanasia with certain provisos which relate to the right of the patient to decide.

The words *wakon yōsai* ('Japanese spirit and Western learning') were a popular slogan in the Meiji period (1868–1912). They signified the attitude that the Japanese would maintain their strong spirituality and actively introduce the best of Western S&T. The result is a hybrid of Japanese 'traditional' culture and Western knowledge. We have seen elsewhere in this book examples of how the Japanese have adapted foreign technology and made it their own. However, Western S&T cannot necessarily simply be grafted on to another culture. Death-hastening technology is one example of a technology that is difficult to transfer, because it originates in Western society where it is assumed that individuals have the right to be autonomous and make their own decisions. There are great dangers in transferring the technology to Japan where physicians ignore the wishes of patients and decide their fate either with or without consulting the patient's family. Much advanced medical care can be viewed as the medical manipulation of life and death. The medical system needs to be rebuilt into one where the rights of the patient are central. Technology and culture are not so easily torn asunder and Japan would do well to consider whether aspects of Western culture (especially attitudes to the body and approaches to medical care) might be usefully introduced as well. While it might be argued that Western bioethics are not appropriate for Japan (Lock & Honde: 1990, 113), the introduction in Japan of medical technologies used in Europe and the United States demands that the cultural contexts from which they have emerged also be given due consideration (Aono: 1995).

Oral Contraceptives

In contrast with the issue of brain death, abortions are not controversial in Japan. As Lock (1998) suggested, this may be because the foetus is considered part of the pregnant woman. Hardacre (1997) pointed out that abortion has long been practised in Japan and is widely accepted. It has been suggested that the prevalence of abortions, and the medical profession that performs them, have discouraged the use of oral contraceptives. The Japan Medical Association has been a longtime supporter of the LDP and had considerable influence on policy-making (*Asiaweek*: 1996). About 350 000 women in Japan are estimated to have abortions each year, and 29 per cent of women have had at least one abortion (Hadfield: 1997; *Medical World News*: 1992; Ogawa & Retherford: 1991).

It has been arged that authorisation of the contraceptive pill would promote sexual promiscuity, discourage condom use and lead to an AIDS epidemic in Japan. The safety of the contraceptive pill, it was said, could not be guaranteed. Some women prefer men to take more responsibility and encourage greater use of condoms. Condoms are the main form of contraception for 80 per cent of Japanese couples (Watts: 1997). Some women would prefer that this remained the situation.

Condom makers would certainly prefer that there was no competition from the pill. While legalisation and greater use of the pill has the potential for women to exert more control over their bodies, both oral contraceptives and abortions place the onus of birth control on women.

Oral contraceptives were banned in Japan for three decades after they had been introduced in most other industrialised nations and they are still not freely available in Japan. This has led some 200 000 women to endanger their health by using high-dose combined pills prescribed for menstrual disorders as a contraceptive, since low-dose oral contraceptives have not been permitted (Nagata et al.: 1997). The high-dose combined pills are rarely used in the West as they contain a higher dose of oestrogen and can have side-effects such as blood clotting (Hadfield: 1997).

Conclusion

This chapter demonstrates that not all people share the same attitudes to life and death, and the body. Many Japanese believe that it is time to bring about a change in attitude in Japan, but controversies surrounding organ transplants have not helped. As this chapter has shown, the government, physicians, and pharmaceutical companies need to respond better to the needs of the public and unless the pharmaceutical companies act as a prompter this may not be possible. As Japan enters the twenty-first century, individual Japanese are increasingly having to take responsibility for their own lives. There is still a strong desire to make Japan a science and technology-oriented nation, but the Japanese public need to ensure that it is also for the public good, as distinct from national benefit.

Conclusions

A central concern of this book has been to survey some of the more significant S&T-related activities in Japan. Of course, this book has been limited in its scope, but we have attempted to describe how S&T is organised in Japan, and who are the major players. We have confronted a number of issues relating to S&T and have shown that people matter. While S&T has largely fulfilled its postwar promise of generating wealth for Japan, not all Japanese have benefited from it. The Japanese people have demanded more from S&T.

As Japan approaches the new millennium, S&T has shifted focus from concerns of national security and economic benefits to the needs of the Japanese people. The fact that these have not necessarily converged in the past reflects the reality that national interest has not been the same as the public good. Symptomatic of the changes has been the proposed reorganisation of Japan's bureaucratic structure, which most likely will be similar to that depicted in Figure 12.1.

The proposed structure is expected to come into effect from January 2001 and will involve the consolidation of the twenty-two existing ministries and agencies into one office, ten ministries, two agencies and a commission for public safety. The number of bureaus will be reduced from 128 to 96 (Daimon: 1999, 7). This reorganisation has been shaped by some of the controversies discussed in this book, and it is part of the process of change which occurred in the 1980s and 1990s. Nuclear technologies (Chapter 4) and aerospace technologies (Chapter 6) were a prominent part of high-tech development during the Cold War, but as we enter the new millennium and become more conscious of issues relating to the global environment, they have become less important aspects of S&T for many people in Japan. Instead, we are witnessing a shift in emphasis to fields which relate directly to the everyday life of the

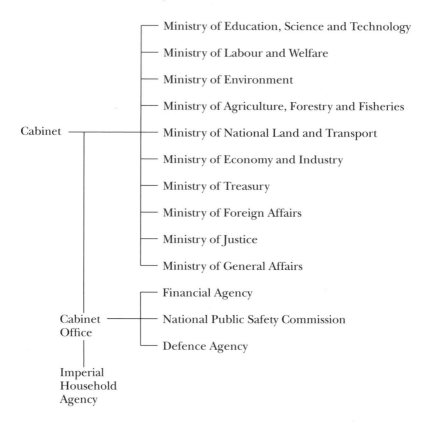

Figure 12.1 Major elements of Japan's proposed bureaucratic structure from 2001
Source: Daimon: 1999, 7.

people. There is a clear preference for S&T that improves the quality of life. People have high hopes that medical science may allow life to be prolonged even further, or that patients, as we saw in Chapter 11, have a right to make an informed choice of whether or not to terminate their own lives.

In bringing a book to a close, there is always the temptation to continually update chapters to take advantage of the latest developments. It is satisfying to know that issues discussed in this book are in the process of being resolved. On 24 February 1999 the Japanese government decided to develop basic guidelines to combat dioxin pollution, but most of the measures proposed have been criticised for offering nothing particularly new (Mainichi Shinbun: 1999). A few days later, on

28 February 1999, a 47-year-old man became the recipient of the first heart transplant operation to have been carried out in Japan in thirty-one years. By 1 March kidneys from the same donor were transplanted to patients in Sendai (Miyagi prefecture) and Omura (Nagasaki prefecture). The donor's corneas were transplanted to patients in Kochi prefecture. Although the transplants were conducted with the approval of the family of the donor, a 44-year-old woman, the family protested at the frenzied nature of media coverage. The heart transplant was conducted by Dr Matsuda Hikaru and his team at the Osaka University Medical School Hospital, and screened live for the waiting media (Lies: 1999; Millett: 1999; *Australian*: 2 March 1999; *Japan Times International*: 1–15 March 1999). Now it seems that it is the media which is overstepping the line, virtually intruding into people's bodies and violating their rights to privacy. A tension has emerged between the rights of the public to access information to ensure that such operations are being conducted in an appropriate manner, and the desire of patients to maintain privacy (Aita: 1999).

Even when information is forthcoming from official sources, such as the Ministry of Health and Welfare, it is sometimes suspect. Official statistics for the number of HIV/AIDS cases in Japan is suspiciously low (Chapter 11); it is now reported that such cases are well above 4000. The ministry has announced that sexually-transmitted diseases are on the rise in Japan, but there seems to be a timidity in dealing with AIDS in Japan (*Japan Times Weekly International Edition*: 14–20 December 1998).

Attitudes to S&T still continue to be gendered (Chapters 9 and 11), especially when it comes to the body and sexuality. The sale of Viagra was quickly approved within six months in Japan, reflecting how it is still a society dominated by men who are willing to license a pill which could be of benefit to them. These same men have been more reluctant to allow young women to have control over their own female fertility and sexuality. Approval for widespread access to oral contraceptives by women has been slow in coming. After nearly four decades, at a meeting in June 1999, a Ministry of Health and Welfare committee agreed to approve the low-dose pill for women, and it was expected to become available later that year (Osedo: 1999, 11).

The passing of Freedom of Information legislation by the Japanese Lower House on 7 May 1999 augurs well for increased public participation in, and scrutiny of, the policy-making process. If the legislation is approved by the Upper House decision-making will, by necessity, become more transparent. Politicians and bureaucrats will be more socially accountable as government ministries and agencies will be required to release information on their activities upon request (Hani: 1999; Sankei Shinbun: 1999). There is a growing perception that the views of local communities are being heeded, and that people's lives are becoming less regulated by government.

In many ways, what is occurring now is a continuation of unfinished business arising from social movements in the period from the late 1960s to the early 1970s. This activity included the anti-Vietnam movement, student unrest, the consumer movement, environment protection groups, and anti-development movements. As a result, the Japanese people gained a heightened sense of the rights which were due to them. The oil shock of 1973 to 1974 and the strengthening of the Japanese yen forced many Japanese to work hard to regain their national competitiveness. Despite the recession of the 1990s Japan remains one of the most prosperous nations but there is a perception that the Japanese still do not enjoy a quality of life which their affluence might suggest. Various scandals involving bribery of politicians and bureaucrats have only confirmed the belief that benefits are not necessarily accruing to the people. Chapter 11 briefly discussed the tainting of blood products and the ineffectiveness of the Ministry of Health and Welfare. Attempts to cover up the seriousness of an accident at the FBR 'Monju' (Chapter 4) was further evidence of S&T not being harnessed to the needs of the people. It is no coincidence that there are plans for the STA and the Ministry of Health and Welfare to merge with others. The fact that MITI will be renamed but remain largely the same, is testimony to its influence and relative success.

As in any other society, we can identify certain groups which exert social, political and economic power. The ruling LDP, bureaucrats of major ministries and big business have been dominant. The administrative reforms and improved environment are but two examples of how public outcry can bring about change. Narita airport (Chapter 10) and the continued pursuit of nuclear power in Japan (Chapter 4) show how opposition by citizens can have mixed success.

One theme which has been present through many of the chapters is how Japanese S&T has become less Japanese and more global, with the manufacturing of products overseas (Chapter 7), and the establishment of think-tanks and laboratories outside Japan which draw on the expertise of non-Japanese. Even environmental concerns have brought global problems into the foreground at the cost of neglecting local pollution (Chapter 5). What has been called 'Japanese' has, in fact, drawn on ideas and technologies from elsewhere (Chapter 3). While the Japanese have made these their own, others in turn have adapted Japanese technologies for their own purposes.

The internationalisation of the private sector in Japan continues with France's auto company, Renault SA, proposing to purchase 35 per cent of Nissan Motor Company, Japan's no. 2 manufacturer of cars. This would effectively cede control of Nissan to Renault as the latter would be able to veto Nissan board decisions. The Asian economic crisis has forced the Japanese corporate sector to open up to foreign interests, with ailing local firms actively seeking potential partners. It is now not so much Japanese auto manufacturers but other players who are leading the globalisation of the automotive industry (Associated Press: 1999).

Corporate restructuring is not isolated to the auto industry. The world's no. 2 consumer electronics company, Sony Corporation, will cut 10 per cent of its workforce and turn three subsidiaries into wholly-owned business units as part of plans to create five in-house companies and eliminate 17 000 jobs by 31 March 2003. Hitachi plans to form ten in-house companies on 1 April 1999 (Bloomberg: 1999).

What can we expect of Japanese innovation in the future? Increases in the government S&T budget suggest many are pinning their hopes on an S&T-oriented future, amid the gloom of the Asian economic crisis. Many nations are encouraging S&T in the hope that it will lead to economic growth and job creation. As this book shows, there is much evidence that S&T will lead to prosperity, but we must be cautious to ensure that the interests of the people are part of the process. Japan is moving in that direction and introducing a system more geared to protecting the basic rights of people. Power remains in the hands of politicians, bureaucrats and big business, and it is up to the Japanese to create an alternative model to this triumvirate, especially if the role of S&T is to be more attuned to social needs. The old model was oriented towards creating a technologically-strong nation which could be self-sufficient and defend itself in times of war (Samuels: 1994). Such ideas have been internalised into S&T in Japan and they have constituted a powerful motivating force in the modernisation of the country, but Japan must change with the times. What is required is a reformatting of Japanese S&T to meet the needs of citizens and the challenges of the twenty-first century (Morris-Suzuki: 1998, 162–7).

Bibliography

Aiba, K., 1995. 'Gender inequality in the Japanese workplace', *Social Science Japan*, no. 4, August, p. 31.

Aita, K., 1999. 'Doctors struggle with privacy issue', *Japan Times International*, 1–15 March, p. 1.

AMPO–Japan Asia Quarterly Review (eds), 1996. *Voices from the Japanese Women's Movement*, Armonk, New York: M. E. Sharpe.

Anchordoguy, M., 1989. *Computers Inc.: Japan's Challenge to IBM*, Cambridge, Mass.: Council on East Asian Studies, Harvard University.

Anderson, A., 1988. 'New US–Japan Science Agreement reached', *Nature*, vol. 332, no. 6164, p. 475.

Andō, Yoshio, 1998. 'Multimedia in Japan: what the future holds for the Telecom industry', *Nomura Research Institute Quarterly*, vol. 7, no. 2, pp. 14–35.

Aono, Yuri, 1995. 'Brain death: doctors have the technology to transplant organs, but is society ready?', *Japan Update*, no. 45, June, pp. 18–19.

Aoyagi, T., 1990. 'Knocking on wood', *Look Japan*, October, pp. 22–3.

Aoyama, M., 1996. 'Beyond software factories: concurrent-development process and an evolution of software process technology in Japan', *Information and Software Technology*, vol. 38, pp. 133–43.

Aoyama, Y., 1991. *Kaden (Home Appliances)*, Tokyo: Nihon Keizai Hyōron sha.

Appiah, K. A., 1995. 'Race', in *Critical Terms for Literary Study*, F. Lentricchia & T. McLaughlin (eds), 2nd edn, pp. 274–87, Chicago: University of Chicago Press.

Apter, D. E. & Sawa, N., 1984. *Against the State: Politics and Social Protest in Japan*, Cambridge, Mass.: Harvard University Press.

Arafune, K., 1991. 'Japan as an environmental pariah', *Economic Eye*, Winter, pp. 13–17.

Arai, K., 1992. 'Rikōkei daigakuin no ryōteki kakudai o kangaeru' ('Reflections on the quantitative development of graduate schools of science and technology'), *Kōdō gijutsu shakai nyūsu (High Technology Society News)*, no. 27, September, p. 13.

Arai, Y., 1998. 'How competitive is Japan's video game industry?', *Nomura Research Institute Quarterly*, Nomura Research Institute, vol. 7, no. 3, pp. 24–35.

Asano, M., 1994. 'Searching for a new generation of research parks', in Japanese, paper presented at the symposium 'The Science City in a Global Context', Kansai Science City, 17–18 October.

Ashihara, Y., 1989. *The Hidden Order: Tokyo through the Twentieth Century*, L. E. Riggs (trans.), Tokyo: Kodansha International.

Asia Inc. Online, 1998. '10,000 people die from Karo–shi', November.

Asiaweek, 1996. 'Just do it: Japan should cut the excuses and legalize the pill', vol. 22, no. 37, 13 September, p. 20.

Associated Press, 1999. 'Japanese car giant cedes to Renault', *Courier Mail*, 18 March, p. 26.

Australia–Japan Economic Institute Economic Bulletin, 1994. Vol. 2, no. 8, August.

Australian, 1999a. 'Nissan admits it's open to all offers', 20 January, p. 24.

—— 1999b. 'Women bound by more than tradition', 29 January, p. 32.

—— 1999c. 'Transplant frenzy', 2 March, p. 8.

Barnhart, M. A., 1987. *Japan Prepares for Total War: The Search for Economic Security*, Ithaca, New York: Cornell University Press.

Barrett, B. F. D. & Therivel, R., 1991. *Environmental Policy and Impact Assessment in Japan*, London: Routledge.

Belderbos, R. A., 1995. 'The role of investment in Europe in the globalization strategy of Japanese electronics firms', in *Japanese Firms in Europe*, F. Sachwald (ed.), pp. 89–167, Luxembourg: Harwood Academic.

Bernstein, G. L., 1988. 'Women in the silk-reeling industry in the nineteenth-century Japan', in *Japan and the World: Essays on Japanese History and Politics in Honour of Ishida Takeshi*, G. L. Bernstein & H. Fukui (eds), pp. 54–77, London: Macmillan.

Bess, J. L., 1995. *Creative R&D Leadership: Insights from Japan*, Westport, Conn.: Quorum.

Bloomberg, 1998. 'Toyota eases lines', *Australian Financial Review*, 17 December.

—— 1999. 'Sony to slash 17,000 jobs', *Australian*, 10 March, p. 30.

Boyd, T., 1998. 'Why IT revolution is passing Japan by', *Australian Financial Review*, 23 December, p. 7.

Bray, F., 1997. *Technology and Gender: Fabrics of Power in Late Imperial China*, Berkeley: University of California Press.

Broadbent, J., 1998. *Environmental Politics in Japan: Networks of Power and Protest*, Cambridge University Press.

Bungei Shunju, 1990. 'Taiketsu! Nichibei no byōkon o tataku', ('Showdown! Thrashing out the cause of US–Japan problems'), January, pp. 148–60.

Buruma, I., 1985. *A Japanese Mirror: Heroes and Villains of Japanese Culture*, Harmondsworth, Middx: Penguin.

Bush, V., 1945. *Science: The Endless Frontier*, Washington, DC: US Government Printing Office.

Business Japan, 1986. 'Japanese enterprises trying to have access to American brains', vol. 33, 6 February, pp. 15–16.

Business Tokyo, 1990. 'Much ado about "No"', February, pp. 26–9.

Business Week, 1984. 'Japan is buying its way into U.S. university labs', 24 September, pp. 72–3.

Callon, S., 1995. *Divided Sun: MITI and the Breakdown of Japanese High-Tech Industrial Policy, 1975–1993*, Stanford University Press.

Castells, M. & Hall, P., 1994. *Technopoles of the World: The Making of Twenty-First Century Industrial Complexes*, London: Routledge.

Chang Jr, Ike Y., 1994. *Technology Access from the FS-X Radar Program: Lessons for Technology Transfer and U.S. Acquisition Policy*, Santa Monica, Cal.: RAND.

Chao, S. J. (comp.), 1994. *The Japanese Automobile Industry: An Annotated Bibliography*, Westport, Conn.: Greenwood Press.

Chester, R., 1999. 'Sony puts a game console in one million Aussie homes', *Courier Mail*, 6 February, p. 3.

Chin, A. & Hayashi, A. (eds), 1995. *Ajia no gijutsu hatten to gijutsu iten (Technology Transfer and the Development of Technology in Asia)*, Tokyo: Bunshindō.

Clennell, A., 1999. 'Global whale sanctuary push', *Sydney Morning Herald*, 30 January, p. 13.

Coghlan, A., 1993. 'The Green Empire', *New Scientist*, 2 October, pp. 48–50.

Coleman, S., 1983. *Family Planning in Japanese Society*, Princeton University Press.

—— 1995. 'Industry–university cooperation at Japan's Protein Engineering Research Institute: a study based on long-term fieldwork', *Human Organization*, vol. 54, no. 1, pp. 20–30.

Collins, K. A., 1989. *Education in Japan: Statistical Comparisons with Australia*, Canberra: Australian Government Publishing Service.

Courchene, T. J., 1995. 'Glocalization: the regional/international interface', *Canadian Journal of Regional Science*, vol. XVIII, no. 1, pp. 1–20.

Cusumano, M. A., 1985. *The Japanese Automobile Industry: Technology and Management at Nissan and Toyota*, Cambridge, Mass.: Council on East Asian Studies, Harvard University.

—— 1991. *Japan's Software Factories: A Challenge to US Management*, New York: Oxford University Press.

Daimon, S., 1998. 'Nissan reports $562.7 million losses', *Japan Times Weekly International Edition*, 12–18 October, p. 13.

—— 1999. 'Government streamlining plan OK'd', *Japan Times International*, 1–15 February 1999, pp. 1, 7.

Dauvergne, P., 1993. 'U.S.–Japan high-tech military cooperation: implications of FSX co-development', *Asian Perspective*, vol. 17, no. 2, pp. 179–210.

—— 1997. *Shadows in the Forest: Japan and the Politics of Timber in Southeast Asia*, Cambridge, Mass.: MIT Press.

David, A. & Wheelwright, T., 1989. *The Third Wave: Australia and Asian Capitalism*, Sydney: Left Book Club.

Davis, N. W., 1992. 'Japan's struggling aerospace industry: issues in bilateral relations', *Journal*, American Chamber of Commerce in Japan, April, pp. 10–17.

Dewitte, L. & Vanhastel, S., 1997. 'FS-X/F-2: Fighter Support Experimental', 17 February, electronic report.

Djerassi, C., 1987. 'The politics of contraception: the view from Tokyo', *Technology in Society*, vol. 9, no. 2, pp. 157–61.

Dore, R., 1986. 'Where will the Japanese Nobel prizes come from?', *Science and Public Policy*, December, pp. 347–61.

Drifte, R., 1990. *Japan's Foreign Policy*, London: Routledge and Royal Institute of International Affairs.

Easlea, B., 1983. *Fathering the Unthinkable: Masculinity, Scientists, and the Nuclear Arms Race*, London: Pluto Press.

Economist, 1986. 'Japanese research: more sci than tech', vol. 301, 22 November, p. 90.

—— 1998. 'Sayonara, secret light?' 8–14 August, pp. 69–70.

Education About Asia, 1997. 'Asian factoids', vol. 2, no. 1, p. 35.

Ekusa, Ato, 1992. 'The rise of women's power', *Journal of Japanese Trade and Industry*, no. 5, 1 October, p. 33.

Elzinga, A. & Jamison, A., 1995. 'Changing policy agendas in Science and Technology', in *Handbook of Science and Technology Studies*, S. Jasanoff, G. E. Markle, J. C. Petersen & T. Pinch (eds), pp. 572–97, Thousand Oaks, Cal.: Sage Publications.

Endicott, J. E., 1975. *Japan's Nuclear Option*, New York: Praeger.

Endo, H., Yokoo, Y., Hirano, Y. & Shimoda, R., 1993. *Josei kenkyūsha no genjō ni kansuru kiso chōsa (Female Researchers in Japan)*, NISTEP Report no. 30, Tokyo: National Institute of Science and Technology Policy.

Far Eastern Economic Review, 1950. 'The Japanese electric power industry', 21 December, pp. 760–6.

Feldman, E. A., 1997. 'Deconstructing the Japanese HIV scandal', *JPRI Working Paper*, no. 30, Cardiff, Cal., Japan Policy Research Institute.

Foray, D. & Freeman, C. (eds), 1993. *Technology and the Wealth of Nations: The Dynamics of Constructed Advantage*, London: Pinter, with the Organisation for Economic Cooperation and Development.

Fransman, M., 1995. *Japan's Computer and Communications Industry*, New York: Oxford University Press.

Fukai, S. N., 1988. 'Japan's energy policy', *Current History*, April, pp. 169–72, 182.

Fukukawa, S., 1992. 'The government's role for a better environment', *Journal of Japanese Trade and Industry*, 1 October, pp. 12–13.

Furihata, S. & Ichinose, K. (eds), 1991. *Sabakareru Narita kūkō (Passing Judgement on Narita Airport)*, Tokyo: Shakai Hyōronsha.

Fushimi, K., 1995. 'Genshi-ryoku heiwa kōsei ni dō taishō suru ka' ('How to deal with the atomic power peace offensive'), *Chūō kōron*, June, pp. 34–42.

—— 1987. *Kagaku-sha to shakai: Fushimi Kōji chosaku-shū 6 (Scientists and Society: The Collected Papers of Kōji Fushimi, Volume 6)*, Tokyo: Misuzu Shobō.

Garran, R., 1997a. 'Japanese women win right to low-dose pill', *Australian*, 18 June, p. 7.

—— 1997b. 'Deflation is all that's left when the bubbles burst', *Australian*, 28 October, p. 30.

Geisler, E. & Furino, A., 1993. 'University–industry–government cooperation: research horizons', *International Journal of Technology Management*, vol. 8, nos. 6–8, pp. 802–10.

Geisler, E. & Rubenstein, A. H., 1989. 'University–industry relations: a review of major issues', in *Cooperative Research and Development: The Industry–University–Government Relationship*, A. N. Link & G. Tassey (eds), pp. 44–62, Boston: Kluwer.

Gijutsu to Ningen (ed.), 1979. *Han-Narita kūkō ron (Anti-Narita Airport Studies)* Tokyo: Gijutsu to Ningen.

Goto–, M., 1992. 'The great divide', *Look Japan*, vol. 38, no. 434, May, pp. 32–3.

Gottlieb, N., 1993. 'Written Japanese and the word processor', *Japan Forum*, vol. 5, no. 1, April, pp. 115–32.

—— 1995. 'Technology and language policy: word processing in Japan', *Asian Studies Review*, vol. 18, no. 3, April, pp. 58–68.

Gyoten, Y., 1992. 'Japanese health care', *Journal of Japanese Trade and Industry*, no. 5, 10 October, pp. 42–5.

Hadfield, P., 1990. 'Covering up cutting criticism', *Look Japan*, October, pp. 34–5.

—— 1996. 'Japan takes its medicine', *New Scientist*, 1 June, pp. 14–15.

—— 1997. 'Japan may finally swallow the pill', *New Scientist*, vol. 153, no. 2074, 22 March, p. 5.

Hall, G. R. & Johnson, R. E., 1970. 'Transfers of United States aerospace technology to Japan', in *The Technology Factor in International Trade: A Conference of the Universities–National Bureau Committee for Economic Research*, R. Vernon (ed.), pp. 305–58, New York: National Bureau of Economic Research.

Hane, G. J., 1995. 'Clearing the fog around R&D consortia in Japan', *Science and Public Policy*, vol. 22, no. 2, April, pp. 85–94.

Hani, Y., 1999. 'Lower House passes Information Disclosure Bill', *Japan Times International*, 16–28 February, pp. 1, 7.

Hardacre, H., 1997. *Marketing the Menacing Fetus in Japan*, Berkeley: University of California Press.

Hartcher, P., 1988. 'The arsenal ready and waiting in the Pacific', *Sydney Morning Herald*, 6 April, p. 17.

Harvey, D., 1989. *The Condition of Postmodernity: An Enquiry into the Origins of Cultural Change*, London: Basil Blackwell.

Hayashi, E., 1985. *Onnatachi no fūsen bakudan (The Women's Balloon Bomb)*, Tokyo: Aki Shobō.

Hayashi, K., 1991. 'High-technology strategies and regional restructuring', *International Journal of Political Economy*, vol. 21, no. 3, pp. 70–89.

Hemmert, M. & Oberländer, C. (eds), 1998. *Technology and Innovation in Japan: Policy and Management for the Twenty-First Century*, London: Routledge.

Hicks, D., 1993. 'University–industry research links in Japan', *Policy Sciences*, vol. 26, no. 4, pp. 361–95.

Hicks, D. & Hirooka, M., 1991. *Nihon kigyō ni okeru kiso kenkyū no teigi oyobi Nihon kigyō ni okeru kagaku: Yobiteki bunseki (Defining Basic Research in Japanese Companies and Science in Japanese Companies: A Preliminary Analysis)*, Tokyo: Science and Technology Agency.

Hicks, D., Isard, P. & Hirooka, M., 1992. 'Science in Japanese companies', *Japan Journal for Science, Technology and Society*, vol. 1, pp. 109–40.

Hicks, D., Ishizuka, T., Keen, P. & Sweet, S., 1994. 'Japanese corporations, scientific research and globalization', *Research Policy*, vol. 23, no. 4, pp. 375–84.

Hilgartner, S., Bell, R. C. & O'Connor, R., 1982. *Nukespeak: Nuclear Language, Visions, and Mindset*, San Francisco: Sierra Club Books.

Hills, B., 1993. 'Martyrs of Minamata', *Age Good Weekend*, 5 June, pp. 36–43.

—— 1994a. 'HIV's land of secrecy and shame', *Age*, 8 August, p. 13.

—— 1994b. 'Made in Japan', *Age*, 13 August, features section, pp. 5–6.

—— 1995a. 'Garbage is choking Fuji's goddess', *Sydney Morning Herald*, 21 February, p. 10.

—— 1995b. 'Island of the damned: Japan confronts its shameful secret', *Age*, 8 July, spectrum, p. 9a.

Hirabayashi Y. & Sasa T., 1996. *ISO 14000*, Tokyo: Nihon Kagaku Gijutsu Rengōkai.

Ho, S. K. M., 1995. *TQM, An Integrated Approach: Implementing Total Quality Through Japanese 5-S and ISO 9000*, London: Kogan Page.

Holley, D., 1997. 'Digital boom puts Japan on top', *Australian*, 10 June, p. 10.

Holliman, J., 1990. 'Environmentalism with a global scope', *Japan Quarterly*, vol. 37, no. 3, July–September, pp. 284–90.

Hunter, J., 1984. 'Labour in the Japanese silk industry in the 1870s: the *Tomioka Nikki* of Wada Ei', in *Europe Interprets Japan*, G. Daniels (ed.), pp. 20–5, Tenterden, Kent: Paul Norbury Publications.

Iacocca, L. A. with Novak, W., 1984. *Iacocca: An Autobiography*, New York: Bantam Books.

Ikenaga M., 1994. *Kanja no kenri (The Rights of Patients)*, Fukuoka: Kyūshū University Press.

Imai, R., 1970. 'Japan and the Nuclear Age', *Bulletin of the Atomic Scientists*, vol. 26, no. 6, June, pp. 35–9.

Ishihara, S., 1989. 'From bad to worse in the FSX project', *Japan Echo*, vol. 16, no. 3, pp. 59–65.

—— 1991. *The Japan That Can Say No: Why Japan Will Be First Among Equals*, New York: Simon & Schuster.

Ishihara, S., Watanabe, S. & Ogawa, K., 1990. *Soredemo 'No' to ieru Nihon: Nichi-Bei kan no konpon mondai (Even So, Japan Can Say No: Basic Problems of the US–Japan Relationship)*, Tokyo: Kōbunsha.

Ishizuka, M., 1985. 'Japan at random: defense chief sums up postwar mind', *Japan Economic Journal*, 9 July, p. 6.

ISO (International Organisation for Standardisation), 1999. 'Introduction to ISO', ISO electronic website, <htttp://www.iso.ch/infoe/intro.html>.

Itō, D., 1991. 'Government–industry relations in a dual regulatory scheme: engineering research associations as policy instruments', in *The Promotion and Regulation of Industry in Japan*, S. Wilks & M. Wright (eds), pp. 51–80, London: Macmillan.

Itō, S., Sakamoto, K., Yamada, K. & Murakami, Y. (eds), 1983. *Kagakushi gijutsushi jiten*, Tokyo: Kōbundō.

Itō, T., 1992. *The Japanese Economy*, Cambridge, Mass.: MIT Press.

Iwasaki, T., 1991. 'Koei: winning strategy in computer games', *Journal of Japanese Trade and Industry*, 1 March, pp. 52–3.

JAIF (Japan Atomic Industrial Forum), 1971. *Nihon no genshi-ryoku: 15 nen no ayumi, jyō (Japanese Nuclear Power: A 15-Year History, Part One)*, Tokyo: Nihon Genshi-ryoku Sangyō Kaigi.

JAEC (Japan Atomic Energy Commission), 1996. *Genshiryoku Hakusho (White Paper on Atomic Energy)*, 1995 edn, Tokyo: Ministry of Finance Printing Bureau.

James, P., 1993. 'Caught between techno-science and global capitalism: images of global warming', *Social Alternatives*, vol. 12, no. 3, October, pp. 31–4.

Japan Science Council, Standing Committee No. 3, 1991. *Nihon no gakujutsu kenkyū kankyō: Kenkyūsha no ishiki chōsa kara (The Research Environment in Japan: A Survey of Researchers)*, Tokyo: Japan Science Council.

Japan Society for Applied Geology, Kansai Branch (ed.), 1993. *Global Environmental Problems and the Role of Japan (Chikyū kankyō mondai to Nihon no yakuwari)*, Tokyo: Kamokawa Shuppan.

Japan Times, 1993. 'Imports of color TVs jump 56% in July', 4 September, p. 7.

—— 1997a. 'Final reform report trims government to 13 entities', 4 December, pp. 1, 9.

—— 1997b. 'Leftists set fire to official's home', 18 December, p. 2.

—— 1997c. 'Honda enjoys new life as no. 2 maker', 20 December, p. 12.

Japan Times International, 1999. 'A medical milestone', 1–15 March, p. 20.

Japan Times Weekly International Edition, 1998. 'The silence on AIDS is deadly', 14–20 December, p. 20.

Japan Washington Watch, 1997a. 'Science and technology', 3 December, electronic version.

—— 1997b. 'Science and technology', 16 December, electronic version.

—— 1997c. 'Toyota's hybrid car goes on sale', 16 December, electronic version.

—— 1998. 'Autos', 9 January, electronic version.

Japanese Government, Ministry of Education, 1991. *Waga kuni no daigakuto ni okeru gakujutsu kenkyū seikato ni kansuru chōsa kenkyū (A Study of Research Achievements in Japanese Universities)*, Tokyo: Ministry of Education.

—— Ministry of Transport, Civil Aviation Bureau (ed.), 1970. *Kōkūkyoku gojūnen no ayumi (The 50-Year History of the Civil Aviation Bureau)*, Tokyo: Civil Aviation Bureau.

—— Ministry of Transport, Civil Aviation Bureau, Airport Section (ed.), 1987. *Hikōjobu nijū nen no ayumi (The 20-Year History of the Airport Section)*, Tokyo: 20th Anniversary Project Committee.

—— Science and International Affairs Bureau, 1994. *Implementation of Joint Research Projects between Academic Institutions and the Private Sector in 1993*, in Japanese, Tokyo: Ministry of Education, courtesy of the Japan Documentation Center, Library of Congress.

—— Science and Technology Agency, 1992. *Kagaku gijutsu hakusho (Science and Technology White Paper)*, Tokyo: STA.

—— Science and Technology Agency, 1994. *White Paper on Science and Technology: Japan in the World in Transition, Summary*, pp. 15–17, Tokyo: STA, courtesy of the Japan Documentation Center, Library of Congress.

—— Science and Technology Agency, 1995. *Survey Report on Japan's Research Activities: A Fact-Finding Survey Covering Researchers in the Advanced Sciences*, in Japanese, Tokyo: STA.

Jehlen, M., 1995. 'Gender', in *Critical Terms for Literary Study*, F. Lentricchia & T. McLaughlin (eds), pp. 263–73, 2nd edn, University of Chicago Press.

Jiji Press, 1997. 'Surfing the next wave of ads', *Japan Times*, 19 July, p. 3.

Johnson, C., 1982. *MITI and the Japanese Miracle: The Growth of Industrial Policy, 1925–1975*, Stanford University Press.

Johnston, W., 1995. *The Modern Epidemic: A History of Tuberculosis in Japan*, Cambridge, Mass.: Council on East Asian Studies, Harvard University.

Kahaner, D. K., 1993. 'Major Western R&D centers of Japanese companies', *Kahaner Report*, 10 April, electronic version.

Kakinuma, S., 1986. 'Oil and yen rock Japan's energy boat', *Tokyo Business Today*, October, pp. 46–50.

Kamata, S., 1993. *Japan in the Passing Lane: An Insider's Account of Life in a Japanese Auto Factory*, T. Akimoto (trans.) with an intro. by R. Dore, London: Allen & Unwin.

Kamioka N., 1987. *Nihon no kōgai shi (The History of Pollution in Japan)*, Tokyo: Sekai Shoin.

Kaplinsky, R. with Posthuma, A, 1994. *Easternisation: The Spread of Japanese Management Techniques to Developing Countries*, Ilford, Essex: Frank Cass.

Katayama, R. with Thomas, M., 1990. 'Japanese civil aviation in the soaring nineties: will it fly?', *Business Tokyo*, February, pp. 18–24.

Kawamoto, T., 1994. 'Partnership among public, academic and private sectors in Tsukuba', in Japanese, paper presented at the symposium 'The Science City in a Global Context', Kansai Science City, 17–18 October.

Kawano, Y., in press. 'Two foci of Japanese NGO activities: technological co-operation and global environmental advocacy', in *Nihon no kagaku gijutsu (The Social History of Science and Technology in Contemporary Japan)*, S. Nakayama, H. Yoshioka, and K. Gotō (eds), in Japanese, Tokyo: Gakuyō Shobō.

Keen, B., 1987. '"Play it again, Sony": the double life of home video technology', *Science as Culture*, no. 1, pp. 6–42.

Kenney, M. & Florida, R., 1993. *Beyond Mass Production: The Japanese System and Its Transfer to the US*, New York: Oxford University Press.

Kinmonth, E. H., 1986. 'Engineering education and its rewards in the United States and Japan', *Comparative Education Review*, vol. 30, no. 3, pp. 396–415.

—— 1989. 'Business–university links in Japan', *Engineering Education*, May–June, pp. 485–9.

—— 1991. 'Japanese engineers and American myth makers', *Pacific Affairs*, vol. 64, no. 3, pp. 328–50.

Kitahara, K., 1996. *Daichi no ran Narita tōsō* (*The Battle for the Land: The Narita Struggle*), Tokyo: Ochanomizu Shobō.

Kōdansha, 1962. *Hōmuraifu, dai ikkan, kurashi no kagaku: kaji gōrika, kaden, rejaa* (*Home Life, Vol. 1: The Science of Home Life: Rationalization of Housekeeping, Household Electrical Goods, and Leisure*), Tokyo: Kōdansha.

—— 1983. *Kodansha Encyclopedia of Japan*, 9 vols, Tokyo: Kōdansha.

Koizumi, K., 1993. 'Historical turning points in Japanese joint research policy', *Science and Public Policy*, vol. 20, no. 5, October, pp. 313–22.

—— 1995. 'The development of industrial technology in Japan: will versus absorptive capacity', *Minerva*, vol. 33, pp. 19–35.

Komatsu, K., 1997. 'Chairman of gov't panel fired over HIV remarks', *Mainichi Daily News*, 17 July, p. 14.

Kotler, P., Fahey, L. & Jatusripitak, S., 1985. *The New Competition*, Englewood Cliffs, NJ: Prentice-Hall.

Kurokawa, K., 1991. *Intercultural Architecture: The Philosophy of Symbiosis*, London: Academy Editions.

Kyodo News, 1998. 'Japan launches its first Mars probe', *Japan Times Weekly International Edition*, 13–19 July, p. 15.

Lapp, R., 1958. *The Voyage of The Lucky Dragon*, New York: Harper & Row.

Levine, S. B. & Kawada, H., 1980. *Human Resources in Japanese Industrial Development*, Princeton University Press.

Lies, E., 1999. 'Japan late starter in transplant stakes', *Courier Mail*, 2 March, p. 13.

Lock, M., 1987. 'Introduction: health and medical care as cultural and social phenomena', in *Health, Illness, and Medical Care in Japan: Cultural and Social Dimensions*, E. Norbeck & M. Lock (eds), pp. 1–23, Honolulu: University of Hawaii Press.

—— 1988. 'New Japanese mythologies: faltering discipline and the ailing housewife', *American Ethnologist*, vol. 15, no. 1, pp. 43–61.

—— in press. 'Deadly disputes: hybrid selves and the calculation of death in Japan and North America', *Osiris*, vol. 13.

Lock, M. & Honde, C., 1990. 'Reaching consensus about death: heart transplants and cultural identity in Japan', in *Social Science Perspectives on Medical Ethics*, G. Weisz (ed.), pp. 99–119, Dordrecht: Kluwer.

Lorell, M., 1995. *Troubled Partnership: A History of US–Japan Collaboration on the FS-X Fighter*, Santa Monica: RAND.

Low, M. F., 1992. 'Towards a gendered approach to teaching the history of Japanese science and technology', in *Gendering Japanese Studies*, V. Mackie (ed.), pp. 71–84, papers of the Japanese Studies Centre, no. 19, Clayton: Japanese Studies Centre, Monash University.

—— 1995. 'The Japan that can say no: the rise of techno-nationalism and its impact on technological change', in *Technological Change*, R. Fox (ed.), pp. 201–14, Luxembourg: Harwood Academic.

Low, M. F. & Yoshioka, H. 1989. 'Buying the "Peaceful Atom": the development of nuclear power in Japan', *Historia Scientiarum*, vol. 38, pp. 29–44.

Luukkonen, T., Persson, O. & Sivertsen, G., 1992. 'Understanding patterns of international scientific collaboration', *Science, Technology, & Human Values*, vol. 17, no. 1, pp. 101–38.

Maddock, R., 1998. 'Environmental politics and policies in the Asia-Pacific', in *Governance in the Asia-Pacific*, R. Maidment, D. Goldblatt & J. Mitchell (eds), pp. 221–47, London: Routledge.

Mainichi Shinbun, 1999. 'Dealing with dioxin', *Japan Times International*, 1–15 March, p. 21.

Matsuda, M., 1966. *Oyaji tai kodomo (Fathers versus Children)*, Tokyo: Iwanami Shoten.

Matsui, Y., 1987. *Women's Asia*, London: Zed Books.

Matsuoka, H., 1981. *Narita kūkō-tte nandarō (What is Narita airport?)*, Tokyo: Gijutsu to Ningen.

McCormack, G., 1996a. *The Emptiness of Japanese Affluence*, with a foreword by N. Field, St Leonards, NSW: Allen & Unwin.

—— 1996b. 'When will Japan stop devouring its world?', *Asahi Evening News*, 19 October.

McIntosh, M., 1986. *Japan Re-armed*, London: Frances Pinter.

McKean, M. A., 1977. 'Pollution and policymaking', in *Policymaking in Contemporary Japan*, T. J. Pempel (ed.), pp. 201–38, Ithaca, Cornell University Press.

—— 1981. *Environmental Protest and Citizen Politics in Japan*, Berkeley: University of California Press.

Meadows, D. H., Meadows, D. L., Renders, J. & Behrens III, W. W., 1972. *Limits to Growth: A Report for the Club of Rome's Project on the Predicament of Mankind*, London: Universe Books.

Medical World News, 1992. 'Japan expected to approve the pill', vol. 33, no. 2, February, p. 14.

Mercado, S. C., 1995. 'The YS-11 project and Japan's aerospace potential', *Japan Policy Research Institute Occasional Paper*, no. 5, Cardiff, Cal.: Japan Policy Research Institute.

Mikami, Y., 1998. 'The seeds of invention: new trends in Japanese technology policy', *Look Japan*, September, pp. 4–8.

Mikesh, R. C., 1973. *Japan's World War II Balloon Bomb Attacks on North America*, Smithsonian Annals of Flight, no. 9, Washington, DC: Smithsonian Institution Press.

Millett, M., 1999. 'Comatose woman in organ donation first', *Sydney Morning Herald*, 27 February, p. 19.

Minear, R. H., 1980. 'Orientalism and the study of Japan', *Journal of Asian Studies*, vol. 39, no. 3, pp. 507–17.

MITI (Ministry of International Trade and Industry), 1996. *Daihenkaku suru Nihon no kenkyū kaihatsu (R&D in a Japan Undergoing Great Change)*, Tokyo: MITI.

Mitsugi, Y., Takimoto, M. & Yamazaki, M., 1998. 'Information technology and new retail strategies in Japan', *Noruma Research Institute Quarterly*, vol. 7, no. 3, pp. 14–22.

Miyahara, M., 1998. 'Supplementary budget for emergency economic package adds 511.1 billion yen for S&T', *Report Memorandum #98–19*, Tokyo: National Science Foundation.

Miyamoto, M., 1996. 'Mental castration, the HIV scandal, and the Japanese bureaucracy', *Japan Policy Research Institute Working Paper*, no. 23, Cardiff, Cal.: Japan Policy Research Institute.

Miyamoto, S., 1988. *Sentan iryō kakumei: sono gijutsu, shisō, seido* (*The Revolution in Advanced Medical Care: The Technology, Concepts, and System*), Tokyo: Chūōkōronsha.

Miyata, S., 1985. *Kagakusha no josei shi* (*A History of Women Scientists*), Tokyo: Sōchisha.

Morimatsu, Y., Saigetsu, K. & Konishi, S. (eds), 1985. *Seikatsu shi III, taikei Nihon shi sōsho 17* (*History of Lifestyle, Part 3, Outline History of Japan, Vol. 17*), Tokyo: Yamakawa Shuppan.

Morita, A. & Ishihara, S., 1989. *'No' to ieru Nihon: Shin Nichibei kankei no kaado* (*The Japan That Can Say No: The New Card to be Played in US–Japan Relations*), Tokyo: Kōbunsha.

Moritani, M., 1995. '"Gijutsu henkaku' no jidai: Nihon ni keikoku suru' ('The era of technological change: a warning to Japan', *Gaikō foramu*, no. 84, September, pp. 12–19.

Morris-Suzuki, T., 1988. *Beyond Computopia: Information, Automation and Democracy in Japan*, London: Kegan Paul International.

—— 1994. *The Technological Transformation of Japan: From the Seventeenth to the Twenty-first Century*, Cambridge University Press.

—— 1998. *Reinventing Japan: Time, Space, Nation*, Armonk, New York: M. E. Sharpe.

Mowery, D. C., 1993. 'Japanese technology and global influence', in *Japan's Emerging Global Role*, D. Unger & P. Blackburn (eds), pp. 171–93, Boulder: Lynne Rienner.

Mowery, D. C. & Rosenberg, N., 1989. *Technology and the Pursuit of Economic Growth*, Cambridge University Press.

Murakami, T., 1998. 'The development of ICT industries and their impact on the macroeconomy', *Noruma Research Institute Quarterly*, vol. 7, no. 1, pp. 54–75.

Murata, H., 1967. 'Nuclear energy: the next 10 years', *New Scientist*, vol. 36, no. 571, 16 November, supplement 3–4.

Nagai S., 1998. 'Appliance Recycling Bill lacks a philosophy', (in Japanese), *Kankyō to Kōgai* (*The Environment and Pollution*), vol. 28, no. 1, p. 1.

Nagata, C., Matsushita, Y., Inaba, S., Kawakami, N. & Shimizu, H., 1997. 'Unapproved use of high-dose combined pills in Japan: a community study on prevalence and health characteristics of the users', *Preventive Medicine*, vol. 26, no. 4, 1 July, pp. 565–9.

Nakamura, Y. & Shibuya, M., 1996. 'Japan's technology policy: a case study of the R&D of the Fifth Generation computer systems', *International Journal of Technology Management*, vol. 12, nos. 5–6, pp. 509–33.

Nakaoka, T., 1992. 'Changes in the attitude of major Japanese corporations towards R&D', *Japan Forum*, vol. 4, no. 1, April, pp. 121–43.

Nakayama, S., 1989. 'Independence and choice: Western impact on Japanese higher education', in *From Dependence to Autonomy: The Development of Asian Universities*, P. G. Altbach & V. Selvaratnam (eds), pp. 97–116, Dordrecht: Kluwer.

—— 1991. *Science, Technology and Society in Postwar Japan*, London: Kegan Paul International.

—— 1995a. 'The development of Japanese style quality control', in *Nihon no kagaku gijutsu* (*The Social History of Science and Technology in Contemporary Japan*), S. Nakayama, K. Gotō & H. Yoshioka (eds), vol. 1, pp. 269–74, Tokyo: Gakuyō Shobō.

—— 1995b. 'The rise of corporate R&D activities: the central laboratory boom', in Japanese, in *Nihon no kagaku gijutsu* (*The Social History of Science and Technology in Contemporary Japan*), S. Nakayama, K. Gotō & H. Yoshioka (eds), vol. 3, pp. 44–9, Tokyo: Gakuyō Shobō.

Nakayama, S. & Low, M. F., 1997. 'The research function of universities in Japan', *Higher Education*, vol. 34, pp. 245–58.

Namihira, E., 1991. 'An update on organ transplants in Japan', *Journal of Japanese Trade and Industry*, no. 2, 1 March.

Narin, F. & Davidson Frame, J., 1989. 'The growth of Japanese science and technology', *Science*, vol. 245, 11 August, p. 604.

Narita Airport Problem Roundtable Conference Record Compilation Committee, 1996. *Narita kūkō mondai entaku kaigi kirokushū.*

Narita Airport Problem Symposia Record Compilation Committee, 1995. *Narita kūkō shinpojiumu kirokushū* (*Record of the Symposia Dealing with the Problems Surrounding Narita Airport*).

National Declaration Drafting Committee, 1984. 'Declaration of the rights of patients', draft proposal, 14 October.

National Defense Counsel for Victims of *Karōshi*, *Karōshi: When the Corporate Warrior Dies*, Tokyo: Madosha.

Negishi, M. & Adachi, J., 1991. 'Overseas acceptance of Japanese scientific papers as seen in a citation analysis', in *Preprints of the Third International Conference on Japanese Information in Science, Technology and Commerce*, 15–18 May 1991, Nancy, France, pp. 243–59, Paris: Centre National de la Recherche Scientifique.

New Tokyo International Airport Authority 20-Year History Compilation Committee (ed.), 1987. *Shin Tōkyō Kokusai Kūkō Kōdan 20 nen no ayumi* (*The Twenty-Year History of the New Tokyo International Airport Authority*), Tokyo: New Tokyo International Airport Authority.

New York Times, 1992. 'Wary Japan maintains ban on the pill', *Age*, 20 March, p. 6.

Nicolas, F., 1995. 'The expansion of foreign direct investment', in *Japanese Firms in Europe*, F. Sachwald (ed.), pp. 5–44, Luxembourg: Harwood Academic.

Nintendō, 1998. 'Nintendō Company History', Nintendō Corporate Info, electronic website: <www.nintendo.com/corp/history.html>.

Nishimura, Hirofumi, 1998. 'The second phase of telecommunications deregulation in Japan', *Noruma Research Institute Quarterly*, vol. 7, no. 3, pp. 2–13.

NISTEP (National Institute of Science and Technology Policy), 1991. Second Policy-oriented Research Group, A. Nishimoto & H. Nagahama, 'The interchange of researchers and engineers between Japan and other countries', *NISTEP Report*, vol. 16, March.

Noble, G. W., 1992. *Flying Apart?: Japanese–American Negotiations over the FSX Fighter Plane*, Berkeley: Institute of International Studies, University of California.

Noguchi, M. Goebel, 1992. 'The rise of the housewife activist', *Japan Quarterly*, July–September, pp. 339–52.

Normile, D., 1993a. 'Japanese universities become magnets for Asian students', *Science*, vol. 262, no. 5132, 15 October, p. 351.

—— 1993b. 'Japan holds on tight to cutting-edge technology', *Science*, vol. 262, no. 5132, 15 October, p. 352.

Nudeshima, J., 1991. 'Obstacles to brain death and organ transplantation in Japan', *Lancet*, vol. 338, 26 October, pp. 1063–4.

Odagiri, H. & Goto, A., 1993. 'The Japanese system of innovation: past, present, and future', in *National Innovation Systems: A Comparative Analysis*, R. R. Nelson (ed.), pp. 76–114, New York: Oxford University Press.

OECD (Organisation for Economic Cooperation and Development), 1994. *OECD Environmental Performance Reviews: Japan*, Paris: OECD.

Ogawa, N. & Retherford, R. D., 1991. 'Prospects for increased contraceptive pill use in Japan', *Studies in Family Planning*, vol. 22, no. 6, November–December, pp. 378–83.

Ohsono, T., 1995. *Charting Japanese Industry: A Graphical Guide to Corporate and Market Structures*, London: Cassell.

Oishi, N., 1990. 'Asia demand fuels N-plant competition', *Japan Economic Journal*, 2 June, p. 17.

Okimoto, D. I., 1989. *Between MITI and the Market: Japanese Industrial Policy for High Technology*, Stanford University Press.

Okimoto, D. I. & Yoshikawa, A. (eds), 1993. *Japan's Health System: Efficiency and Effectiveness in Universal Care*, New York: Faulkner & Gray; Washington, DC: Healthcare Information Center.

Olson, L., 1959. 'Atomic cross-currents in Japan', *American Universities Field Staff Reports: East Asia Series*, vol. 7, no. 5, April.

Ōmine, Akira, 1991. 'Right and wrong in the brain-death debate', *Japan Echo*, vol. 18, no. 1, pp. 68–71.

Ormonde, T., 1990. 'The silent charade of a "Cold"', *Age*, 28 September, p. 7.

Osedo, H., 1999. 'Japan set to lift ban on contraceptive pill', *Courier Mail*, 5 March, p. 11.

Ōtsuki, S., 1990. 'The FSX problem resolved?', *Japan Quarterly*, January–March, pp. 70–83.

Patrick, H. & Rosovsky, H. (eds), 1976. *Asia's New Giant: How the Japanese Economy Works*, Washington, DC: Brookings Institution.

Pearson, E. S., 1935. *The Application of Statistical Methods to Industrialisation and Quality Control*, London: British Standards Institution.

Peck, M. J. with Tamura, S., 1976. 'Technology', in *Asia's New Giant: How the Japanese Economy Works*, H. Patrick & H. Rosovsky (eds), Washington, DC: Brookings Institution.

Pempel, T. J., 1975. 'Japan's nuclear allergy', *Current History*, vol. 68, no. 404, pp. 169–73, 183.

Peters II, R. A., 1993. 'Blue sky research: cooperation between a Japanese company and a US university', *Japan Technical Affairs*, vol. 1, no. 3, pp. 13–19.

Popham, P., 1991. 'Quicksilver's ghosts', *Age Good Weekend*, 24 August, pp. 63–9.

Prestowitz, C., 1988. *Trading Places: How We Allowed Japan to Take the Lead*, New York: Basic Books.

Provenzo Jr, E. F., 1992. 'What do video games teach?', *Education Digest*, vol. 58, no. 4, December, pp. 56–8.

—— 1997. 'Video games and the emergence of interactive media for children', in *Kinderculture: The Corporate Construction of Childhood*, S. R. Steinberg & J. L. Kincheloe (eds), pp. 103–13, Boulder, Colorado: Westview Press.

Puffert, Douglas J., 1997. 'Technical standards and access to the Japanese cellular communications equipment market', in *Japan's Technical Standards: Implications for Global Trade and Competitiveness*, J. R. McIntyre (ed.), pp. 87–92, Westport, Conn.: Quorum Books.

Raitberger, F., 1994. 'UNESCO finds research is growing in secret', *Age*, 15 February, p. 16.

Rappaport, C., 1993. 'Japan to the rescue', *Fortune International*, vol. 128, no. 9, 18 October, pp. 30–2.

Ray, T. & Buisseret, T., 1995. 'Japan's use of collaborative research to build a computer industry: lessons for the UK?', *Prometheus*, vol. 13, no. 1, June, pp. 90–106.

Sachwald, F., 1995a. 'The decision of Japanese firms to produce in Europe', in *Japanese Firms in Europe*, F. Sachwald (ed.), pp. 45–87, Luxembourg: Harwood Academic.

——— (ed.) 1995b. *Japanese Firms in Europe*, Luxembourg: Harwood Academic.

Said, E. W., [1978] 1985. *Orientalism*, London: Routledge & Kegan Paul; Harmondsworth, Middx: Penguin.

Sakakibara, K. & Westney, D. E., 1985. 'Comparative study of the training, careers, and organization of engineers in the computer industry in the United States and Japan', *Hitotsubashi Journal of Commmerce and Management*, vol. 20, pp. 1–20.

Sakamura, K., 1996. 'The TRON project', *Information and Software Technology*, vol. 38, pp. 239–51.

Samuels, R. J., 1987. *The Business of the Japanese State: Energy Markets in Comparative and Historical Perspective*, Ithaca: Cornell University Press.

——— 1994. *'Rich Nation, Strong Army': National Security and the Technological Transformation of Japan*, Ithaca: Cornell University Press.

Sankei Shinbun, 1999. 'We need to know', *Japan Times International*, 16–28 February, p. 21.

Saphir, A., 1994. 'A policy of science', *Look Japan*, August, pp. 4–8.

Sato, T., 1990. 'Mitsubishi heavy industries makes a comeback', *Tokyo Business Today*, January, pp. 50–2.

Sawada, Y., 1996. 'The Fifth Generation computer project', unpublished manuscript.

Saxonhouse, G., 1976. 'Country girls and the Japanese cotton spinning industry', in *Japanese Industrialization and Its Social Consequences*, H. Patrick (ed.), pp. 97–126, Berkeley, Cal.: University of California Press.

Schaede, U., 1995. 'The "old boy" network and government–business relationships in Japan', *Journal of Japanese Studies*, vol. 21, no. 2, pp. 293–317.

Science and Technology in Japan, 1995. 'Current R&D in science and technology: from the NISTEP Report', vol. 14, no. 53, January, pp. 23–41.

Science and Technology Policy Research Institute, Science and Technology Agency, Japan (ed.), 1991. *Taikei kagaku gijutsu shihyō: Nihon no kagaku gijutsu katsudō no taikeiteki bunseki* (*Science and Technology Indicators: A Systematic Analysis of Japanese Activities in Science and Technology*), Tokyo: STA.

Sega, 1998. 'History of Sega of America, Inc.', Sega of America Inc. Company Background, electronic website: <www.sega.com/central/culture.html>.

Serapio, Jr, M. G., 1994. 'A comparative study of US–Japan cross-border direct R&D investments in the electronics industry', *Kahaner Report*, 5 March, electronic version.

Shear, J., 1994. *The Keys to the Kingdom: The FS-X Deal and the Selling of America's Future to Japan*, New York: Doubleday.

Shibuya, T., 1997. 'Does Japan need the pill?: a three-decade debate may be near an end', *Japan Times*, 16 December, p. 3.

Shillony, B., 1986. 'Universities and students in wartime Japan', *Journal of Asian Studies*, vol. 45, no. 4, pp. 769–87.

Shimoda, M., 1994. 'Kansai Science City and regional development policy', in Japanese, paper presented at the symposium 'The Science City in a Global Context', 17–18 October, Kansai Science City.

Shimokawa, K., 1994. *The Japanese Automobile Industry: A Business History*, London: Athlone Press.

Shimura, Y., 1993. *Nihon no gijutsu ga sekai o seiha suru riyū* (*The Reason Why Japanese Technology Dominates the World*), Tokyo: PHP Kenkyūjo.

Shioda, S., 1994. 'Innovation and change in the rapid economic growth period', in *Technology Change and Female Labour in Japan*, M. Nakamura (ed.), pp. 161–92, Tokyo: United Nations University Press.

Shirahase, S. & Ishida, H., 1994. 'Gender inequality in the Japanese occupational structure: a cross-national comparison with Great Britain and the United States', *International Journal of Comparative Sociology*, vol. 35, nos. 3–4, pp. 188–206.

Sievers, S. L., 1983. *Flowers in Salt: The Beginnings of Feminist Consciousness in Modern Japan*, Stanford University Press.

Sigurdson, J., 1992. 'Internationalising research and development in Japan', *Science and Public Policy*, vol. 19, no. 3, June, pp. 134–44.

Sigurdson, J. & Anderson, A. M., [1984] 1991. *Science and Technology in Japan*, 2nd rev. edn, Essex: Longman.

Skelton, R., 1996. 'Professor with blood of 400 on his hands', *Sydney Morning Herald*, 2 March, p. 22.

—— 1998. 'Japan's jobless soar to 2.9 m', *Sydney Morning Herald*, 30 May, p. 19.

Slaughter, S., 1993. 'Beyond basic science: research university presidents' narratives of science policy', *Science, Technology and Human Values*, vol. 18, no. 3, pp. 278–302.

Smilor, R. W. & Gibson, D. V., 1991. 'Accelerating technology transfer in R&D consortia', *Research Technology Management*, vol. 34, no. 1, pp. 44—9.

Smilor, R. W., Kozmetsky, G. & Gibson, D. V. (eds), 1988. *Creating the Technopolis: Linking Technology Commercialization and Economic Development*, Cambridge, Mass.: Ballinger.

Smith, T. C., 1959. *The Agrarian Origins of Modern Japan*, Stanford University Press.

Sollors, W., 1995. 'Ethnicity', in *Critical Terms for Literary Study*, F. Lentricchia & T. McLaughlin (eds), 2nd edn, pp. 288–305, University of Chicago Press.

Spar, D., 1992. 'Co-developing the FSX fighter: the domestic calculus of international co-operation', *International Journal*, vol. 47, no. 2, pp. 265–92.

STA (Science and Technology Agency), 1997. *Kagaku gijutsu hakusho* (*Science and Technology White Paper*), Tokyo: Ministry of Finance Printing Bureau.

STA Today, 1991. 'Significant shortage of researchers expected in 2005: survey of research personnel by STA', vol. 3, no. 11, p. 8.

—— 1995. 'First decline of R&D expenditures: report on the survey of research and development', vol. 7, no. 1, January, p. 6.

—— 1998. 'Survey report on research activities of private companies in FY1997', vol. 10, no. 9, September, p. 9.

Stokes, A., 1999. 'Japan's jobless rise to record', *Weekend Australian*, 1–2 May, p. 34.

Sugaya, A., 1981. *Nihon no byōin* (*Hospitals in Japan*), Tokyo: Chūōkōronsha.

Sugimoto, M. & Swain, D. L., [1978] 1989. *Science and Culture in Traditional Japan*, Cambridge, Mass.: MIT Press; Vermont: Tuttle.

Sullivan, Kevin & Jordan, Mary, 1999. 'Move over Nintendo, let's dance', *Sydney Morning Herald*, 6 February, p. 30.

Sumiya, M., 1996. *Narita no sora to daichi: Tōsō kara kyōsei e no michi* (*The Sky and Ground of Narita: The Road from Struggle to Co-existence*), Tokyo: Iwanami Shoten.

Sunagawa, K., in press. 'The rise of the video game industry: another aspect of the history of computer technology and industry in Japan', in *Nihon no kagaku gijutsu* (*The Social History of Science and Technology in Contemporary Japan*), S. Nakayama, K. Gotō & H. Yoshioka (eds), Tokyo: Gakuyō Shobō.

Suttmeier, R. P., 1981. 'The Japanese nuclear power option: technological promise and social limitations', in *The Politics of Japan's Energy Strategy*, R. A. Morse (ed.), pp. 106–33, Berkeley: Institute of East Asian Studies, University of California.

Swinbanks, D., 1988. 'Classified US technology for transfer to Japan', *Nature*, vol. 332, no. 6164, p. 669.

—— 1994. 'OECD gives Japan mixed score on environment', *Nature*, vol. 369, 5 May, p. 5.

Tada, M., 1978. 'The glory and misery of "My Home"', in *Authority and the Individual in Japan: Citizen Protest in Historical Perspective*, J. Victor Koschmann (ed.), pp. 207–17, Tokyo, University of Tokyo Press.

Takagi, T., 1997. 'Japanese Internet development since 1995', paper presented at the 10th Biennial Conference of the Japanese Studies Association of Australia, Melbourne, 6–10 July, p. 4.

Takahara, S., 1991. 'Women's power in Japan's economy', *Journal of Japanese Trade and Industry*, no. 2, pp. 28–30.

Takayoshi, H., 1995. 'The distressing hollowing out of industry', *Journal of Japanese Trade and Industry*, no. 1, pp. 36–7.

Takeshita, T., 1996. 'Software technologies created in Japan', *Information and Software Technology*, vol. 38, pp. 229–38.

Taketani, M. & Nakamura, S., 1950. *Genshi-ryoku* (*Atomic Energy*), Tokyo: Mainichi Shinbunsha.

Talcott, P., 1996. 'The poisoned body politic: the AIDS case and the erosion of trust in MHW', *Social Science Japan*, no. 7, August, pp. 16–18.

Tanabe, K., 1997. 'Globalization and the role of standards', in *Japan's Technical Standards: Implications for Global Trade and Competitiveness*, J. R. McIntyre (ed.), pp. 67–73, Westport, Conn.: Quorum.

Tanagaki, S., 1998. 'Reshaping Japan: role of science and technology', paper presented at 23rd Annual American Association for the Advancement of Science Colloquium on Science and Technology Policy, 1 May, Washington, DC.

Tanaka, M., 1990. 'Everybody's fault', *Look Japan*, October, pp. 26–7.

Thee, K. W., 1992. 'Technology transfer from Japan to Indonesia', paper prepared for the Second Conference on the Transfer of Science and Technology, 3–6 November, Kyoto, Japan.

Tokyo Business Today, 1993. 'Japanese high-tech manufacturing is on the move – out of Japan', October, pp. 44–6.

Tōkyō Shibaura Denki Kabushiki Gaisha, 1977. *Tōshiba hyakunen shi* (*A One-Hundred Year History of Tōshiba*), Tokyo: Daimondosha.

Tōkyō Shinbun Chiba Branch & Ōtsubo, K. (eds), 1978. *Dokyumento Narita kūkō* (*Narita Airport Documented*), Tokyo: Tokyo Shinbun Press.

Toyoda, T., 1984. 'Scientists look at peace and security', *Bulletin of the Atomic Scientists*, vol. 40, no. 2, pp. 16–19.

Tsugawa, A. & Kanomi, S., Kiraku, 1996. *Nihon no josei kagakusha no kiseki* (*Pioneering Science: Tracing the Paths of Japan's Women Scientists*), Tokyo: Domesu Shuppan.

Tsukahara, S., 1995. 'The expansion of government research activity into the forefront of research', in *Nihon no kagaku gijutsu* (*The Social History of Science and Technology in Contemporary Japan*), S. Nakayama, K. Gotō & H. Yoshioka (eds), vol. 3, pp. 51–60, Tokyo: Gakuyō Shobō.

Tsukahara, S. & Kamatani, C., 1995. 'MITI's national program of large scale R&D projects', in *Nihon no kagaku gijutsu* (*The Social History of Science and Technology in Contemporary Japan*), S. Nakayama, K. Gotō & H. Yoshioka (eds), vol. 3, pp. 61–71, Tokyo: Gakuyō Shobō.

Tsurumi, E. P., 1990. *Factory Girls: Women in the Thread Mills of Meiji Japan*, Princeton University Press.

Tsutsui, W. M., 1996. 'W. Edwards Deming and the origins of quality control in Japan', *Journal of Japanese Studies*, vol. 22, no. 2, pp. 295–325.

Tuathail, G. O., 1992. '"Pearl Harbor Without Bombs": A Critical Geopolitics of the US–Japan FSX Debate', *Environment and Planning A*, vol. 24, no. 7, 1 July, pp. 975–94.

Tyson, L. D'A., 1992. *Who's Bashing Whom: Trade Conflict in High Technology Industries*, Washington, DC: Institute for International Economics.

Uchiyama, H., in press. 'History of environmental science in Japan: formation and progress', in Japanese, in *Nihon no kagaku gijutsu* (*The Social History of Science and Technology in Contemporary Japan*), S. Nakayama, K. Gotō & H. Yoshioka (eds), Tokyo: Gakuyō Shobō.

Ueno, C., 1994. 'Women and the family in transition in postindustrial Japan', in *Women of Japan and Korea: Continuity and Change*, J. Gelby & M. Lief Pally (eds), pp. 23–42, Philadelphia: Temple University Press.

UNCTAD (United Nations Conference on Trade and Development), 1974. *The Role of the Patent System in the Transfer of Technology to Developing Countries*, New York: United Nations.

Unger, J. M., 1987. *The Fifth Generation Fallacy: Why Japan is Betting Its Future on Artificial Intelligence*, New York: Oxford University Press.

US Government, National Science Foundation, Division of Science Resource Studies, 1991. 'Scientists, engineers, and technicians in manufacturing are highly concentrated in high technology industries', J. P. Gannon (comp.), *Science Resource Studies Data Brief*, 29 November.

—— National Science Foundation, Division of Human Resource Development, 1992a. *Gateway to Diversity in the Scientific and Technological Workforce*, Washington, DC: National Science Foundation.

—— National Science Foundation, Division of Science Resource Studies, 1992b. 'Foreign citizens continue to increase US ranks of Science and Engineering doctorate recipients', S. T. Hill (comp.), *Science Resource Studies Data Brief*, no. 4.

—— National Science Foundation, Directorate for Education and Human Resources, 1993a. *Proceedings of the National Conference on Diversity in the Scientific and Technological Workforce, 25–26 September 1992*, Washington, DC: National Science Foundation.

—— National Science Foundation, Division of Science Resource Studies, 1993b. 'Asian Science and Engineering degrees top 700,000', J. M. Johnson (comp.), *Science Resource Studies Data Brief*, no. 93-316.

—— 1997. 'US–Japan Fighter Aircraft: Agreement on F-2 production', General Accounting Office report number NSIAD-97-76, 11 February, electronic version.

Uzawa, H., 1992a. *Sanrizuka ansoroji* (*Sanrizuka Anthology*), Tokyo: Iwanami Shoten.

—— 1992b. *'Narita' towa nanika: Sengo Nihon no higeki* (*What is 'Narita'?: A Postwar Japanese Tragedy*), Tokyo: Iwanami Shoten.

van Wolferen, K., 1989. *The Enigma of Japanese Power: People and Politics in a Stateless Nation*, New York: Vintage Books.

Wada, E., 1931. *Tomioka nikki* (*Tomioka Diary*), Nagano: Shinano Kyōikukai.

Wajcman, J., 1991. *Feminism Confronts Technology*, Sydney: Allen & Unwin.

Wakamatsu, Y., 1995. 'The growth of scientific journalism', in *Nihon no kagaku gijutsu* (*The Social History of Science and Technology in Contemporary Japan*), S. Nakayama, H. Yoshioka & K. Gotō (eds), vol. 3, pp. 396–406, Tokyo: Gakuyō Shobō.

Walsh, J. R., 1993. 'Technonationalism in US–Japanese security relations: the FSX controversy', *Armed Forces and Society*, vol. 19, no. 3, pp. 377–91.

Watanabe, M., 1990. *The Japanese and Western Science*, O. T. Benfey (trans.), Philadelphia: University of Pennsylvania Press.

—— 1998. 'Public health service reforms and the growth of private health care', *Noruma Research Institute Quarterly*, vol. 7, no. 2, pp. 38–57.

Watts, J., 1997. 'Japan is close to approving "the pill"', *Lancet*, vol. 350, no. 9088, 8 November, p. 1377.

Weekend Australian, 1996. 'Japanese firms apologise for selling HIV-tainted products', 16–17 March, p. 15.

Welfield, J., 1988. *An Empire in Eclipse: Japan in the Postwar American Alliance System: A Study in the Interaction of Domestic Politics and Foreign Policy*, London: Athlone Press.

Westney, D. E., 1986. 'The military', in *Japan in Transition: From Tokugawa to Meiji*, M. B. Jansen & G. Rozman (eds), pp. 168–94, Princeton University Press.

—— 1987. *Imitation and Innovation: The Transfer of Western Organizational Patterns to Meiji Japan*, Cambridge, Mass.: Harvard University Press.

Westney, D. E. & Sakakibara, K., 1986. 'Designing the designers: computer R&D in the United States and Japan', *Technology Review*, April, pp. 25–31, 68–9.

White, J. C., 1997. 'AIDS in Japan: an unacceptable diagnosis', unpublished MA thesis, Department of Japanese and Chinese, University of Melbourne.

Wilkinson, E., 1983. *Japan Versus Europe: A History of Misunderstanding*, Harmondsworth, Middx: Penguin Books.

Wise, J., 1997. 'Japan to allow organ transplants', *British Medical Journal*, vol. 314, no. 7090, 3 May, p. 1298.

Yagi, E., Matsuda, H. & Narita, K., 1997. 'Toshiko Yuasa (1909–1980), and the nature of her archives at Ochanomizu University in Tokyo', *Historia Scientiarum*, vol. 7, no. 2, pp. 153–63.

Yamada, S., 1982. *Kaden ima mukashi monogatari* (*Household Electrical Goods: Then and Now*), Tokyo: Sanseidō.

Yamamoto, S., 1993. 'Reorganization of research in the mass higher education system in Japan: will Japan create centers of excellence at universities?', in *R&D Strategies in Japan: The National, Regional and Corporate Approach*, H. Eto (ed.), pp. 177–88, Amsterdam: Elsevier.

Yamashita, A., 1983. *Kindai Nihon josei shi: Kagaku* (*A History of Modern Japanese Women: Science*), Tokyo: Kajima Shuppankai.

Yanaga, C., 1968. *Big Business in Japanese Politics*, New Haven: Yale University Press.

Yanagawa, Y., 1992. 'The greening of corporate Japan', *Journal of Japanese Trade and Industry*, 1 October, pp. 14–16.

Yoshioka, H., 1995. 'The high-speed growth of civil air transport', in Japanese, in *The Social History of Science and Technology in Contemporary Japan*, S. Nakayama, K. Gotō & H. Yoshioka (eds), vol. 3, pp. 278–91, Tokyo: Gakuyō Shobō.

—— 1996a. 'The rise and fall of fast breeder development in Japan', *Science Studies*, vol. 6, no. 2, pp. 14–26.

—— 1996b. 'Monju jiko no sekaishi-teki imi', *Kanagawa Daigaku hyōron*, vol. 24, pp. 87–98.

Yoshioka, Y., 1995. 'Nihon ni okeru katei denki seihin no tōjō to fukyū no rekishi' ('A history of the spread of household electrical goods in Japan'), in *The Social History of Science and Technology in Contemporary Japan*, S. Nakayama, K. Gotō & H. Yoshioka (eds), vol. 2, pp. 416–25, Tokyo: Gakuyō Shobō.

Yoshizawa, J., Oyama, Y., Yamamoto, T. & Gonda, K., 1995. *Comparative Studies on Science and Technology Parks for Regional Innovation throughout the World*, in Japanese, NISTEP Report no. 38, Tokyo: National Institute of Science and Technology Policy.

Yunomae, T., 1996. 'Commodified sex (sexism): Japan's pornographic culture', in *Voices from the Japanese Women's Movement*, AMPO–Japan Asia Quarterly Review (eds), pp. 101–10, Armonk, New York: M. E. Sharpe.

Zampetti, A. B., 1996. 'Globalisation in the consumer electronics industry', Organisation for Economic Cooperation and Development, *Globalisation of Industry: Overview and Sector Reports*, Paris: OECD, pp. 207–50.

Ziman, J., 1984. *An Introduction to Science Studies: The Philosophical and Social Aspects of Science and Technology*, Cambridge University Press.

Index

abortions, 153, 187, 188
academic argument, 21–2
academic journals/articles, 20–1, 22–3, 25, 27, 33, 34, 135
academic sector, 13, 19–20, 21–2, 23, 24–32, 33, 34, 36, 42, 43–4, 46, 47, 58, 107; *see also* universities
acid rain, 91
acupuncture, 175
Advanced Telecommunications Research Institute International, 47, 48
advanced thermal reactors, 47, 48, 70, 77, 79, 80
Aerospace Industries Association of America, 115
aerospace industry, 81, 107–18, 189
Against the State, 160
'Agenda 21', 101
agriculture, 22, 147, 150
Aiba, K., 150
AIDS, 102, 175, 177, 187, 191
air accidents, 163–4
Air Self-Defence Force, 110
air travel growth, 160–2, 163
airconditioners, 82, 88
airport noise pollution, 163, 164, 165, 172
airports, 159–73
All-Nippon Airlines, 161, 162–3
amakudari, 176, 177
American Electronics Association, 115
Anchordoguy, M., 35
Anderson, A. M., 4
Andō, Y., 139
anti-nuclear movement, 152
anti-pollution movement, 62, 90, 91, 92, 93, 95, 96, 152
anti-Vietnam movement, 192

Aoyama, M., 140
apartment dwellers, 86
applied and basic research, 11–34, 42, 43, 66, 121
architecture, 43, 153–4
ASEAN, 125, 126–7
Ashihara, Y., 154
Asia
    and atomic energy industry, 128
    and 'brain reverse', 156
    and class, 128, 156
    and female workers, 151
    and manufacturing, 127–8, 158
    and technological gap, 126
    and technology transfer, 32, 107, 123, 126, 127, 151
    doctoral students from, 27, 155–6
    dynamic growth of, 11
    engineering students from, 27
    environmental problems in, 83, 90, 128
    exports to, 55, 56, 83
    herbal medicines of, 175
    industrial investment in, 83
    industry relocation to, 32, 33, 64, 121, 122, 125, 128
    Japanese investment in, 125
    medical techniques of, 175
    multinational firms in, 122
    quality control in, 60
    S&T workforce from, 46, 146, 155
    wealth levels in, 158
Asian economic crisis, 4, 5, 11, 36, 49, 128, 193
Association for the Promotion of New-Generation Network Services Pilot Project Key Station, 47
Atomic Energy Commission (US), 70, 71